PRESENTED TO:

FROM:

DATE:

THE
Believer's
CODE

365 Devotions
to Unlock the
Blessings in
God's Word

O. S. Hawkins

COUNTRYMAN®

A Division of Thomas Nelson Publishers

THOMAS NELSON
Since 1798

Published in Nashville, Tennessee, by Thomas Nelson. Thomas Nelson is a registered trademark of HarperCollins Christian Publishing, Inc.

Thomas Nelson titles may be purchased in bulk for educational, business, fundraising, or sales promotional use. For information, please e-mail SpecialMarkets@ ThomasNelson.com.

ISBN: 978-0-7180-9953-4

Printed in China

19 20 21 DSC 6 5 4

TO JOHN JONES

For over twenty years, John has been by my side, helping to navigate through the waters of leading a multibillion-dollar ministry we call GuideStone "with the integrity of our hearts and the skillfulness of our hands" (Psalm 78:72). This talented COO could lead any Fortune 500 company. But what makes him special is his heart for those we serve every day, especially those in need, served through Mission:Dignity. John's dedication, along with that of his wife, Ann, is a constant source of inspiration to me personally and to all who come in contact with his Christ-filled life.

Along with John, and like all the other "Code" volumes, this book is dedicated to all those faithful servants who labored a lifetime and ministered with dedication and determination in those seemingly out-of-the-way places where they often wondered if they had been forgotten. They lived on meager pastors' salaries with even less to prepare for their declining years. As all the author's royalties and proceeds from The Believer's Code *go to support them, you have had a part in being Christ's hand extended by purchasing this book. Mission:Dignity is here to enable them, their wives, and their widows to live out their final years with the kind of security and dignity they so richly deserve. Find out more at www. guidestone.org, and click on Mission:Dignity.*

INTRODUCTION

Many believers who are serious about personal devotions and spiritual growth seem to think it is the volume of Scripture one can devour daily that is most important. For years I have sought to read the Bible through every year, which involves the reading of several chapters a day. However, *The Believer's Code* is designed to guide readers through each day of the year with one particular verse upon which they can "meditate" both "day and night" (Joshua 1:8). You will find a verse for each day, accompanied by a devotional thought, a "Code Word," and a sentence prayer.

When teaching us how to pray, Jesus instructed that we should ask God to "give us this day our daily bread" (Matthew 6:11). Note it is DAILY bread. Just as the manna fell each day for the children of Israel in the wilderness, we need a daily portion of God's Word to sustain us. Yesterday's victories will never suffice for today's devotion. It was said of those in Thessalonica that they "searched the Scriptures daily" (Acts 17:11). In defining the demands of discipleship, Jesus called upon us to "take up [our] cross daily" (Luke 9:23). Our own personal devotion demands a daily discipline.

The Believer's Code is designed to be used each morning . . . and to live with you and in you throughout your day. Each devotion embodies a "Code Word" that serves to unlock the truth of the daily devotion. Write it down. Keep it with you. Think about it throughout the day as it stirs you to put into practice each daily devotion so that, as James said, you will become a "doer of the word and not a hearer only" (James 1:22). Each day also includes a sentence prayer. Keep this prayer in your heart, and pray it repeatedly throughout your day.

Thus, we begin the journey to make our own personal devotion a part of our daily routine throughout the year. Yes, "This Book of the Law shall not depart from your mouth, but you shall meditate in it day and night, that you may observe to do according to all that is written in it. For then you will make your way prosperous, and then you will have good success" (Joshua 1:8). We have a God who still speaks to you and me through His Word and by His Spirit. Turn the page and begin to unlock the blessings of God's Word through . . . *The Believer's Code.*

JANUARY

---

*By this we know love,
because He laid down
His life for us. And we
also ought to lay down
our lives for the brethren.*

1 JOHN 3:16

You have not passed this way before. . . . Sanctify yourselves, for tomorrow the LORD will do wonders among you.

JOSHUA 3:4–5

New Year's Day provides us with a new beginning, so . . .

Be flexible. Don't be afraid of change. Change can be your friend and not your foe.

Be focused. Enter the new year with your eyes on the Lord.

Be faithful. Commit yourself to stay pure in mind, motives, and morals.

Be futuristic. Don't let memories of yesterday be more important than visions of tomorrow.

Be fearless. Jesus is your Good Shepherd, and great is His faithfulness.

At this new beginning, we come to the water's edge. We might be tempted to say, "Lord, just let those waters part, and then I will step in." But—like the priests taking the ark across the Jordan River—we often have to get our feet wet before God begins to "work wonders among us."

CODE WORD: NEW

"New" is one of those words that almost always finds the welcome mat out at our heart's front door. God is the giver of many wonderful new things. And now He is giving you a new start, a new beginning, a new year!

Lord, You said, "Old things pass away, and all becomes new." As I turn the page to this new year, help me seize the new opportunities it may bring. In Jesus' name, amen.

Who may ascend into the hill of the LORD?
Or who may stand in His holy place?
He who has clean hands and a pure heart.

PSALM 24:3–4

P salm 24 prompts us to look toward Calvary, toward that "hill of the LORD" where Christ was crucified and died, an atonement for the sins of the world.

We will be able to "ascend into the hill of the LORD" because of the one Person in all of history whose hands were clean and heart was pure. Knowing I was without hope, He descended from heaven so that I could one day ascend. His clean hands became dirty with the sin of the world, with my sin and yours. Why? So that our dirty hands could become clean and our sinful hearts could be made pure.

So we join the psalmist's praise! We welcome the King of glory to take up residence within us, so that "it is no longer I who live, but Christ lives in me" (Galatians 2:20).

CODE WORD: PURE

Pure—that is one word that you and I are not. We have dirty hands and impure hearts. Your only hope of ascending eternity's hill is in your substitutionary Savior, who took your place.

Lord, help me get out of the way so that "Christ [who] lives in me" may also live through me today. In Jesus' name, amen.

"For God so loved the world that He gave His only begotten Son, that whoever believes in Him should not perish but have everlasting life."

JOHN 3:16

When he was thirteen, Angel Martinez (1922–1995) became a follower of Jesus—and he preached his first sermon two months later. Besides saving souls during his sixty-year ministry, the evangelist memorized the entire New Testament. So of course Angel clearly knew salvation's cause: our holy God's love for us, His sinful, straying people.

The motivating factor behind God's redemptive plan is His love for us, a love with a "breadth, and length, and depth, and height" that are hard to comprehend (Ephesians 3:18 KJV). The apostle John declared, "God is love" (1 John 4:16) and celebrated "how great a love the Father has bestowed on us, that we would be called children of God" (1 John 3:1 NASB). God's unfathomable and never-ending love for you is the motivating cause of salvation.

CODE WORD: CAUSE

We know that everything has a cause and effect. And we know well the story of the cross. Focus today on what really caused Jesus to die on that cross: God's amazing love for *you*!

Father, You loved me so much You gave Your "only begotten Son." Help me this day to love others as You have loved me . . . sacrificially. In Jesus' name, amen.

The righteousness of God apart from the law is revealed . . . the righteousness of God, through faith in Jesus Christ, to all and on all who believe.

ROMANS 3:21–22

J esus died for all.

Jesus never shows favoritism. He reaches out to each of us—to you and to me whom He created, whom He loves, and whose brokenness and pain He sees. Jesus knows you—including all those hidden thoughts of your heart. And He loves you—deeply. He loves you so much that He took all your sin upon Himself, suffered, and died your death so you could live forgiven of your sin and in relationship with Him. Admit. Confess. Forsake. Mercy still triumphs over judgment.

May we live as if Christ died yesterday and the cross is still standing tall atop Golgotha. May we live as if Christ rose this morning and we can still see His grave clothes, folded neatly, inside the empty tomb. And may we live as if He is coming back tomorrow! Come quickly, Lord Jesus!

CODE WORD: FRESH

Is the gospel story still fresh to you? If not, seek to live today as if the cross is still standing, the tomb is still empty, and He is coming tomorrow.

Lord, come near. May I sense the aroma of Your presence in a fresh way today. In Jesus' name, amen.

You were bought at a price.

1 CORINTHIANS 6:20

For followers of Jesus, *salvation* refers to being saved from judgment for our sin. God's righteous wrath—and the consequent eternal separation from our holy God—is the appropriate consequence for our sin. But God mercifully provided deliverance from that sentence. This salvation—the free pardoning of our sin and the promise of eternal life—did not come without cost.

Freedom is never free, and in God's economy, freedom from sin is always bought with blood. Starting in Genesis and woven throughout Scripture, a scarlet thread indicates the blood atonement God requires for the forgiveness of sin. This condition for salvation is ultimately fulfilled in the final sacrifice for sin: Jesus died on a cross outside the gates of Jerusalem. Jesus not only spoke of His love for us, "but God demonstrates His own love toward us, in that while we were still sinners, Christ died for us" (Romans 5:8). Our salvation came at a great cost: God "gave His only begotten Son" (John 3:16). That is the gospel.

CODE WORD: COST

The value of an object is determined by its cost. Your salvation came at a high cost: the death of the Father's only Son—in your place! How very valuable you are to God!

Father, no one's love for me compares to Your love. Help me this day to live worthy of the tremendous price You paid. In Jesus' name, amen.

John the Baptist came preaching in the wilderness of Judea, and saying, "Repent, for the kingdom of heaven is at hand!"

MATTHEW 3:1–2

There seems to be a forgotten word in our Christian vocabulary. The word? *Repentance.* The call to repent is strangely absent today, yet it was the message of all the prophets. It was the message of John the Baptist when he preached in the wilderness (Matthew 3:1–2). It was the message with which the Lord Jesus commenced His ministry (Matthew 4:17). It was the message of the apostles as they preached throughout the known world (Mark 6:12). It was the message that birthed the church at Pentecost (Acts 2:37–38). It was the missionary message of the apostle Paul (Acts 17:30). In the final book of the Bible, it is John's message to the churches of Asia (Revelation 2:5). In fact, this call to repent is woven throughout Scripture, appearing on almost every page.

Repentance involves recognizing your sin, acknowledging it before God, receiving His forgiveness, and turning away from that behavior and attitude.

CODE WORD: TURN

Repentance is not a right turn or a left turn at an intersection of life. It is a U-turn, turning around from your own selfish desires and heading in the direction of Christ and His plan for your life.

Lord, as an act of my will I turn to You and seek only Your face today. In Jesus' name, amen.

Weeping may endure for a night,
But joy comes in the morning.

PSALM 30:5

Is our Lord weeping with you or over you today? There is a huge difference between the two.

If He is weeping over you, it's time to repent of your sin.

If He is weeping with you in your pain, be encouraged by the promise of Revelation 21:4. We read that in heaven "God will wipe away every tear from [our] eyes." King David put it this way: "His anger is but for a moment, His favor is for life; weeping may endure for a night, but joy comes in the morning" (Psalm 30:5). This is our hope: one day our compassionate God will wipe away all our tears.

We have a Lord who is not far off and removed. He is very near. He is touched by our broken hearts, and He weeps with us. And He is troubled by our blinded eyes, and He weeps over us.

CODE WORD: EXPECTANCY

What a promise—weeping may endure for a night. *But* joy comes in the morning! God can see past today. Can you?

Lord, help me live today in light of what is coming—joy in the morning. In Jesus' name, amen.

"A certain man went down from Jerusalem to Jericho, and fell among thieves, who stripped him of his clothing, wounded him, and departed, leaving him half dead. . . . A certain Samaritan, as he journeyed, came where he was. And when he saw him, he had compassion."

LUKE 10:30, 33

This Samaritan could have passed by the bleeding man, but he didn't. The Samaritan carried the man to an inn, left him in the care of the innkeeper, paid his bill in advance, and promised to return in a few days to pay for any extra expenses.

Consider that each of us has been the wounded man. Jesus saw us beaten, battered by sin, and lying on the side of the road. Overwhelmed by compassion and love for us, He left heaven, came into our world, and provided for us. He died on the cross for our sins so that we could know complete spiritual health and wholeness as well as eternity with Him.

Praise God for our compassionate and gracious Lord!

CODE WORD: NEED

Open your eyes today. There are needs all around you. Learn from this Samaritan. See the need, feel the need, meet the need.

Lord, help me to really "see" the needs of others who cross my path today and meet them. In Jesus' name, amen.

"He who believes in Me has everlasting life."

JOHN 6:47

The promise of everlasting life is stated in John 3:16, which one wise believer expanded this way:

> For God . . . the greatest Lover
> so loved . . . the greatest degree
> the world . . . the greatest company
> that He gave . . . the greatest act
> His only begotten Son . . . the greatest gift
> that whoever . . . the greatest opportunity
> believes . . . the greatest simplicity
> in Him . . . the greatest attraction
> should not perish . . . the greatest promise
> but . . . the greatest difference
> have . . . the greatest certainty
> everlasting life . . . the greatest possession

CODE WORD: CONSEQUENCE

Much of the time we associate consequences with some type of unpleasant cause and effect. In this case, however, the consequence is the positive outcome that when you put your trust in Christ, you will not "perish but have everlasting life."

Father, I am aware that this amazing consequence of placing my faith and trust in You for salvation came at a high cost: You gave Your only Son for me. I thank You with all my heart. In Jesus' name, amen.

*There is a lad here who has five barley loaves and two small
fish, but what are they among so many?*

JOHN 6:9

Given the situation you face and the seemingly inadequate
resources at your disposal, maybe you are asking, "What are
they among so many?"

The loaves and fish didn't seem like much if you looked at them
and at the crowd from a human perspective. But Christ wasn't limited by the number of loaves or fish. He had big plans, and He fed
five thousand men, plus women and children, with the boy's lunch.

Have you considered that this lad left home that morning with
the potential to feed thousands of people with his little lunch—and
he didn't even know it? Maybe you who are reading these words
right now have incredible potential for serving God, and you don't
even realize it.

Yes, little is much when you factor Christ into the equation of
your life. Similarly, "all things" are used for our good when we factor in Christ.

CODE WORD: POTENTIAL

You are like that little lad with the lunch. You start out this day
with the potential to be used by God to do incredible things for His
glory. Christ is IN you right now!

*Lord, help me live today not in light of what I see in myself
but in light of the potential that You see in me. Live Your life
through me today. In Jesus' name, amen.*

By grace you have been saved through faith, and that not of yourselves . . . lest anyone should boast.

EPHESIANS 2:8–9

S cripture says our salvation is by God's grace and through our faith—and faith means trusting in God alone for forgiveness. As the Greek word for *through* suggests, our faith is the channel through which God's saving grace flows to us. Salvation from punishment for our sins comes through faith that Jesus suffered our punishment with His death.

Paul emphasized that salvation is "not of yourselves" and "not of works" (Ephesians 2:8–9), but not everyone has heard this message. How much clearer could Paul be than this? Salvation is "by grace . . . through faith . . . not of yourselves; it is the gift of God."

No amount of human effort, no magic number of good deeds, and no level of giving can earn us God's favor. Salvation is God's work ("by grace") in God's way ("through faith").

CODE WORD: CHANNEL

Just as an aqueduct channels water to those who are thirsty, so our faith is the channel through which God's amazing grace—that far exceeds our sin and our guilt—flows into our thirsty hearts.

Lord, I am aware that You have saved me not because of any good words I have spoken or any good works I have done. I have received salvation through the channel of Your grace, through my faith in You, and through that faith alone. In Jesus' name, amen.

Having been justified by faith, we have peace with God through our Lord Jesus Christ, through whom also we have access by faith into this grace in which we stand, and rejoice in hope of the glory of God.

ROMANS 5:1–2

E ven before we put our trust in Christ alone for our salvation, most of us believed the facts of Christ's story. Few of us were bona fide atheists or agnostics.

Yet many people today believe that Jesus died on a cross in much the same way that we think of George Washington being the first president of the United States. They acknowledge that Jesus existed as a real person. They may even accept the wisdom of His teachings, but they do not trust their lives and eternal destiny to Him.

The tragedy is that these people don't realize that their "faith" is false and futile. Yet without true saving faith—which is putting our trust in Christ alone for our salvation rather than relying on any effort of our own—our faith is false and futile.

CODE WORD: ASSENT

Many give intellectual assent to the claims of Christ without ever being converted. Even the devil believes. Examine your own heart today. Do you have the assurance that your faith is real?

Lord, You have searched me and You know me. Give me the assurance of my salvation. In Jesus' name, amen.

Jesus began to preach and to say, "Repent, for the kingdom of heaven is at hand."

MATTHEW 4:17

This call from the lips of our Lord is not an option; it is a command. Obedience, then, calls us to fully understand what repentance is.

First, note what it is not. Repentance is not remorse. It is not simply being sorry for our sin. The rich young ruler went away "sorrowful," but he didn't repent (Luke 18:23). Repentance is not regret, or merely wishing that the deed had not happened. Pontius Pilate washed his hands in regret over his turning Christ over to the crowds (Matthew 27:24). Repentance is not resolve. It is not like a New Year's resolution where we resolve to take on new moral standards. And repentance is not reform. Judas Iscariot took the thirty pieces of silver, the payment for betraying Jesus, and flung them down the corridors of the temple. Judas reformed, but he did not repent (Matthew 27:3).

Repentance calls for a change of behavior, not just a change of thought or attitude.

CODE WORD: REMORSE

Although simply being remorseful is not repentance, it is a step in that direction. Godly sorrow over your sin will lead you to true repentance.

Lord, soften my heart so that it will be broken today over the same things that break Your heart. In Jesus' name, amen.

God is our refuge and strength,
A very present help in trouble.

PSALM 46:1

Oh, the significance of the two-letter word *is* in both Psalm 46:1 and Psalm 23:1!

Our preeminent Lord is with us right now: He is our Refuge, Strength, Help, and Shepherd. David did not write in past tense— "The LORD was my shepherd"—or future tense—"The LORD will be my shepherd." David wrote about present-tense reality: "The LORD is my shepherd." He is with us at this very moment to meet our present needs.

Also, when God spoke to Moses in the desert, the Almighty identified Himself in the present tense: "I AM WHO I AM" (Exodus 3:14). Unlike the world's other religions, we do not have a god who has long since departed the scene or one who is yet to come. Our God is not the great "I WAS" or the great "I WILL BE." Our God is the great "I AM."

CODE WORD: PRESENT

The Lord is with you always. He is with you everywhere you will go this day. He does not live in the past tense; He is always in the present. Right now, as you read these words, Jesus is with you.

Lord, please keep me mindful that You are with me in every minute of this day and with every step I take. You are listening to my every word, knowing my every thought, and watching my every deed. In Jesus' name, amen.

"My sheep hear My voice, and I know them, and they follow Me."

JOHN 10:27

There is a huge difference between David, the author of Psalm 23, saying, "The LORD is a shepherd" and saying, "The LORD is my shepherd." It's the difference between hearing about someone's child who is deathly sick and having our own child be deathly sick. The genuine compassion we feel for that parent pales next to our intense concern for our child.

Similarly, David spoke not about just any shepherd, but about "my shepherd." David realized—as you and I can—that we are not insignificant specks of protoplasm in God's vast array of solar systems. The fact that the God of this universe is concerned about me personally gives purpose and meaning to my short sojourn on this planet. And that God is my Shepherd!

When we place our trust in Christ, we are blessed to know Him the way sheep know their shepherd. We who are Christ's sheep know His voice, and of course we follow Him: He is our Shepherd.

CODE WORD: HEAR

We have a God who speaks to us. Do you hear His voice speaking to your heart through His Word and by His Spirit even right now? God's voice is recognizable to His sheep. Ask Him to help you hear it.

Speak, O Lord, and direct me to fulfill all Your purposes this day. You are my Shepherd, and I want to hear Your voice and follow You. In Jesus' name, amen.

[You were redeemed] with the precious blood of Christ, as of a lamb without blemish and without spot.

1 PETER 1:18–19

R ecently, while hurrying through the hustle and bustle of the always-busy DFW International Airport, I witnessed a scene that brought tears to every onlooker's eye . . . including my own. A small boy passed me running at full speed into the waiting arms of his father, who had just stepped off an airplane returning from the Middle Eastern conflict. Tears of joy flowed freely as the little lad nestled his head on the neck of his strong and grateful dad.

You and I are a bit like that father and son. We, too, are away from home. But one day, we, ourselves, will run into the strong and loving arms of our heavenly Father who redeemed us with the precious blood of His only begotten Son.

CODE WORD: WELCOME

What a warm and wonderful feeling to be genuinely welcomed by someone! Jesus, with His arms outstretched, welcomes you, promising, "Whoever comes to me I will never drive away" (John 6:37 NIV).

Lord, I run to You right now . . . into Your waiting and welcoming arms. In Jesus' name, amen.

[The Jews] asked [the healed man], "Who is the Man who said to you, 'Take up your bed and walk'?"

JOHN 5:12

For thirty-eight years, the man had been unable to walk—and now he was walking. What had happened? How? Who? Who had healed him?

When we praise Jesus for the gracious, kind, wonderful, or amazing things that He has done in our lives—when we share our stories with others—those people will also wonder and often even ask out loud, "What happened? How? Who?"

Who transformed your life? Who put your family back together? Who brought you peace in the midst of such tragedy? Who enabled you to be victorious over your addiction? Who gave you hope in the darkness of your circumstances? Who?

When they ask, we can tell them about Jesus, who blesses His people with transformation, healing, peace, strength, hope; who brings good out of apparent bad.

You have experienced Jesus' power and love, so now extol Him and extend Him to others.

CODE WORD: WHO

Challenge yourself today to live your life in such a way that others see Jesus in you and begin to ask, "Who is this that gives you such purpose, joy, and peace, even in the midst of struggle?"

Lord, use my weaknesses and my challenges today as an opportunity for others to see You in me so they might ask, "Who?" And I might answer, "Jesus!" In Your name, amen.

"Bring all the tithes . . . and try Me now in this . . . if I will not open for you the windows of heaven and pour out for you such blessing that there will not be room enough to receive it."

MALACHI 3:10

D o we truly trust that our Shepherd's gracious care will continue?

Our finances generally indicate the level of our trust and the condition of our spiritual pilgrimage.

One-third of Jesus' parables address our stewardship of the income and material possessions He blesses us with, yet God never emphasizes our giving. He always focuses on our receiving, even here in His instruction about the tithe. God said, "Bring all the tithes" (Malachi 3:10). Why? To support the church or missionary work? No! At issue is God's desire to open for us "the windows of heaven" and pour out His blessings on us.

God promises to provide abundantly for those people faithful in their stewardship of the blessings He gives them.

CODE WORD: TRUST

Your own personal stewardship of all God blesses you with begins with trusting Him. You came into this world naked, and you will not take a single one of your possessions with you when you leave this world. Everything belongs to the One you can trust completely to continue to provide what you need.

Lord, I trust You today to meet all my needs, not according to my riches, but "according to [Your] riches in glory by Christ Jesus," my Lord (Philippians 4:19). In His name, amen.

We know that all things work together for good to those who love God, to those who are the called according to His purpose.

ROMANS 8:28

J ust because you are in a storm doesn't mean you aren't in the middle of God's will. You see, God uses storms to refine His disciples' faith. Still, when difficulties come we can find ourselves asking a multitude of questions that have no satisfying answers.

One evening some time ago, I woke up in the night feeling very nauseated. I went into the bathroom and grabbed a bottle of that famous pink medicine. Just before taking a dose, I noticed the red letters on the side of the bottle: SHAKE WELL BEFORE USING. And what does that have to do with life's storms?

From time to time we get too settled in our everyday life, too focused on ourselves, or too unaware of the Lord's presence with us or desires for us. Then our loving God comes along. Why? To shake us well before using us!

CODE WORD: SHAKE

Our top priorities in life have a way of settling at the bottom of our everyday activities and responsibilities. If you are being shaken today, maybe God is realigning your priorities—and maybe He is doing so because He is about to use you in an amazing way.

Lord, help me keep You as my top priority even though the busyness of life constantly swirls all around me. In Jesus' name, amen.

It is good for me that I have been afflicted,
That I may learn Your statutes.

PSALM 119:71

O ne of the most comforting thoughts in all of Scripture is the truth that—by God's gracious and sovereign power—things that happen in our life work together for our good.

As we each look back over our lives, how many disastrous events actually, in the end, worked out for good? Realize that these happy endings occurred neither by accident nor by blind chance, but because of God Himself at work in each of our lives.

In this fallen world where we make poor and sinful choices, we experience many things that are bad. But God can take our mistakes and messes and work them together for our own good (see Romans 8:28). King David realized this truth. The poignant words of Psalm 119:71 show that he learned that God has purpose in our afflictions. And that purpose is our good.

CODE WORD: RETROSPECT

Look back over your life. Do you see that many of those things that were so unpleasant at the time actually worked together for your good? Trust God, that whatever you are going through right now will end up working to make you more like Jesus and more trusting of the Father.

Lord, not everything that comes my way is good. But I thank You that You still weave even the afflictions in my life together for my good and for Your ultimate glory. In Jesus' name, amen.

Three times I was beaten with rods; once I was stoned; three times I was shipwrecked.

2 Corinthians 11:25

Today's Scripture is just the beginning of the list of the hardships Paul suffered as he preached the message of Jesus. In Romans 8:28 Paul said, "We know that all things work together for good to those who love God." Had he said "some things," "many things," or even "most things" work for our good, it would be more palatable. But "all things"?

Yes, all things. Individually, those things are hard. Eating a bowl of baking soda or flour would be disgusting, but put them together, add a few other ingredients, stir them up, put them in the oven, and they turn into biscuits. And I love biscuits!

Similarly, when worked together in the tapestry of the cross, all things—not necessarily good in and of themselves—come out for our good and God's glory.

Code Word: COMPREHENSIVE

This word means "encompassing everything"—and everything includes the good, the bad, and, yes, the ugly. Our great God takes every aspect of your life—in all three categories—and works them in you and through you for your own good. May that truth help you choose hope.

Lord, help me choose to see my own struggle and today's difficulties as tools in Your hands as You mold me into Your own image for my own good and for Your glory. In Jesus' name, amen.

"You are the salt of the earth. . . . You are the light of the world."
MATTHEW 5:13–14

Scripture says we are to confront our culture with His truth spoken in love. And that is not an easy assignment, because our culture is schizophrenic.

We listen as ministers pray at presidential inaugurations and then punish high schoolers who want to pray at football games or valedictorians who want to end a graduation speech with a prayer. We cry out for law and order in the streets yet in our classrooms teach kids that there are no moral absolutes. We speak of the dire need to keep families together while we liberalize divorce laws. And on . . . and on . . . and on.

And this is the culture we believers are called to confront with God's truth spoken in love. Too many of us believers remain hunkered down behind stained glass walls, isolating ourselves from the world. But Christ has called upon us to be salt and light in this dying and dark world—before He returns.

CODE WORD: FLAVOR

It only takes a little salt to flavor a huge mass. Think baked potato! You can make a difference. Flavor someone's life today.

Lord, while some speak the truth but not in love, and others speak in love and not the truth . . . help me speak Your truth in love today. In Jesus' name, amen.

Let the words of my mouth and the meditation of my heart
Be acceptable in Your sight,
O LORD, my strength and my Redeemer.

PSALM 19:14

Too many times (but maybe fewer as we get older?) we hear words coming out of our mouths that we can't believe we actually said. Oh, to be able to hit a "delete" key for our spoken words.

Even more appalling is the thought that those words reflect our hearts. Thankfully, Jesus, through His work on the cross, can transform our hearts at the same time that He helps us learn to better control our tongues. Only Jesus in us can help us honor Him and bless others with our words. Once we have surrendered our will to His, our words and our heart work together in beautiful harmony.

And by God's grace that harmony will yield actions that bless people around us and bring Him glory. When we focus on God and on following Him, God-glorifying rather than salvation-earning actions follow.

CODE WORD: WORDS

What comes out of your mouth today is really issuing from what is in your heart. And your words can hurt or heal even more than your actions. Watch your words!

Lord, put a guard over my mouth and a seal over my lips that today what comes forth verbally might honor You and be a blessing to others. In Jesus' name, amen.

"Unless one is born of water and the Spirit, he cannot enter the kingdom of God."

JOHN 3:5 ESV

How are we initially filled with the Spirit? How are we "born of . . . the Spirit"?

First, we confess. We acknowledge to God that, in our thoughts, words, and deeds, we have fallen far short of His standards. But 1 John 1:9 says, "If we confess our sins, He is faithful and just to forgive us our sins and to cleanse us from all unrighteousness."

Next, we crown Jesus the Lord of our lives. Romans 14:9 says, "Christ died and rose and lived again, that He might be Lord of both the dead and the living." Remove yourself from the throne of your heart and welcome Him there.

Finally, we are to claim by faith that God's love and forgiveness are real. As Romans 3:28 says, "A man is justified by faith apart from the deeds of the law."

Confess! Crown! Claim! "Be filled with the Spirit" (Ephesians 5:18)—and then be a blessing to those around you.

CODE WORD: POWER

The power for fueling a purposeful, joyful life is not in a program, a plan, or a procedure. That power is in a Person: the Holy Spirit is in you right now. Think of it. All power in *you*!

Lord, mold me, make me, fill me, use me so that others might see You in me today. In Jesus' name, amen.

"I am the good shepherd."

JOHN 10:11

Almost every animal has some type of defense mechanism. Rabbits can run. Cats can scratch. Dogs can bite. Bees can sting. Goats can butt. Skunks . . . well, you get the point. But sheep? They are defenseless. They are totally unprepared for fight or for flight. They cannot fight other animals, and they cannot outrun those who seek them for prey. They are virtually helpless.

The person without the Lord Jesus Christ is like a sheep, helpless to get to the sheepfold of salvation on his own. The man without the Lord Jesus Christ is on his own against "the wiles of the devil" (Ephesians 6:11), and he is ill equipped for fight or flight. A person without Jesus cannot defeat the devil, with his subtle deceit and perfectly tailored temptations.

We all need a Good Shepherd to protect us.

CODE WORD: HELPLESS

You and I are helpless. Not only are we hopeless without Christ, but we are helpless to ward off temptations and the enemy that constantly seeks to keep us defeated. Be encouraged. You have a Good Shepherd who is leading you and protecting you from your enemy even when that enemy is you!

Lord, without You I am helpless against the enemy. I can do nothing in my own strength to stand strong in the face of temptations. But with You I can be strong—and I thank You for Your strength and protection. In Jesus' name, amen.

"Ask, and it will be given to you; seek, and you will find; knock, and it will be opened to you."

MATTHEW 7:7

God speaks to us through His Word, making Scripture memorization and meditation essential to our relationship with Him, and we speak to God through our prayers of praise, petition, and intercession. Without the Bible, our prayer has no solid direction. And without prayer, the Bible is only half a conversation. Like ham and eggs, the Bible and prayer go hand in hand.

In the Sermon on the Mount, Jesus encouraged us to "ask . . . seek . . . knock." Prayer is effective when it is aligned with God's will for our lives. If we know His will in a matter, we ask according to His will. If we do not know God's will, we are to seek to know it. If we know God's will but the answer has not come, we are to knock until the door opens.

Ask. Seek. Knock.

CODE WORD: COMMUNICATION

Communication is a huge part of our everyday lives, especially in this day of social media. Whatever the means we use, communication is a two-way street. That is true about communication between you and God: He speaks to you through the Bible, and you speak to Him through prayer.

Lord, thank You for the times I hear Your voice as I read Your Word. Thank You for the times You clearly reveal Your will and Your way for me. In Jesus' name, amen.

Let the word of Christ dwell in you richly.

COLOSSIANS 3:16

J esus first commands us to ask, to simply present our petition before God. Then He commands us to press our petition. This is the prayer we pray when we do not know the will of God, and we seek until we find it. This is a deeper, more mature level of prayer because we put self aside.

We are motivated not by self-interest but by a deep desire to know God's will. Pressing our petition involves an intense search for the heart of God, and that search involves Bible reading. That is one reason why Paul admonished us to "let the word of Christ dwell in you richly" (Colossians 3:16).

God's promise is that we will find His perfect will if we don't give up. He does not want to veil His will from us; He desires that we know it and walk in it.

CODE WORD: SEEK

Again, God has no intention of veiling His will from you. Whatever situation or decision you face, He wants you to know His will even more than you yourself want to know it! Remember that you have His promise that you will find . . . when you seek with your whole heart.

Father, I want to know Your perfect will for my life. Thank You for the promise that I can know Your will when I seek it. In Jesus' name, amen.

Hear my prayer, O Lord,
And give ear to my cry.

PSALM 39:12

Ask. Seek. Knock—and to continue knocking requires tremendous perseverance. We pray—we persist with a petition—when we feel certain we know the will of God in a matter but have not seen it come to fruition yet. We keep on asking . . . keep on seeking . . . keep on knocking and hold to the promise that "it will be opened to you" (Matthew 7:7).

In a sense, God deals with us the way we deal with our own children. When they are small, we teach them to ask for what they want. When they get older, we teach them to seek after their own desires. And when they are young adults, they best learn how to knock. We encourage them to show real earnestness and to knock until doors are opened for them.

After all, Jesus promises: "It will be opened to you."

CODE WORD: KNOCK

Perhaps you have a vague sense that a certain thing may be God's will for your life. If so, then keep on knocking. Don't give up! Keep knocking at the door, and God promises that in His good and perfect time, He will open the door to you.

Lord, I believe You will reveal to me the specifics of Your will. I am knocking, and I will continue to knock—as You encourage me to do—until the door is opened. In Jesus' name, amen.

"Though [the neighbor] will not rise and give [three loaves of bread] to him because he is his friend, yet because of his persistence [the neighbor] will rise and give him as many as he needs."

LUKE 11:8

A t times in our Christian experience, we ask God in prayer for certain things, and it seems He does not answer us—but He always answers in one way or another.

Sometimes God's answer is direct: we pray and almost immediately and/or quite specifically we see the answer we requested. Other times our request is denied: God answers, but He denies our request because He knows what is best for us. There are also times when the answer is delayed: God seems to put us in a holding pattern, and the answer eventually comes according to His timetable instead of ours. And then there are answers that are different from what we expected. Just because He answers our prayers in a different manner than we anticipated does not mean our prayers are not answered. Bottom line, keep asking.

CODE WORD: ANSWER

Have you ever asked somebody for something and gotten no response, positive or negative? That never happens when God is the Someone you are asking. God always answers prayers.

Lord, thank You that You can see past today and answer my prayers according to the big picture of Your good plans for my life. Help me to always line up my requests with Your Word and Your will for my life. In Jesus' name, amen.

The king [Darius] spoke, saying to Daniel, "Your God, whom you serve continually, He will deliver you [from the lions]."

DANIEL 6:16

We meet the Old Testament hero Daniel as a young Jewish boy in exile, and we watch him grow up, serve God with steadfast devotion, and impact both a pagan Babylonian culture and a pluralistic Persian one.

Daniel lived out a message of hope in God, confident that the Lord would protect him, provide for him, and save him. Today we call this message about God's grace "the gospel," and it still impacts lives and transforms cultures. In fact, the apostle Paul called the gospel the "power of God" (Romans 1:16), and the Greek word for *power* is the word from which we derive *dynamite*. This power is God's free gift to us. We can do nothing to save ourselves.

This gospel power—not pickets, petitions, protests, or politics—is our only hope today.

CODE WORD: DYNAMITE

There is supernatural power within each of us just waiting to be released. It is the life-changing power—the dynamite power—of the gospel, of the good news of Jesus' death and resurrection.

Lord, my journey of faith is not about my getting more of You, but Your getting more of me. May I walk through this day fully yielded to and guided by You. Help me to live in Your power and to love with Your love. In Jesus' name, amen.

And they were all filled with the Holy Spirit.

ACTS 2:4

T he outward evidence that we are filled with the Holy Spirit manifests itself in our relationships with others. One of those manifestations is the countercultural trait of submission.

Now, this element of submission does not involve any sense of inferiority; it is not a matter of weakness or unworthiness. Submission is what the apostle Paul was driving at when he said we who follow Jesus should "esteem others better than [ourselves]" (Philippians 2:3). This attitude was never more beautifully illustrated than in the Upper Room when our Lord Himself became the Servant and washed His disciples' feet. Consider, then, whom God has placed in your life. Ask God to give you His eyes and His heart as well as His guidance regarding both whom to serve and how.

Believers who are being controlled by God's Spirit within will have a song in their hearts, will be thankful always for all things, and will be willing to submit in their dealings with others.

CODE WORD: SUBMIT

Many people shudder at the word *submit*. It goes against our very nature to "line up under" someone else. But doing a simple—yet not necessarily easy—sacrificial act is a way to be like Jesus. If we want to be great in God's kingdom, we must—as Jesus said—learn to be servant of all.

Lord, help me today to look for ways to serve those with whom I come into contact. I am never more like You than when I am washing someone's feet. In Jesus' name, amen.

FEBRUARY

And the peace of God, which surpasses all understanding, will guard your hearts and minds through Christ Jesus.

PHILIPPIANS 4:7

The fruit of the Spirit is love, joy, peace, longsuffering, kindness, goodness, faithfulness, gentleness, self-control. Against such there is no law.

GALATIANS 5:22–23

Fruit is the delectable product created in us by the life-giving energy of the Vine.

The Lord Jesus taught that we cannot bear fruit unless we abide in Him (John 15:4). The fruit we bear as believers is evidence of His abiding in us and His sitting on the throne of our lives.

Before we get to that fruit, do you notice what appears to be a grammatical error in today's verse? Note carefully: "The fruit of the Spirit is love, joy, peace. . . ." The truth is, the fruit of the Spirit is love. Period. The nine fruits listed are evidence of the life of Christ—the love of Christ—within us.

Furthermore, the fruit reveals who we are rather than listing what we do. Here we see the principle of being before doing. What we do is determined by who—or whose—we really are!

CODE WORD: ABIDE

The dictionary defines *abide* as "to make one's abode, to dwell, to reside, to continue." Your Christian character and your Christlike conduct are the results of Christ abiding in you and your abiding in Him.

Lord, only by Your abiding in me can I bear fruit for Your kingdom. Keep me, I pray, continuously abiding in You that fruit may be abundant. In Jesus' name, amen.

FEBRUARY 2

"Peace I leave with you, My peace I give to you."
JOHN 14:27

S ome people seem to radiate the love, joy, and peace of Jesus. Paul, in Galatians 5:22, said that the "fruit of the Spirit is love, joy, peace . . ." The word translated "love" here is *agape*, God's own love, the highest level of love, a love that always seeks the other's good. Everything good—including the other fruit of the Spirit—issues out of God's love.

Next comes joy, and it is the inner joy Christ spoke about on His last night with His disciples: "These things I have spoken to you, that My joy may remain in you, and that your joy may be full" (John 15:11).

Peace is another characteristic obvious in the life of the Spirit-controlled believer, and inner peace is God's very special gift to us (see John 14:27). The Spirit's presence in us gives us peace, and so does knowing that we are loved and forgiven by God and that we will spend eternity in heaven with our Lord.

When we abide in Jesus, the love, joy, and peace of His Spirit become obvious in how we live.

CODE WORD: COUNTENANCE

Look in the mirror. What does your countenance say about your life in Christ? Do people see His warm love in your eyes? Do you smile with His joy? Are your muscles relaxed in His peace? When Jesus is Lord of your life, that truth will be written on your face by His very presence in you.

Lord, may I so abide in You that others will see in me Your love, Your joy, and Your peace. In Jesus' name, amen.

Jesus . . . went about doing good.

ACTS 10:38

O ne fruit of the Spirit, longsuffering (Galatians 5:22–23), is synonymous with patience or, in Greek, "far from anger." Like all the other fruit, longsuffering arises from love. Love's greatest triumph is not always in what love does but—more often than not—in what love refrains from doing.

The conduct of one who is abiding in Christ is also characterized by kindness. Since Christ shows His kindness to us (Ephesians 2:7), we are to pass this kindness on to others.

Paul then introduced the fruit of goodness. Jesus "went about doing good" (Acts 10:38). There is a genuine sense of goodness about those who are abiding in Christ and being controlled by His Spirit.

This orderly conduct is seen in the lives of many who have come to Christ. Where once they may have been impatient, now they have supernatural patience. Where once they were self-centered, now they show kindness toward others. Where once they may have been self-seeking, now their actions are characterized by goodness.

A Spirit-filled person truly glorifies God.

CODE WORD: CONDUCT

Our patience, our kindness, and our goodness manifesting themselves in our actions speak louder than any words we could say about who God is.

Lord, in the normal traffic pattern of my life today, please show me someone to whom I may show kindness . . . for Your sake. In Jesus' name, amen.

"Blessed are the meek, for they shall inherit the earth."

MATTHEW 5:5

C an anything better be said of someone than that he or she is faithful to God? Such faithfulness is a fruit of the Spirit (Galatians 5:22–23). When the Spirit enables us to be faithful to our ever-faithful God, we please and glorify Him.

Another fruit of abiding in Christ is gentleness (translated "meek" in Matthew 5:5), and this Greek word speaks of power on a leash. The powerful animal has come under the control of its master. The wild stallion can be ridden.

Finally, we come to self-control. Only the Spirit can help us, for—like Paul—"the good that I will to do, I do not do; but the evil I will not to do, that I practice" (Romans 7:19). Like all the fruit, self-control is the result of the Holy Spirit's life within us.

When we come to know Christ as our personal Savior, the Father sends the Holy Spirit not only to seal us, indwell us, and fill us, but also to produce fruit in us.

CODE WORD: CHARACTER

Faithfulness, gentleness, and self-control are fruit of a character grounded in the Word of God and obedient to His commands. Ask yourself, then, "Am I faithful? Am I gentle? Do I exhibit self-control?" These traits all issue forth when we abide in Christ and His love.

Lord, like an animal that has come under control of its master, I surrender to Your lordship over me today. I will come when You call and go where You send me. In Jesus' name, amen.

The effective, fervent prayer of a righteous man avails much.

JAMES 5:16

When we pray, we should first thank God for all He has done for us. Next we praise Him for who He is. We tell God that we love Him. We praise Him for His goodness, patience, mercy, and grace.

Prayers of intercession follow praise. Here we approach God's throne on behalf of others. We pray for family members, friends, political leaders, people we know who need Christ, and even people who have spoken against us.

After intercession, we move to petition. We ask God for whatever He has put on our hearts.

Then, we arrive at the prayer of communion. This is prayer that goes beyond mere words; this is when, with an open Bible, we are still and listen for God to speak to us.

One more note: the Bible and prayer are inseparable. When you call to Him as you read His Word, He will answer you and teach you "great and mighty things, which you do not know" (Jeremiah 33:3).

CODE WORD: INTERCEDE

To intercede means to intervene on behalf of someone else. Pick out a person today for whom you will intercede in prayer on their behalf.

Lord, bring that "someone" to my mind right now who is in need of intercessory prayer today. In Jesus' name, amen.

FEBRUARY 6

*If you confess with your mouth the Lord Jesus and believe in
your heart that God has raised Him from the dead, you will be
saved.*

ROMANS 10:9

What do you need to do in order to be saved?
Admit your sin. In humility, acknowledge to yourself and
to God that you don't live up to your own standards, much less His.

Believe that Jesus is the Son of God who suffered the punishment for your sins when He died on the cross and who, rising from the dead, defeated sin and death.

Confess your faith that God raised Jesus from the dead after He took on the consequences of your sin and died on the cross in your place.

Salvation has been accomplished: Jesus was perfect and yet sacrificed His life so that His shed blood would guarantee the forgiveness of every single one of our sins (see Hebrews 9:22). Our part is to believe!

CODE WORD: ABC

Unlocking the door of salvation is as easy as ABC. A—Admit you are a sinner. B—Believe in Christ, that He was crucified to save you from eternal punishment for your sins, and that He rose again, Conqueror of sin and death. C—Confess to others that Jesus Christ is your Savior and Lord.

*Lord, I A—admit that I have sinned and fallen short of
Your glory. So I place my B—belief, in You right now. And
I C—confess that You are the one and only Lord. In Jesus'
name, amen.*

We do not know what we should pray for as we ought, but the Spirit Himself makes intercession for us with groanings which cannot be uttered.

ROMANS 8:26

W hen we get alone with God, it is crucial that we pray with integrity.

As you probably know, prayers that get results are not long, drawn-out orations. They are pointed and powerful, asked with intensity and approached with integrity. They are prayers like that of the publican: "God, be merciful to me a sinner!" (Luke 18:13). These fervent prayers are like the one Simon Peter prayed while sinking in the sea: "Lord, save me!" (Matthew 14:30). They are prayers like Jacob's: "I will not let You go unless You bless me!" (Genesis 32:26).

It is not the length of your prayers but the depth of your prayers that makes them effective—the depth of your trust that God hears you and that He will answer according to His good and perfect will. It is not the prayers that issue forth from your head, but the prayers that spring from your heart that are effective as you are genuine and vulnerable. So approach God with integrity, do those things He commands, and then pray with passion and intensity.

CODE WORD: PASSION

God is not so much interested in the purity of your words as He is in the passion of your heart. Words are just that . . . words . . . unless they issue from a burning heart.

Lord, I will not let You go unless You bless me today. In Jesus' name, amen.

The Word became flesh and dwelt among us, and we beheld His glory, the glory as of the only begotten of the Father, full of grace and truth.

JOHN 1:14

W ho is this "Word" spoken of in the opening verses of John's gospel? Was it another prophet or a holy angel? No, this Word is God Himself, stepping out of heaven, clothing Himself in human flesh, and entering human history.

Other Scripture passages expand on this truth about Jesus, the God-man. Paul, for instance, wrote that Christ "is the image of the invisible God. . . . For by Him all things were created . . . and in Him all things consist . . . that in all things He may have the preeminence" (Colossians 1:15–18). And the writer of Hebrews related that He "purged our sins [and] sat down at the right hand of the Majesty on high" (1:3).

The incarnation, that period of thirty-three years when God invaded earth clothed in flesh, is one of the most amazing displays of divine love ever.

CODE WORD: INCARNATION

Think of it—Christ set aside His own glory and clothed Himself in human flesh to identify with you. Amazing condescension.

Lord, I am never more like You than when I humble myself and serve others. In Jesus' name, amen.

We do not have a High Priest who cannot sympathize with our weaknesses, but was in all points tempted as we are, yet without sin.

HEBREWS 4:15

F or forty days Jesus fasted and was tempted by the devil. Jesus overcame each of three temptations by quoting Scripture to the enemy. Knowing God's Word will also keep us from sinning when we are tempted.

Besides, God promises to "make the way of escape, that [we] may be able to bear [the temptation]" (1 Corinthians 10:13). The word picture is of a mountain pass: soldiers who are surrounded by an enemy suddenly see an escape route to safety through a mountain pass.

Similarly, none of us needs to succumb to the temptations when we feel surrounded. Jesus will make a way of escape. Many who have fallen into sin did so willfully because they refused to take the path of escape that the Lord put before them.

"Blessed is the man who endures temptation" (James 1:12)—and the Lord will help him do exactly that.

CODE WORD: ESCAPE

When temptation comes knocking today—and it will—there will always be a way of escape. Watch for it, and be sure to take it.

Lord, thank You for rescuing me time and again from circumstances and situations that could well have resulted in a fall. In Jesus' name, amen.

"Watch and pray, lest you enter into temptation."

MATTHEW 26:41

O n the evening before His crucifixion, Jesus agonized in prayer in Gethsemane's garden. It was the ultimate decision point: would Jesus do His own will or the will of His Father and go to the cross? Before He entered into that spiritual wrestling match, Jesus gave us some good advice when He said to His disciples, "Watch and pray, lest you enter into temptation" (Matthew 26:41).

Prayer has to do with the internal source of temptation, our own desires. Prayer keeps us connected with God so that His desires are our desires. Watching has to do with the external force of temptation, the deception. We are to be alert, to watch out. The bait has a hook in it. If we look closely enough, we will see the enticement for what it is—a trap!

God is not the author of temptation. Nor is Satan (James 1:13–14). Nor is any situation. As God's Word teaches, the root of our temptation lies within us.

CODE WORD: WATCH

As you pray today, make equally sure that you also "watch." Watch and pray. Why? So that you do not enter into temptation.

Lord, help me today to not simply look but to see, to watch. Guide me. Lead me. In Jesus' name, amen.

Do not be deceived.

GALATIANS 6:7

P aul and James were very direct: "Do not be deceived" (Galatians 6:7; James 1:16). The Greek word we translate as "deceived" describes a ship that strays from its designated route.

It is possible for us to be deceived about our sin—even blind to it—and get off course. We can't minimize our sin by saying it's not as bad as other people's, and we can't dismiss our sin by saying that everyone else is doing it. Sin—any and all sin—is so serious that it required Jesus to die on the cross.

Also, don't be deceived about salvation. We are saved not because of our own good works or sincere efforts, but entirely by God's grace when we simply put our faith in Christ (Ephesians 2:8–9).

And, finally, don't be deceived about Jesus. God in human flesh, Jesus paid the penalty for our sin by dying on a cross. Then He rose from the grave on the third day, victorious over sin and death! Hallelujah! What a Savior!

CODE WORD: DECEPTION

Satan is the father of all lies and the master of all deception. So be on guard today and do not believe his lies about your sin, your salvation, or your Savior.

Almighty God, today and every day may I submit to Your lordship, resist the devil, and hold to Your promise that he will flee from me. In Jesus' name, amen.

FEBRUARY 12

I am doing a great work, so that I cannot come down. Why should the work cease while I leave it and go down to you?

NEHEMIAH 6:3

Those were the words of Nehemiah when his longtime nemesis made a final attempt to derail him from completing reconstruction of the walls of Jerusalem.

So often—and whatever the task—something seemingly harmless comes along, and we can lose focus. We get off on side streets. I often did that literally when my family and I lived in Fort Lauderdale. Called the "Venice of America," the city has more than two hundred miles of waterways. Each time I tried to beat the (car) traffic by taking a side street, I ended up on a cul-de-sac, going in a circle, or—worse—sitting in a dead end at a canal.

A side street may appear to be a good thing, but the good is the enemy of the best. So keep focused—a laserlike focus like Nehemiah—and stay off the side streets!

CODE WORD: ENEMY

Remember that often something that is good is the enemy of God's best for you. Stay off the side streets and don't settle for anything less than God's best.

Lord, as I come to intersections today, help me stay on the main road. In Jesus' name, amen.

"My food is to do the will of Him who sent Me, and to finish His work."

JOHN 4:34

N o one ever finished his assigned race stronger than the Lord Jesus. When the finish line for His race was in sight, He said to His Father, "I have finished the work which You have given Me to do" (John 17:4).

The enemy tried his best to get Jesus sidelined from His divine purpose. A tool of Satan, the crowd jeered, mocked, spat, and shouted, "If You are the Son of God, come down from the cross" (Matthew 27:40). But Jesus kept focused and faithful. And in the end, He solemnly proclaimed victory: "It is finished!" (John 19:30). And, to prove it, three days later He arose from the grave.

Finish strong! Maybe you have fallen down on the track. Get up. Stay focused. And finish the race. Our Lord is standing at the finish line with His arms outstretched. Keep running toward Him!

CODE WORD: FINISH

This word can bring great satisfaction. In many ways it is not so much how you start the race—or even how you run it—as much as it is how you finish.

Lord, help me as I run my own race to keep my eye on the finish line and finish strong. In Jesus' name, amen.

*"Blessed are those who hunger and thirst for righteousness,
For they shall be filled."*

MATTHEW 5:6

Jesus' Sermon on the Mount begins with a series of verses we know as the Beatitudes. Our verse for today is planted squarely in the middle of this section. All the Beatitudes coming before it point to it, and all the ones following it issue out of it. It is important to understand what our Lord is driving home here: these are the Be-attitudes and not the Do-attitudes. Being comes before doing, for what we do is always determined by who we are.

The Beatitudes are not a set of rules, like the Ten Commandments, by which we are to live. The Ten Commandments have to do with actions; the Beatitudes have to do with attitudes. The Ten Commandments have to do with conduct; the Beatitudes have to do with character. Why is it imperative that we believers incarnate these Beatitudes into our very being? It is because our actions flow from our attitudes, and our conduct issues out of our character.

CODE WORD: BE

It is more important who you are—and whose you are—than what you do. Why? Because the attitudes of our hearts determine the actions of our hands. Being comes before doing . . . always.

Father, help me remember who I am today—a child of the King! You love me, Christ lives in me, and You refine my character for Your glory and my good. In Jesus' name, amen.

As [Jesus] prayed, the appearance of His face was altered, and His robe became white and glistening. . . . Two men talked with Him, who were Moses and Elijah, who appeared in glory and spoke of His decease which He was about to accomplish at Jerusalem.

LUKE 9:29–31

Of Christ's incarnation, the apostle John wrote, "We beheld His glory, the glory as of the only begotten of the Father" (John 1:14).

John was undoubtedly reminiscing about the Transfiguration when he penned these words. He had been there with his brother, James, and Simon Peter when our Lord was transfigured: "His face shone like the sun, and His clothes became as white as the light" (Matthew 17:2).

The incarnation of Christ should not be thought of only as a past, historical phenomenon. In a sense, Jesus' amazing incarnation can be a continuing experience, because this same Jesus who was born in Bethlehem, who took on human flesh, longs to be born again in our hearts. His desire is to take up residency in you, to dwell in your heart today. Have you invited Him?

CODE WORD: RESIDENCE

Where do you live? What is your address? When you go about your home today, think about this—Christ lives in you! That is His residence. Make Him feel welcome and at home in you today.

Lord, thank You for the realization that You are truly alive in me today. In Jesus' name, amen.

As by one man's disobedience many were made sinners, so also by one Man's obedience many will be made righteous.

ROMANS 5:19

God placed Adam and Eve in a beautiful garden and gave them dominion over it. But then they listened to the devil's lie and disobeyed God. As a result, they were expelled from the garden. Gone was the significance they once enjoyed as its caretakers. Ever since then, human beings have been searching for significance. Not all the world's possessions, power, or prestige can satisfy. We can find significance only in a restored relationship with our Creator.

And that relationship is possible because of the gift of God's only Son, the Lord Jesus Christ. Jesus laid aside His glory and clothed Himself in human flesh. He who had never sinned became sin for us. He died our death . . . so we could live His life. He took our sin . . . so we could take His righteousness. If you are looking for significance, your search for significance will end only when you look to Jesus.

CODE WORD: SEARCH

We are all on a search; some of us just haven't realized it yet. We are in search of our lost estate, a search for meaning and significance in life. God said, "You will seek Me and find Me, when you search for Me with all your heart" (Jeremiah 29:13).

Lord, before I ever thought about searching for You, You were searching for me. You said in Luke 19:10 that You came to seek and save those who are lost. In Jesus' name, amen.

[We are] justified freely by [God's] grace through the redemption that is in Christ Jesus . . . that He might be just and the justifier of the one who has faith in Jesus.

ROMANS 3:24–26

O nly the work of Jesus on the cross makes us able to stand before our holy God. In an act of indescribable grace, God credited to our account the righteousness of Christ. A human court of law may acquit or pardon, but only a righteous God can—and will—take someone guilty like me, justify me, and treat me as if I have never sinned.

We are "justified freely by His grace through the redemption that is in Christ Jesus" (Romans 3:24).

And God extends this gift of salvation not in response to any of our human efforts. Paul taught that grace is "the gift of God" (Ephesians 2:8), a blessing freely given by the Father.

CODE WORD: JUSTIFIED

No court of law can justify a person. A court may acquit or pardon someone, but it is powerless to justify anyone, to make that person's life just as if the crime never happened. But God can . . . God did . . . and God still does justify us: He treats us as if we have never sinned.

Lord, You will not—in fact, You cannot—see my sin, for I have been cleansed and justified by the blood of Your Son, my Lord, Jesus. Your unmerited favor truly is amazing grace! In Jesus' name, amen.

Give to Your servant an understanding heart to judge Your people, that I may discern between good and evil.

1 KINGS 3:9

When God asked him what he wanted, Solomon knew what he needed most if he was to govern effectively, so he asked God to give him "an understanding heart" (1 Kings 3:9). Aware of what he lacked, Solomon humbly said, "I need wisdom."

Solomon had the greatest education money could buy, but he recognized the difference between knowledge and wisdom. Knowledge is the accumulation of facts; wisdom is the ability to use those facts to make good decisions.

Solomon could have asked for anything, but he knew that what he needed most was for God to work in him. And isn't that true for all of us?

Solomon said, "Lord, I know You have spoken to David, but I want an 'understanding heart' so that I, too, might hear Your voice and be guided by Your wisdom." If we have a heart that can hear from God, what else would we ever need to live life well?

CODE WORD: DIFFERENCE

Think today of the difference between knowledge and wisdom. Almost anyone can acquire knowledge if they study enough. But wisdom comes from God. There is a huge difference.

Lord, You said if anyone lacked wisdom, that person could ask of You, and You would give it liberally. I take You at Your word and ask now for "an understanding heart." In Jesus' name, amen.

As you therefore have received Christ Jesus the Lord, so walk in Him.

COLOSSIANS 2:6

By God's grace, we come to recognize ourselves as sinners in need of a Savior—and that is the beginning of walking through this life with Jesus.

I remember when our first child was first learning to walk. She would reach up her chubby little hand, grab my index finger, and hang on tight. She would take a step or two, let go, and fall to the ground. I learned right away an important lesson about my role: instead of just letting her hold my finger, I needed to hold her hand. Then, when she stumbled, I could hold her up and keep her from falling.

In the same way, our salvation is not a matter of our holding on with all our might. God holds us with His strong hand. When we stumble, He keeps us from falling. We are secure. If Christ can give us new life—and He did—He can surely keep us in that new life.

CODE WORD: HOLD

Can you see yourself right now being held securely in the arms of Christ? It is not about you holding on to Him. He is holding you.

Lord, thank You for Your promise that You will never let me go. Hold me tight. In Jesus' name, amen.

"They will see the Son of Man coming on the clouds of heaven with power and great glory."

MATTHEW 24:30

We are secure in this life because God holds us, and by His grace, we are also secure in the next life. The Lord will keep us until that grand and glorious day when He will come again—"on the clouds of heaven"—to receive us as His own. On that day the church—the body of Christ—becomes the bride of Christ.

We are living now in the great "until." Until Jesus, sacrificed on Calvary, returns as the almighty and eternal King. Until then, we can trust Him and know we are secure in the now life and in the next life.

Your salvation is, from first to last, all the doing of Him who loves you and gave Himself for you. Since He is the origin of it all, you can trust Him with the outcome of it all. As songwriter Fanny Crosby once said, "Blessed assurance, Jesus is mine!"

CODE WORD: UNTIL

Live today in this word—*until!* Keep looking for that day; your blessed hope is His glorious appearing!

Lord, it may be at dawn when the day is awakening or when the blackness of midnight will burst into light at the sign of Your coming. "Even so, come, Lord Jesus." In Jesus' name, amen.

The LORD is my shepherd;
I shall not want.

PSALM 23:1

Have you ever thought about the fact that Psalm 23:1 does not say, *"A lord is my shepherd"*? The psalm says, *"The LORD is my shepherd."* There is no other Lord; He has no peer.

You speak of Washington, and I can speak of Lincoln. You speak of Beethoven, and I can speak of Handel. You speak of Alexander, and I can speak of Napoleon. But when it comes to Christ, He stands alone—without peers. There is only one Lord!

And only the records of heaven will verify how many individuals through the centuries have laid down their lives and gone to their deaths, martyred because they insisted on the truth of these first two words in Psalm 23: "The LORD." These faithful gave their lives because they were convinced there was only one Lord, and His saving name is Jesus.

Our God is still preeminent: He is the one and the only Lord.

CODE WORD: ONE

Everyone and everything lines up behind this number—One. Jesus is the Alpha. He is the only Lord. And Jesus plus nothing always equals everything you need. Is Jesus number One in your life?

Father, in all I say and do today, may I acknowledge You as my one and only Lord. Rule today from the throne of my heart, and where You lead, I will follow. In Jesus' name, amen.

There was a man of the Pharisees named Nicodemus, a ruler of the Jews. This man came to Jesus by night.

JOHN 3:1–2

Nicodemus waited until dark before going to Jesus. Why? We don't know. Maybe he didn't want to invite the criticism of his ecclesiastical colleagues. Perhaps so many people wanted an audience with Nicodemus that he was busy from sunrise to sundown. Or maybe Nicodemus desired uninterrupted time with Jesus, who, during the day, was often surrounded by massive crowds. I like to think that Nicodemus was so consumed with seeking truth that he simply couldn't wait until morning.

Whatever the reason, one thing is certain. Underneath his long robes was a heart—perhaps like yours—hungry for something more. This good Pharisee had an abundance of head knowledge, and he was doing all he knew to do to keep God's law. What Nicodemus needed was a new heart that honored Jesus as Savior and Lord, a new heart that rested in God's love so he could stop trying to earn both God's acceptance and his way into heaven.

CODE WORD: URGENCY

There will not always be adequate time for you to come to Jesus. Like Nicodemus, be so consumed with a passion for truth that you sense the urgency right now!

Lord, thank You that anytime, anywhere I can approach You, and You are always there. Forgive me for not being more urgent in simply coming to You, even at night. In Jesus' name, amen.

"I am the good shepherd. The good shepherd gives His life for the sheep."

JOHN 10:11

Jesus, our preeminent and perfect Shepherd, is protective. Without a shepherd, sheep cannot find their way to clean water or nourishing pastures. The shepherd keeps a constant vigil for wild animals and other threats to his flock's safety. A good shepherd also goes after the single sheep that strays from the fold.

Furthermore, without a shepherd, sheep are virtually helpless. They cannot defend themselves, make their way through treacherous mountain passes, or run fast enough to escape a predator. And just as sheep need a shepherd, we human beings need our Good Shepherd.

One more thing. Have you ever noticed that a shepherd is always out in front of the sheep, never behind them? Shepherds lead sheep; they do not drive sheep the way cattle ranchers drive their cattle. Our Lord will never force us or drive us against our will. Instead, He will lead us. And we can—in faith—follow the Shepherd who gave His life for us, His sheep.

CODE WORD: PROTECTION

Live today in the reality that this great and good Shepherd is your Protector.

Lord, thank You for protecting me physically, emotionally, and spiritually. I know that nothing enters my life without passing through God the Father and God the Son—and if what I experience gets that far, there must surely be a good purpose in it. In Jesus' name, amen.

When Jesus saw [Peter], He said, "You are Simon, son of John.
You will be called Cephas" (which means "Rock").

JOHN 1:42 HCSB

When Jesus first met Simon Peter, He performed a play on words in Greek. *Simon* means "a small pebble." The fisherman was rather a small pebble. But Jesus knew that Peter would become a great rock in His kingdom. Jesus saw Peter's potential, and He sees yours. God sees us not so much for what we are now but for what we could be—if, that is, we receive a vision from Him and rely on Him to help us fulfill it.

In fact, one of the spiritually beneficial things that a vision brings to a person's life is a greater dependence on the Lord. Our visions should be so God-sized that there is no way for us to accomplish them unless God intervenes.

We don't need to fear having too big a vision when God is calling us, guiding us, and empowering us to achieve that vision.

CODE WORD: POSSIBILITY

Jesus is not looking at you today for who you are or what you are, but for who you could be and what you could accomplish. There is so much possibility in you, and He sees it.

Lord, I am amazed that You see possibility in me. Help me let it out for Your glory. In Jesus' name, amen.

Give thanks to the Lord, for he is good;
his love endures forever.

1 Chronicles 16:34 niv

From time to time on life's journey, we find ourselves standing at temptation's corner, that place where we are called to make a decision as to which way we should turn.

Whenever we find ourselves at the intersection, we can be sure the tempter is always there seeking to lure us into making a wrong turn. To keep from doing so, we should ask ourselves, "If I go this way, say this thing, or do this deed, will I thank God afterward?"

The Bible says, "In everything give thanks; for this is the will of God in Christ Jesus for you" (1 Thessalonians 5:18). We are called upon to give thanks "in everything." (Not *for* everything but *in* everything, and that's an important distinction.) If we are tempted toward an attitude or action for which we could probably—or even definitely—not give God thanks in the aftermath, then we should avoid it.

Code Word: THANKS

If you are tempted to turn a certain way at one of life's intersections today and you cannot give thanks for doing so in the aftermath, then don't do it.

Lord, help me get to the place where I can thank You "in" everything, not necessarily "for" everything. In Jesus' name, amen.

"Let your light so shine before men, that they may see your good works and glorify your Father in heaven."

MATTHEW 5:16

As we've seen, Paul admonished the believers—and us—to give thanks to God in all things, despite the frustration, grief, loneliness, or pain we're experiencing. Second, Paul said, we are to do all things "in the name of the Lord Jesus" (Colossians 3:17).

Imagine ourselves, standing on temptation's corner, prayerfully asking ourselves, "Can I do it in Jesus' name?" Can I speak what I'm about to speak in Jesus' name, as His representative? Can I do what I want to do in Jesus' name, as His representative? Am I representing Jesus well in what I'm reading, watching, or listening to?

Asking ourselves, "Can I do it in Jesus' name?" would make a huge difference in what came out of our mouths, in what we did, and in what we watched, what we read, and what we listened to. So much of what we say and do might be quite different—for our good and God's glory!

CODE WORD: NAME

You bear the very name of Jesus Christ. This is why you are called "Christian." Wear His name with honor, and guard against anything that can't be done "in His name."

Lord, Your name is my name. Help me reflect Your character today in all I say and do. In Jesus' name, amen.

Whatever you do, do all to the glory of God.

1 Corinthians 10:31

True believers find joy in giving glory to God through their attitudes, their actions, and their words—and that is a helpful guideline when we face a decision. Will what we might say and what we're tempted to do glorify God? Asking ourselves that question would undoubtedly keep us from doing some of the things we do and saying some of the things we say!

When you find yourself at temptation's corner—and that happens several times a day—stop. Don't just rush through the intersection or make a hasty and potentially wrong turn. Ask yourself three important questions: Can I thank God for what these words or actions will result in? Can I do or say this in Jesus' name? Can I do or say this for God's glory?

Asking ourselves these questions will enable us to more readily give thanks in all things, be God's light in this world, and give Him glory in all we say and do.

Code Word: GLORY

His glory is at stake. Remembering this will help you make right decisions. Ask yourself today when decisions come your way, "Can I do this for God's glory?"

Lord, help me bring glory to Your matchless name in what I say and do today. In Jesus' name, amen.

"But when he came to himself, he said, 'How many of my father's hired servants have bread enough and to spare, and I perish with hunger!'"

LUKE 15:17

R epentance comes from a Greek word that literally means "to change one's mind." It is a change of mind that affects a change of will and, in turn, brings about a change of action. This process is beautifully illustrated in Jesus' story of the prodigal son.

After finding himself broke and broken, in the company of a bunch of hogs in a pigpen, the son "came to himself" (Luke 15:17). This change of mind brought about a change of will: "I will arise and go to my father" (v. 18). Once he had changed both his mind and his will, his actions were sure to change as well. Thus, we read, "he arose and came to his father" (v. 20).

Repentance is a change of mind . . . that leads to a change of will . . . that leads to a change of actions. That was certainly the case for the young prodigal.

CODE WORD: MIND

Repentance begins in your mind. Think on this today. A true change of your mind will result in a change of your will, and a change of action will follow.

Lord, give me the mind of Christ today. Think through my mind and change any thought processes that need changing in me. In Jesus' name, amen.

I [Nehemiah] told [the people in Jerusalem] of the hand of my God which had been good upon me, and also of the king's words. . . . So they said, "Let us rise up and build."

NEHEMIAH 2:18

N ehemiah was able to form a team of workers because, first, his goal of rebuilding was conceivable. He made sure those around him could easily understand the plan and picture where they were going and how they were going to get there. Next, Nehemiah made sure his goal of rebuilding was believable. These men and women had been discouraged for years and needed to believe in something again. Hear his challenge: "Let's do it. We can get this done. The hand of our God is with us" (author's paraphrase). The people not only conceived the goal, but they believed it could be accomplished. One reason is because Nehemiah made sure his goal was achievable. This goal was not outside their reach: they definitely could rebuild the broken walls. It was conceivable, believable, and, importantly, achievable.

CODE WORD: GOAL

What are you striving to become? Do you have any God-given goals? Conceive it. Then believe it. You can achieve it.

Lord, You said without faith it is impossible to please You. Help me believe that I might achieve for Your glory. In Jesus' name, amen.

MARCH

"Have I not commanded
you? Be strong and of
good courage; do not be
afraid, nor be dismayed,
for the LORD your God
is with you wherever you
go."

JOSHUA 1:9

We put bits in horses' mouths that they may obey us, and we turn their whole body.

JAMES 3:3

F aith begins with knowing Christ, and it continues with sowing consistent behavior that honors and glorifies our Lord. This consistency manifests itself in our talk and our walk, our conversation and our conduct.

Too often, however, our speech does not honor God because we don't have control over our tongues. A horse controlled by a bit can be of great use, but an unbroken horse can do great damage. Just as a horse needs to come under its master's control, our tongues need to come under our Master's control. A horse can't bridle itself. The one who mastered it puts the bridle on.

Try as we might, we can't control our tongue through our own efforts. After all, what we say actually originates in our hearts, not our mouths. When we yield ourselves to the control of our Master, the Lord Jesus Christ, our speech can honor Him as well as bless others.

CODE WORD: CONSISTENCY

Watch carefully your conversation and your conduct today. Make sure they are consistent.

Lord, bridle my tongue today for my good and for Your ultimate glory. In Jesus' name, amen.

"Not one of them falls to the ground apart from your Father's will."

MATTHEW 10:29

Jesus was talking about tiny field sparrows, two of which sold for a single copper coin, yet our gracious Lord—our Good Shepherd—provides for them. And, Jesus pointed out, He who provides for the birds—and who cares infinitely more about you and me—will also provide for our needs.

Are you living free and joyful in the knowledge that you have a heavenly Father who is attentive to your needs?

CODE WORD: ATTENTIVE

If our great God sees a sparrow fall to the ground, how much more aware is He of what you need today? Find peace in knowing that His eyes are on you. He is waiting to show Himself strong and faithful.

Lord, as I go about this day, please remind me in a hundred ways that You are much more attentive to me than I am to You—and teach me to live more attentive to You. In Jesus' name, amen.

Flee from idolatry.

1 Corinthians 10:14

You shall have no other gods before Me" (Exodus 20:3). God could not be more specific. He demands preeminence. Allowing Him to rule on the throne of our hearts is to be the priority of every believer's life. When we love the Lord with all our heart, soul, and mind, we are amazed by how our faithful God provides "all these [other] things" (Matthew 6:33).

The ancient Hebrews, however, tended to stray from God and worship other gods. A "god" is anyone or anything that enjoys our primary devotion. Some make a god of their possessions; there is nothing wrong with possessing things unless they begin to possess us. Others find their god in promiscuity; sex has become the god many worship in our modern world. Politics is the god of some. Others bow at the altar of pleasure in our sports-mad and entertainment-crazed world. But God warns, "You shall have no other gods before Me." He must have priority over everything in our lives.

Code Word: PRIORITY

Search your heart today. Are there any "gods" in your life taking priority over the Lord? He does not share His glory.

Lord, as I go about this day, You are my priority in life. May the meditations of my heart and the words of my mouth honor You. In Jesus' name, amen.

"If you love Me, keep My commandments."

JOHN 14:15

L ove is something we do. In the Bible, love is always equated with action. What evidence of our love for God do people see when they look at us? Do they see us obeying Jesus' commands to love God and other people, to forgive, to live with integrity, or to treat others the way we want to be treated?

Only those of us who love God and choose to trust that there is purpose in life can understand the deep truth of Romans 8:28, which tells us "that all things work together for good to those who love God." Only those of us who love God can rejoice always and give thanks in all circumstances (1 Thessalonians 5:16, 18).

When we love God, we know He is using all the circumstances of our lives for our good.

CODE WORD: MODEL

Despite the Hollywood portrayals, love is something we do, not something we feel. In fact, love is always equated with action. God models His love—and continues to love us—with His actions: He gave Jesus to die for us, and He gave His commandments to guide us. We show our love when we act in obedience to His commands.

Lord, I love You—and I want to love You today not just with my words but also with my actions. Help me be Your hand of love extended to someone today. In Jesus' name, amen.

God, who is rich in mercy, because of His great love with which He loved us, even when we were dead in trespasses, made us alive together with Christ (by grace you have been saved).

Ephesians 2:4–5

Remember the childhood excitement of opening gifts around the Christmas tree? We did not pay for those gifts. We did nothing to earn them. We simply received them. In contrast, we earn and deserve our wages; we don't earn or deserve a gift. If we did, it would be a reward, not a gift.

"The wages of sin is death" is the bad news in Romans 6:23, and the good news is this: "The gift of God is eternal life in Christ Jesus our Lord."

How is this good news possible in light of the bad news? Because Jesus dealt with the bad news. Sin means death, but Jesus died our death on the cross, paying the penalty for our sin. So our part is to receive this God-provided and free gift by faith, because we have been saved by grace.

Code Word: GIFT

Many miss Christ for the simple reason that they are too proud to receive a free gift. The gift of eternal life cannot be earned and is not deserved. Accept it.

Lord, I humbly accept Your free gift . . . no strings attached. In Jesus' name, amen.

When all our enemies heard of it . . . they perceived that this [successful rebuilding] work was done by our God.

NEHEMIAH 6:16

The walls of Jerusalem had been broken down, and Nehemiah led the rebuilding effort. What exactly was his motive? He did not keep it a secret: "that we may no longer be a reproach" (Nehemiah 2:17). Nehemiah's primary motive was to honor and bring glory to God, not to himself.

There are a lot of broken-down walls in what were once vibrant personal relationships. It is possible to rebuild those walls by, first, acknowledging your personal responsibility in the wreckage. Then work with the person you're reaching out to. You cannot rebuild a relationship alone. Once you've reestablished that relationship, keep working to protect and further strengthen it.

Relationships are hard work. The truth is, all of us need help from outside ourselves. We all need to acknowledge that the hand of our God is good upon us, and our ultimate purpose should always be to bring Him glory.

Just as Nehemiah gave God glory for the rebuilt walls.

CODE WORD: RECOGNITION

Live your life so that others will recognize that God is working in you and through you.

Lord, let others see You in me. I want You to do something through me, not for me. In Jesus' name, amen.

Submit yourselves to every ordinance of man for the Lord's sake, whether to the king as supreme, or to governors.

1 Peter 2:13–14

W hat are we to do when our king—or congress or president— makes a decree that contradicts God's commandments? After all, our Lord admonished us to be subject to those governmental authorities that He, in His sovereignty, allows to rule over us. The apostle Paul was clear: everyone should "be subject to the governing authorities" (Romans 13:1).

Yet the Bible gives clear instructions: we are compelled to disobey civil law when it is in direct opposition to God's laws. Remember Exodus 1: civil law—the Pharaoh's edict—called for the Hebrew midwives to destroy the lives of all Hebrew boys at their birth, but that was in direct contradiction to all the Bible says about the gift of life. So the midwives disobeyed: they delivered the Hebrew babies and protected them.

We are to honor God by refusing to obey any directive that is diametrically opposed to His laws.

Code Word: LAW

You are a citizen of a nation of laws. But, first and foremost, your "citizenship is in heaven." God's laws in His Word always trump all others.

Lord, like those before me, I must obey You rather than men. Guide me. In Jesus' name, amen.

"Shall not the Judge of all the earth do right?"
GENESIS 18:25

Y es! Absolutely! Our holy God can only judge fairly, wisely, and rightly: there is no partiality, deceit, or bias in Him.

And our holy God judges not on superficial externals. Certain judgments may not look "right" to us, but this matter of God's right judgments calls for a spiritual EKG for you and for me and for every Christ-follower. After all, who are we to judge anyone about anything—and to judge wisely? We would depend mostly on the externals—and our fickle hearts could impact our judgment as well.

Only God sees and knows what is really in the heart of man. That's why there will be many people in heaven some of us never thought would be there. And there will be some people we expected to see in heaven but may not. Yet, when all is said and done, we can be confident that "the Judge of all the earth" will do what is right!

CODE WORD: EKG

Perhaps you have been wired up and had an EKG exam to monitor your heart. Allow God to give you a spiritual EKG upon your heart today.

Lord, You examine my heart in light of Your Word, and I am in need. I never have to wonder that You will do what is right. In Jesus' name, amen.

MARCH 9

[Jesus] began to be sorrowful and deeply distressed.

MATTHEW 26:37

S oon after arriving at Gethsemane, Jesus spoke to His disciples from His heart: "My soul is exceedingly sorrowful, even to death. Stay here and watch with Me" (Matthew 26:38). Jesus, who had already done so much for His disciples, made this simple request in the hour of His greatest need.

Knowing His death was but hours away, Jesus went only a few steps before He fell to the ground, lay prostrate, and started to pray: "O My Father, if it is possible, let this cup pass from Me; nevertheless, not as I will, but as You will" (v. 39).

After a while, Jesus returned to the disciples—and they were sound asleep. Then came from Jesus' mouth these piercing words that issued forth from a breaking heart: "What! Could you not watch with Me one hour?" (v. 40).

We see in Gethsemane the intellect, the emotion, and the volition of this God-man's heart. What a Savior!

CODE WORD: NEVERTHELESS

Have you arrived at this word in your own experience? Lord, let this pass from me, *nevertheless*, not my will but Yours be done.

Lord, help me live in this word today—nevertheless. Not as I will, but as You will. In Jesus' name, amen.

"He who hears My word and believes in Him who sent Me has everlasting life, and shall not come into judgment, but has passed from death into life."

JOHN 5:24

First, if you have named Jesus as your Savior and Lord, the judgment of sin has already taken place. Our sins were judged in Christ as He hung on Calvary's cross. He suffered in our place, bore the wrath of God's judgment of sin in His own body on the cross, and paid the penalty for our sins: "[God] made Him who knew no sin to be sin for us" (2 Corinthians 5:21).

God judged the believer's sin outside the city walls of Jerusalem when Christ died our death so that we could eternally live His life. That's why the apostle Paul could say, "There is therefore now no condemnation to those who are in Christ Jesus" (Romans 8:1). No condemnation! No judgment! I want to shout my thanks to God! Christ died in my place and took in His own body the punishment of my sins. Because of His sacrifice, I am acquitted.

CODE WORD: ACQUIT

I'm sure the two most welcome words of someone on trial are "not guilty." Because of Christ these are the words each believer will one day hear.

Lord, remind me throughout the day of the price paid that I may hear these words "not guilty." In Jesus' name, amen.

One thing I do, forgetting those things which are behind and reaching forward to those things which are ahead, I press toward the goal for the prize of the upward call of God in Christ Jesus.

PHILIPPIANS 3:13–14

The powerful FedEx company, headquartered in Memphis, Tennessee, exploded into worldwide prominence by focusing on one service: overnight deliveries. Southwest Airlines is one of the nation's leading air carriers today primarily because of its single focus on low-cost coach travel with on-time performance. And who could talk about the importance of focus without mentioning Starbucks? When other coffee shops were busy dispensing a variety of food services, Starbucks opened coffee shops that focused on— of all things—coffee!

Focus is fundamental to spiritual success as well as business success. Keeping the main thing the main thing in the midst of a multitude of other things is always a challenge for a follower of the Lord Jesus Christ. A key element to spiritual growth, however, is that ability to keep focused on Jesus—and it's a skill we can sharpen.

CODE WORD: FOCUS

"Set your mind on things above" (Colossians 3:2). Focus! Focus on Christ today, and everything else will come into clearer view.

Lord, guard my mind today from anything or anyone that might take my focus off of You. In Jesus' name, amen.

Let us run with endurance the race that is set before us.

HEBREWS 12:1

Why is focusing on Jesus so important? First, focus puts our priorities in order. Notice that Paul said, "This one thing I do . . ." (Philippians 3:13, KJV). Not ten things, not five things, not even two things. But "this one thing I do." What is your top priority in life? Once you define your priorities, they begin to define you.

Second, focus gives us a forward mindset. Too many of us spend too much time looking around or, worse yet, looking behind. Focus enables us to, like Paul, be "reaching forward to those things which are ahead" (v. 13). Paul's focus resulted in a wise forgetfulness about the past and enabled him to make sure his reach continued to exceed his grasp.

Third, focus brings passion to our lives. Paul said, "I press" (v. 14). This word *press* communicates an intense endeavor, like a hunter pursuing his prey. Paul was pressing because he had focus; he had "one thing" as the main priority in life.

CODE WORD: FIRST

Make sure your priorities are in proper order today, that He is your first priority. Join Paul in saying, "One thing I do . . ." and run your race "with endurance" (v. 13) toward your goal.

Lord, I seek You first today . . . and whatever is next is a distant second. In Jesus' name, amen.

Let us run . . . looking unto Jesus.

HEBREWS 12:1–2

I n addition to putting our priorities in order, giving us a forward mindset, and bringing passion to our lives, focus helps us know where we are headed. Paul said he was pressing toward "the goal." The Greek for "goal" is *skopos*, from which we get our word *scope*. Like the scope on a rifle, focus enables us to get our goals and priorities in the crosshairs. Focus enables us to know where we are going and how we are going to get there.

Focus is the fountainhead of successful living. It helps us to begin our task with the end in mind. So what is your goal in Christian living? What is in the crosshairs of your scope? When we begin to focus on Christ alone, He will help us put our priorities in order, give us a forward look, fuel our passion, and let us clearly see the end from the beginning.

Keep your life in focus by keeping Christ in the center of it.

CODE WORD: SCOPE

Keep this word picture in your mind today—the crosshairs of a scope. And make certain Jesus's priorities remain at the center of your target.

Lord, I am keeping Your priorities square in the middle of my focus today. In Jesus' name, amen.

If the LORD is with us, why then has all this happened to us?

JUDGES 6:13

Nothing was going right for Paul and Silas. They had been arrested, beaten, and jailed (Acts 16:16–26). It would have been easy for them to ask, "If the LORD is with us, why then has all this happened to us?" (Judges 6:13).

But instead of railing at the Lord, assuming the martyr's role, or feeling sorry for themselves, Paul and Silas chose to sing a song of praise, and doing so changed their perspective. Often when things are not going our way, our own attitude can make a tough situation even more difficult. But giving thanks to God and singing His praises will alter our perspective.

When we find ourselves in our own prisons at midnight, let's choose to sing a song in the night. There is power in praise. Singing a song in the night will change our perspective, improve our attitude, and strengthen our trust in God, who will use even these circumstances for our good.

CODE WORD: WHY

Often when we are in a difficult situation, the question is not "why?" but "what?" Ultimately we learn from this to grow in grace.

Lord, help me to "sing a song in the night" even when things do not seem to be going my way. In Jesus' name, amen.

Where there is no revelation, the people cast off restraint;
But happy is he who keeps the law.

PROVERBS 29:18

O r, as the King James Version says, "Where there is no vision, the people perish." In other words, individuals who have no vision—no perception of what they could be—seem to have no real direction in their Christian pilgrimage.

Before every great undertaking, someone has a vision for the task ahead. The football coach has a game plan before the kickoff, a vision of what he wants his team to accomplish. The army commander develops a battle plan before the fighting begins. Artists have a conception in their minds before they start putting paint on the canvas.

What a difference vision makes in life. Too many of us Christians are just going to meetings, following schedules, simply existing—and something is missing. That something is a vision, a perception of what God wants us to be and do, and vision is vital to a life that honors God and fulfills you.

CODE WORD: VISION

Where are you headed? Think about it. Without a personal vision of what God wants you to be and do, you will lack direction in life. God has a purpose and a plan just for you.

Lord, make known to me Your purpose and Your plan for my life. In Jesus' name, amen.

"'You shall love the LORD your God with all your heart, with all your soul, and with all your mind.' . . . 'You shall love your neighbor as yourself.'"

MATTHEW 22:37, 39

W hen we truly capture the vision of what God wants us to be and do, that vision serves to define our activity, both short-term and long-term. Many people find it helpful to formulate a one-sentence vision statement for their lives. This becomes the lens through which they view their choices and make their decisions.

Churches need such vision statements as well. For example, one church's vision statement says they are making "a great commitment to the Great Commandment and the Great Commission." This guideline enables church leaders to keep their ministries moving in the decided-upon direction. The vision statement reminds ministry leaders that if something does not foster loving God, loving others, and leading men and women to a saving faith in Jesus Christ, that activity does not make their priority list.

Even as vision brings definition to our lives—to our paths through life—it also defines the decisions we need to make along the way.

CODE WORD: DEFINITION

When you know where you are going and how you are getting there, it brings definition to your life. It defines your task, who you are, and why you are here.

Lord, use me to help others desire Your purpose and plan for their lives. In Jesus' name, amen.

Your eyes have seen my unformed substance;
And in Your book were all written
The days that were ordained for me,
When as yet there was not one of them.

PSALM 139:16 NASB

The birth of a vision is like the birth of a baby. The first step is conception: the Holy Spirit plants in our hearts a seed of what God wants us to be. The next stage is gestation: we think about the vision and pray about it for a period of time. After a while those close to us see that something is happening, that we are pregnant with a vision.

Next comes the birth: the vision is out there for all to see. Then comes the most important step for leaders, the stage of adoption, when the vision is adopted by others. Leaders know the next stage is growth, and growing a vision costs time and money. Next follows maturity, when all we dreamed of and prayed for reaches maturity. Finally there comes the stage of reproduction, when previous visions are reproduced into newer and more expanded visions, and the dream goes on.

CODE WORD: CONCEPTION

Your vision can never grow to maturity unless it is first conceived in the secret place alone with God. Ask Him to plant the seed of His plan for your life in your heart and mind.

Lord, I am wide open to You. Make Your perfect will for me known. I will follow. In Jesus' name, amen.

You will show me the path of life;
In Your presence is fullness of joy.

PSALM 16:11

I n this life—for nonbelievers and believers alike—not much of significance really happens without a vision. Energy and motivation are lacking. The broken-down walls of Jerusalem were rebuilt when Nehemiah's vision gave him a purpose and a plan. The dynamic efforts of a construction work party kicked in when he returned to lead in the rebuilding of the destroyed walls. Vision is what brings a dynamic and a sense of purpose to our work as well as to our witness as believers.

In addition to a definition, a design, and a dynamic, a personal, God-given, and prayed-over vision gives direction to a person's life and a path for that person to follow. "Where are you headed?" is a valid and important question for everyone. We have an answer to that question when we have a personal vision, and when a personal vision is guiding our lives, bringing a new sense of dynamic, we also experience a new sense of purpose and direction.

CODE WORD: DYNAMIC

God wants you to be energized with a fresh sense of a new dynamic in life. It comes with a clearly defined vision of who you are and what you can become.

Lord, when I am in the middle of Your will, there is not only full joy but a new dynamic for living. In Jesus' name, amen.

By grace you have been saved through faith, and that not of yourselves; it is the gift of God.

EPHESIANS 2:8

Ours is a "do it yourself" culture, and I don't mean just building bookcases. I mean salvation: many people today believe they can earn God's favor by their own good deeds. But biblical truth about salvation is countercultural.

Paul was very direct: God "chose us" (Ephesians 1:4). Salvation is both God's work and His gift. In other words, our salvation is "by grace" (2:8). God does not save us in response to any good works we perform, any bad things we avoid, or any prayerful begging we do. We receive salvation wholly because of His grace: He chooses to bless us with His unmerited and undeserved favor.

God sending His Son to die was purely an act of His grace.

CODE WORD: GRACE

What is grace? We define *grace* as "unmerited favor," and we define G-R-A-C-E more specifically as God's Riches At Christ's Expense. And the good news is, it's His free gift to us.

Lord, You didn't send Your Son to die on the cross for any other reason than Your amazing grace. Thank You for not giving me what I deserve—punishment for my sins—and thank You for giving me what I don't deserve—mercy and forgiveness. In Jesus' name, amen.

"He who believes and is baptized will be saved; but he who does not believe will be condemned."

S alvation is a great and gracious provision, and every person responds to it in one of three ways: reject, accept, or neglect.

Some individuals flat-out reject the gospel message. They deliberately refuse the gift of eternal life.

Other people accept the free gift of eternal life. They hear the gospel message, believe it, receive it by faith, repent of their sins, and trust in His finished work to save them. Though undeserving, I thank God that I am counted among these.

Finally, some individuals neither reject the gospel nor accept it. They simply neglect the divine offer of salvation; they simply put off the decision. They think there will always be adequate time to name Jesus as their Savior before they die. They are deceived.

We who were dead in our sin have been saved only "because of [God's] great love with which He loved us" (Ephesians 2:4).

CODE WORD: NEGLECT

Neglect is the deadliest of all deceptions . . . not to decide is to decide!

Lord, how shall I escape if I neglect so great a salvation You offer? In Jesus' name, amen.

Cleanse me from secret faults.

PSALM 19:12

Every sin we try to cover up, God will uncover. Aware of that fact, Paul reminded us that when "the Lord comes, [He] will both bring to light the hidden things of darkness and reveal the counsels of the hearts" (1 Corinthians 4:5). But the good news is this: every sin we uncover, God will cover. Consider this Old Testament promise: "He who covers his sins will not prosper, but whoever confesses and forsakes them will have mercy" (Proverbs 28:13). So go ahead! Confess and forsake your sin, and God will cover it with the blood of Christ. There is no good reason to wait!

God cannot and will not see our sins after we have been cleansed by the blood of Jesus Christ. That's why, in his powerful, penitent prayer, David did not long for his salvation to be restored, but his joy. "Restore to me the joy of Your salvation" was his passionate desire and plea to God (Psalm 51:12).

Confession, forgiveness, joy, revival—it's a divine progression!

CODE WORD: SECRET

Is there a secret sin hidden in your heart today? Get it out now. Confess it to Christ and forsake it. God is waiting to separate it from you in the sea of His forgetfulness.

Lord, restore to me the joy of my salvation. In Jesus' name, amen.

"I am the resurrection and the life. He who believes in Me, though he may die, he shall live."

JOHN 11:25

T his one statement is among the boldest and most definitive acknowledgments of our Lord's deity—and Jesus Himself spoke these words to Martha, the grieving sister whose brother, Lazarus, had just died.

Jesus' proclamation to Martha is hugely significant to us because the resurrection is what separates our Lord from a thousand other gurus and prophets who have come down the pike. This bold declaration is followed, in the next verse, by life's bottom-line question. After declaring Himself to be the Resurrection and the Life, the Victor over death, our Lord turned to His hearers—and to us—and asked, "Do you believe this?" (John 11:26).

Have you ever wondered how Jesus spoke this question? Did He ask, "Do YOU believe this?" Or did He ask, "Do you BELIEVE this?" Or perhaps He asked the question thus: "Do you believe THIS?" Whatever way He said it, His question is personal, pointed, and precise . . . because He loves us.

CODE WORD: INFLECTION

I often wonder how Jesus inflected the sentences recorded from His lips by the gospel writers. Think about it. He most likely asked, "Do YOU believe this?"

Lord, Yes, I do believe . . . help my unbelief. In Jesus' name, amen.

Believe on the Lord Jesus Christ, and you will be saved.

ACTS 16:31

Jesus wants to know more than if we give intellectual assent to his claims. He wants to know if we believe He is God's Son, if we will name Him the Lord of our lives, and if we will love and serve Him with all our heart, soul, mind, and strength.

It is one thing to know the gospel story intellectually. It is another to attempt to conform to its moral standards. One can even offer apologetics and solid arguments for Christianity's legitimacy. It is, in fact, possible to do any of these things without being transformed by grace and through faith. We can know a lot about Jesus without truly knowing Him.

Jesus said, "I am the resurrection and the life" (John 11:25). Do you *believe* this? Have you transferred your trust from relying on your own human efforts to trusting in Him alone for salvation, purpose, fulfillment, and joy?

CODE WORD: ON

"Believe ON the Lord Jesus Christ." Do you believe IN Him or ON Him? You believe *in* Abraham Lincoln but not *on* him; you don't trust your life to him. There is a world of difference between believing in something or someone and believing on them.

Lord, I do believe ON You. I trust You totally with every detail of my life today. In Jesus' name, amen.

O Death, where is your sting?

1 CORINTHIANS 15:55

D o you believe Jesus' claim about deity? Whenever our Lord used the phrase *I am*—and John included seven such statements in his gospel—people around Jesus recognized it as an expression of His deity. He was the same God, named "I AM," who spoke to Moses from the burning bush (see Exodus 3). The most fundamental belief in the Christian faith is that Jesus Christ is God Himself clothed in human flesh. Jesus is not merely a figure from history or a good moral teacher. Jesus is God.

Do you believe Jesus' claim about death? Jesus said, "He who believes in Me, though he may die, he shall live" (John 11:25). Many people live in total denial of their coming appointment with death. It is a fact: we are going to die! But Jesus has conquered death. Do you believe this?

CODE WORD: APPOINTMENT

Some of us are unable to keep appointments from time to time. But there is a date already fixed on God's calendar for you. You can't hasten it or halt it. It is one appointment you will keep, and right on time.

Lord, thank You that when I stand before You on that day, I have an Advocate, the Lord Jesus, pleading my case. In Jesus' name, amen.

I have been crucified with Christ; it is no longer I who live, but Christ lives in me.

GALATIANS 2:20

This new life in Christ is not a reformed life or an improved life or even a changed life. It is an exchanged life. We give God our old life, and He gives us one that is brand-new. The apostle Paul had died to his old self-centered life and awakened to a new life in Christ. Now filled, guided, and empowered by the Spirit, Paul was no longer persecutor, but preacher. He no longer said, "Not Christ, but I." Paul—like believers for the past two thousand years—said, "Not I, but Christ!"

Think of this awesome truth: "Christ lives in me." If we could awaken to this revelation, we would be on the way to turning our "world upside down" like those who went before us in the early church (Acts 17:6). There is no way to defeat a man who truly believes that Christ is alive and has taken up permanent residency in him.

CODE WORD: ALIVE

Arrive at this truth today: Christ is really alive in you. Let it sink in. It will make a difference in what you say, what you do, where you go, and what you watch.

Lord, not I but Christ today. Thank You for the realization that You are truly alive in me. In Jesus' name, amen.

I indeed baptize you with water unto repentance, but He who is coming after me is mightier than I, whose sandals I am not worthy to carry. He will baptize you with the Holy Spirit and fire.

MATTHEW 3:11

R epentance and faith are both gifts of God's grace. They are different sides of the same coin. They are like conjoined twins . . . vitally joined together and born at the same time.

Repentance and faith are inseparable. Repentance alone will not get you to heaven, but you cannot get to heaven without repenting. Jesus' personal mandate commands it: "Repent, for the kingdom of heaven is at hand!" (Matthew 3:2). But notice the positive motivation He gives His listeners for repenting. Jesus did not offer a "Turn or burn!" message. Instead, He emphasized the goodness of God's grace: "Repent and then enjoy fellowship with Me now and for eternity."

CODE WORD: COIN

When you handle money today, let it be a reminder to you that repentance and faith are two sides of the same coin . . . and both are the gifts of God's grace to you.

Lord, although I can't physically see You, I believe, and with "joy inexpressible." In Jesus' name, amen.

"Will You not revive us again, that Your people may rejoice in You?"

PSALM 85:6

For too many of us, it has been too long since we have experienced a visitation from heaven, a personal revival. While revival comes from the hand and heart of a sovereign God, He still invites us to pray to this end: "If My people . . . will humble themselves, and pray and seek My face, and turn from their wicked ways, then I will hear . . . and will forgive their sin" (2 Chronicles 7:14).

When what used to slither down our back alleys now parades proudly down our main streets, is it not time to pray, "Lord, visit us again with Your sovereign power"? When from much of the entertainment industry and social media we hear the raucous cries of a thousand voices calling our children to lifestyles of godlessness, we should be moved to pray for revival. And, when we can imagine hearing the sobs of our Savior, who wept over Jerusalem, weeping over our own sins, is it not time to join Isaiah of old, "Oh, that You would rend the heavens and come down" (Isaiah 64:1 NASB)?

CODE WORD: REVIVAL

This may be one of the most misunderstood words in the Christian vocabulary. Revival is that strange and supernatural visitation from God restoring us to the fullness of God's blessing and opening the door to a new beginning for each of us.

Lord, as You have in times past breathed upon our fallen world with a fresh breath of Your power, do it again . . . and let it begin in me. In Jesus' name, amen.

"Why do you look at the speck in your brother's eye, but do not consider the plank in your own eye? . . . First remove the plank from your own eye, and then you will see clearly to remove the speck from your brother's eye."

MATTHEW 7:3, 5

R evival is conditional upon the actions and heart attitude of God's people. History shows that revival begins when God's own people become convicted of sin and pray for a fresh wind of His Spirit.

God's problem today is not with the lost but with His own people. Yes, our culture is decaying, our moral fabric is tearing, and secular, godless factors pressure us from all around. But God reveals that the real issue is not with them, but with us. As Jesus said, we should not try to get a small splinter out of someone else's eye until we first remove the large beam from our own eye.

God's design for revival begins with His own people's repentance.

CODE WORD: PLANK

Today, when looking at the faults of others, let it be a reminder to look into your own life first and remove any planks that might be affecting your vision. Your standard of righteousness is never measured against anyone else's but only Christ's.

Lord, remove any plank in my own eye today so I can see others clearly through Your eyes. In Jesus' name, amen.

A broken spirit,
A broken and a contrite heart—
These, O God, You will not despise.

PSALM 51:17

God does not keep it a secret: if we want revival, we need to humble ourselves. We need to recognize our sinfulness and confess it to Him. We need to seek Him and obey Him in all things. We must also confess our spiritual pride and self-centeredness. True humility involves a broken spirit before the Lord.

Second, if we want revival, we are to pray—and not a mere recitation of prayers, but an earnest calling out to the Lord. Too many Christians can describe their prayer life with four words from Ephesians 6:12—"we do not wrestle."

Every true revival in history has resulted from heartfelt, committed prayer. That was, in fact, true from the very beginning. We read of the early church that "when they had prayed, the place where they were assembled together was shaken; and they were all filled with the Holy Spirit, and they spoke the word of God with boldness" (Acts 4:31).

CODE WORD: BROKEN

Does this word say anything about you today? When the back of pride is broken, you can soar into regions you have never known.

Lord, mold me, make me, and, if necessary, break me today that I might be more conformed to Your image. In Jesus' name, amen.

Let all those who seek You rejoice and be glad in You.

PSALM 40:16

If we desire true revival, in addition to humbling ourselves and praying, we need to "seek [God's] face" (2 Chronicles 7:14). If we spent as much time seeking God's face as we do seeking His hand, we would be on the way to revival. Much of our praying seems to be focused on seeking something from God's hand in the way of material or physical needs. Perhaps too little of our praying is consumed with simply seeking His face for spiritual revival, both personal and corporate.

God's requirements for revival also include turning from our "wicked ways." Sin that is unconfessed and therefore unforgiven is a great obstacle to revival. As Solomon reminded us, "He who covers his sins will not prosper, but whoever confesses and forsakes them will have mercy" (Proverbs 28:13). Note that it is not enough to simply be sorry for and confess our sins; we must also forsake them.

Seeking God and forsaking sins are key to revival.

CODE WORD: EXAMINE

Time for an examination. Examine your own prayer life. Think about it. Is much of it taken up with asking God to DO something for you or others? Focus today on simply seeking His lovely face.

Lord, I stand in awe before You and Your awesome love and majesty. You alone are worthy of praise. In Jesus' name, amen.

All have sinned and fall short of the glory of God.

ROMANS 3:23

The bad news in Romans 6:23 clearly stated: "The wages of sin is death." The Greek word for *sin* is an archery term meaning "missing the mark." The archer shoots his arrow at the target and misses the bull's-eye, and that describes every single one of us, for "all [of us] have sinned, and come short of the glory of God" (Romans 3:23 KJV). We have all missed the mark of our holy God's standards of behavior, and the cost of doing so is death.

A wage is what we get for doing something. It is something we have earned, something we deserve. It is something we have coming to us. The Bible says, "The wages of sin is death." Satan might try to convince you otherwise, but Satan is a liar. Sin pays its wage all right, but its wage is death, which is separation from all that is good.

When we miss the mark, the cost is great.

CODE WORD: TARGET

We all have something in common. We have all missed the target of perfection. But God has provided a remedy in Christ.

Lord, You walked this way without being contaminated by sin. Live Your life through me today. In Jesus' name, amen.

APHIL

But those who wait on
the Lord
Shall renew their strength;
They shall mount up with
wings like eagles,
They shall run and not be
weary,
They shall walk and not
faint.

Isaiah 40:31

APRIL 1

Wash me thoroughly from my iniquity,
And cleanse me from my sin.

PSALM 51:2

First John 1:7 says, "If we walk in the light as He is in the light . . . the blood of Jesus Christ His Son cleanses us from all sin." Note that *sin* is singular: it refers to our inherent sin nature that we deal with when we recognize ourselves as sinners, acknowledge Jesus as God's Son, and welcome Him as our Savior and Lord.

First John 1:9 says, "If we confess our sins, He is faithful and just to forgive us our sins and to cleanse us from all unrighteousness." Note that *sins* is plural: just because we name Christ our Savior and Lord doesn't mean we cease sinning. Although our sin was paid for by Jesus' death on the cross and we received salvation by trusting in Christ, we need to confess and forsake our personal sins in daily prayer. When we confess our sins, we open ourselves to the revival God longs to bless us with.

CODE WORD: DISTINCTION

Note that there is a distinction between your "sin" and your "sins." Your sin nature was dealt with at your conversion. You are forgiven! Your sins (plural) should be daily confessed to restore not your relationship with Christ but your fellowship with Him.

Lord, thank You that the blood of the Lord Jesus Christ cleanses me from ALL sin. In Jesus' name, amen.

*Or do you despise the riches of His goodness, forbearance, and
longsuffering, not knowing that the goodness of God leads you
to repentance?*

ROMANS 2:4

When our daughters were young, we rented a house deep
in the Smoky Mountains. One night my wife and I were
awakened by the cries of our little seven-year-old at the top of the
stairs. I bounded up the stairs, where I found her disoriented by
the darkness. Taking her by the hand, I led her downstairs into the
security of our bed, where she soundly slept the night away.

Similarly, our Lord finds us in the dark, often disoriented by
the issues of life. Then He takes us by the hand and "leads [us] to
repentance" (Romans 2:4) and relationship with Him.

In the end, what difference does it make if we drive a luxury
car, wear expensive clothes, live in a mansion, and are buried in
a mahogany casket . . . only to, in judgment, meet a God we do
not know?

If you haven't already, repent: turn to your loving heavenly
Father.

CODE WORD: KINDNESS

It is the kindness of God that leads us to repentance (Romans 2:4).
Put your hand in His hand and let Him lead you to true repentance
today.

*Lord, thank You for Your kindness to me so often when I am
least deserving. In Jesus' name, amen.*

Show me Your ways, O Lord;
Teach me Your paths.

PSALM 25:4

When we want to find God's will, it is essential that we know our Bible. After all, God will never lead one of His followers to do anything that is contrary to the Scriptures. That's one reason Paul exhorted us believers to "let the word of Christ dwell in you richly in all wisdom" (Colossians 3:16). When we know Christ, are being led by His Spirit, and are abiding in His Word, we will be more sensitive to God's guidance in our life.

For instance, God will not call you to a certain endeavor without first planting a desire within your heart to do that very thing (see Psalm 37:4). Second, just because we have a desire does not necessarily mean it is God's will for us. If it is God's will, the desire will be accompanied by an opportunity. Third, we are to keep walking according to our desires and opportunities, trusting that God will shut the door if this path is not His will.

CODE WORD: DESIRE

If a certain thing is God's will for you, then you can be sure He will plant a desire within your heart to do it. "In [His] presence is fullness of joy" (Psalm 16:11).

Lord, align my own desires with Your Word today. In Jesus' name, amen.

APRIL 4

After [Paul and Timothy] had come to Mysia, they tried to go into Bithynia, but the Spirit did not permit them.

ACTS 16:7

God does not want to veil His will from you. He is more desirous of your finding it and walking in it than you are yourself. Yes, He has a wonderful plan for your life, and He longs to make His will known to you.

God made His plan known to Paul during his second missionary journey. Paul had both the desire and the opportunity to go to Asia and Bithynia. But God shut the door: "the Spirit did not permit [him]" (Acts 16:7). God was not rebuking Paul; it was simply not God's will at the moment. Instead, God called Paul to Macedonia, and he went straight there—straight to Philippi and a great revival.

Paul sought God's will, recognized God's guidance, and yielded to it. He lived what Jesus prayed: "Not My will, but Yours, be done" (Luke 22:42). May we pray as Jesus did. May we seek and yield as Paul did.

CODE WORD: DOOR

When you open or shut a door today, let it be a reminder that sometimes God shuts doors in our lives because He has something better for us. Keep trying the doorknobs. God has His ways of opening doors we can never open ourselves.

Lord, lead me into open doors of opportunity today. In Jesus' name, amen.

"The Son of Man will come in the glory of His Father with His angels, and then He will reward each according to his works."

MATTHEW 16:27

I f we are believers, we know that Jesus stood in our place for the judgment of sin. We will, however, stand before Him, the righteous Judge, for the judgment of the saints. Paul wrote this in 2 Corinthians: "We must all appear before the judgment seat of Christ, that each one may receive the things done in the body, . . . whether good or bad" (5:10).

At this judgment—that will take place immediately after Christ's return—our works will be judged, not our sins. Our sins were judged at the cross. At this judgment, our eternal salvation is not at issue. That, too, was resolved at the cross. At this judgment, every one of us believers will give an account of ourselves before Jesus, and He will determine our rewards. And Jesus said, "I am coming quickly, and My reward is with Me, to give to every one according to his work" (Revelation 22:12).

CODE WORD: REWARD

Anyone who competes in athletics, music, or other type of competition knows the joy of receiving a reward because the most cherished awards are often a lifetime of dedication.

Lord, any reward I may receive will immediately be laid at Your feet. You alone are worthy. In Jesus' name, amen.

"I will be like the dew to [my people] Israel."

HOSEA 14:5

God promises to "be like the dew" to us, His people. What special meaning could this possibility have to be left for all posterity as a precious promise?

Where does dew come from? Think about it. You get up in the morning and step outside to get the newspaper, and all the grass in your front yard is wet with the morning dew. Does dew rise? Or does dew fall?

The answer is neither. It doesn't fall from above. Nor does it rise from below. It simply appears when certain conditions are right. We call it *condensation*.

Note that promise again—"I will be like the dew" to My people. We pray, "O Lord, fall on us with your mighty power." We pray, "O Lord, rise up to meet us." But the truth is, He is like the dew. God just shows up in power when certain conditions are right within our lives. When we are right with God and right with each other, as the disciples in the Upper Room, God manifests Himself to us in power. Yes, He is like the dew to His people.

CODE WORD: DEW

Think about this word today and let it remind you that God is like the dew. It is not that He falls on us or rises to meet us. He simply has a way of showing up, just like the dew, when certain conditions are right in our lives.

Lord, help me live today in such a way before You that Your presence and power, like the dew, show up in my life. In Jesus' name, amen.

APRIL 7

The Son of God . . . loved me and gave Himself for me.

GALATIANS 2:20

There are two truths I wish the whole world could know: God loves you, and He gave Himself for you. At a specific point in time, God's great love took Him to the cross, and there He willingly gave Himself for you.

Think of it: "He loved me." If I asked Paul how I can know that Jesus loved me, he would fire back, "He gave Himself for you." Jesus proved His love: He died in my place. His love took my sin so that I could take His righteousness. His love died my death so that I could live His life. He gave Himself for me! What a Savior!

Consider these words written by Elizabeth Clephane over one hundred fifty years ago:

I take, O cross, thy shadow for my abiding place . . .
Content to let the world go by, to know no gain or loss;
My sinful self, my only shame; my glory—all the cross.

CODE WORD: GAVE

Allow this Code Word to sink into your heart. He gave Himself away for you! Can we do less for Him? Give yourself away to someone else today.

Lord, no one has ever loved me as You love me, right now.
Love so amazing, so divine demands my soul, my life, my all!
In Jesus' name, amen.

"Do not worry beforehand, or premeditate what you will speak. But whatever is given you in that hour, speak that; for it is not you who speak, but the Holy Spirit."

MARK 13:10–11

The group of believers Jesus spoke to before His return to heaven became effective preachers of the gospel for one reason and one reason only: the Holy Spirit came upon them. When you receive Christ, the Holy Spirit comes upon you as well. In fact, He takes up residency in you. Thus, you have His power within you. There truly is no such thing as a Christian without power.

The Holy Spirit within us enables us—empowers us—to be witnesses to Jesus Christ. That is the very reason why Jesus gave us His Spirit. If we are saved, we have Christ. If we have Christ, we have the Holy Spirit. If we have the Holy Spirit, we have power. And if we have power, we will be effective witnesses of Jesus. There should be no such thing as a Christian who is not a witness.

CODE WORD: RESIDENT

Think about it. If you have trusted in Christ, He is living in you right now. All power—in you. If He is resident, allow Him to be president also.

Lord, all I need You have already provided . . . Christ in me! In Jesus' name, amen.

They stoned Stephen as he was calling on God and saying, "Lord Jesus, receive my spirit."

ACTS 7:59

What is a witness? A witness is a person who simply tells others what he has seen and heard; he shares with others about his firsthand experience. That is what we are to do: as our Lord's witnesses, we are to simply tell others about our firsthand experience with Jesus Christ. We are not recruiters trying to get people to join our club. We are not salesmen trying to persuade folks to buy our product. We are simply to be Jesus' witnesses.

Yet many people at the time of Acts marveled that God had entrusted His holy gospel to such common men and women, to individuals who had no formal training in theology or elocution. But they were true witnesses: the word translated *witness* is the same word from which we get our English word *martyr*. And many of these early believers were witnesses in the truest sense: like Stephen, they lost their lives because of their uncompromising witness to Jesus Christ.

CODE WORD: MARTYR

Let Christ's question in the gospels linger in your mind today: "Will you lay down your life for Me?"

Lord, help me live today so that others see You in my life and hear You from my lips. In Jesus' name, amen.

"I ordained you a prophet to the nations."

JEREMIAH 1:5

J ust as God ordained Jeremiah, God has also ordained you for a special task for which He has uniquely gifted you. *Ordain* means "to assign; to designate." This word is used to describe how God "set [the stars] in the firmament" (Genesis 1:17). Each one of the billions of stars has its own appointed place set by God. Just as God has set each star in the heavens, He has a job for you that no one can do quite like you can.

Ask God to show you the job He has for you: "Lord, what do You want me to do?" Are you willing to be what He wants you to be and to do what He wants you to do? If not, are you willing to be made willing? He has a plan for you that was in place even before you were born!

Know that true success and genuine fulfillment in life come with discerning God's will for your life . . . and doing it.

CODE WORD: ASSIGNMENT

Somewhere there is something for you to do that no one else can do quite like you can. You have a God-given assignment. Find it.

Lord, what would You have me to do? Where do You want me to do it? In Jesus' name, amen.

See, I have inscribed you on the palms of My hands.

ISAIAH 49:16

What walls of protection in your life have been destroyed? What burned-down gates have left you vulnerable?

The Lord Jesus left heaven to rebuild where we are broken. Through the prophet Isaiah, Jesus said, "Can a woman forget her nursing child, and not have compassion on the son of her womb? Surely they may forget, yet I will not forget you. See, I have inscribed you on the palms of My hands" (Isaiah 49:15–16).

Our Lord sees the walls of our lives that need rebuilding. What did He do about it? He came to rebuild them. Just as Nehemiah wept over the broken walls of Jerusalem, Jesus came and wept over us. Then He acted: He took our sin in His own body and died our death so we could live His life; He took our sin so we could take His righteousness.

Jesus left heaven, laid aside His glory, and came to earth in order to rebuild the broken walls of your life.

Code Word: REMEMBER

Remember, God has not forgotten you. He loves you so much that your name was inscribed on His hands when they were nailed fast to the cross. He has a long memory. He has not forgotten you.

Lord, I am overcome that when You were on the cross, I was on Your mind. In Jesus' name, amen.

APRIL 12

With God nothing will be impossible.

LUKE 1:37

W hen Jesus began His ministry, why did He call fishermen to join Him?

I have an idea, because during the fifteen years I lived on the Atlantic Coast, I got to know the legendary "Bonefish Sam" Ellis. On one fishing trip with him, I realized that what I saw in Bonefish Sam is what Jesus is looking for in His followers today.

As we left the dock, Sam always exclaimed something like, "Today's the day! A world-record bonefish is out there, just waiting for us to catch him!" This attitude is characteristic of all real fishermen. A real fisherman is always just one cast away from landing the big one.

And this is the type of person Jesus calls to follow Him. Jesus wants followers who are positive, people who see an answer in every problem, not those who look for a problem in every answer. Jesus wants followers who agree with the angel Gabriel: "With God nothing will be impossible."

A real fisherman is positive.

CODE WORD: POSITIVE

What about you . . . really? Do you usually look for a problem in every answer or an answer in every problem? Jesus uses people who are positive believers.

Lord, often my problems are indications You have a blessing for me for which I have been too busy to ask. So problems come to prompt me to ask You for what You have wanted to give me all along. In Jesus' name, amen.

"This gospel of the kingdom will be preached in all the world as a witness to all the nations, and then the end will come."

MATTHEW 24:14

My fisherman friend, Bonefish Sam, was persistency personified! By noon one day, we had been blistered by the sun and battered by the waves, and had not seen a single bonefish. I was ready to call it a day. Not Sam! We kept at it until late afternoon, until we landed a big one.

Jesus needs persistent people to transform the world. So He calls folks who have a "never give up" attitude, who keep on keeping on, regardless of the circumstances or situation. A real fisherman is persistent.

Sam was also patient, willing to try different methods. If one bait was not working, he put on another.

Jesus knew that those who followed Him would have to be patient when the situation appeared hopeless. And Jesus is still looking for people who are willing to try different methods as we fish for the souls of men. Jesus knows that a real fisherman is patient.

CODE WORD: PERSISTENT

Don't give up. God has His own ways of rewarding those who are persistent in their faith, regardless of what seems to be. It is never wrong to keep doing right.

Lord, like Jacob of old, "I will not let You go unless You bless me" (Genesis 32:26). In Jesus' name, amen.

"Go into all the world and preach the gospel to every creature."

MARK 16:15

E arlier that afternoon, Sam and I had fought a large bonefish for almost half an hour. Finally, when it was within ten feet of the boat and a few hours from the taxidermist, it jumped out of the water, spit the hook in our direction, and swam away. Sam had a fisherman's fit. I learned that day that a real fisherman is passionate. He hates to lose one!

This is exactly the type of person Jesus wants on His team. He is still calling passionate people to follow Him. He longs for His followers to—like Bonefish Sam—always hate to lose one.

The Lord Jesus still uses ordinary people like you and me to do extraordinary things for His glory. Be positive: start looking for an answer in every problem. Be persistent: never give up. Be patient: try some different methods. And be passionate: always hate to lose one!

Follow Jesus, and He will make you a fisher of men.

CODE WORD: ZEAL

Do you need to kindle the fire of passion, the zeal, that once burned in your heart? Are you really passionate about the things of God? If not, why not?

Lord, I may be ordinary, but I believe You can still do extraordinary things through people like me. In Jesus' name, amen.

Now abide faith, hope, love, these three; but the greatest of these is love.

1 CORINTHIANS 13:13

O nce someone approached Jesus of Nazareth and asked Him to identify the greatest of all God's commandments. In a single statement, Jesus reduced the Ten Commandments, not to mention all of the six hundred thirteen commandments in the Torah, down to two. Jesus said, "'You shall love the LORD your God with all your heart, with all your soul, and with all your mind.' This is the first and great commandment. And the second is like it: 'You shall love your neighbor as yourself.' On these two commandments hang all the Law and the Prophets" (Matthew 22:37–40). Those two commands address both the vertical relationship we have with God (Exodus 20:1–11) and the horizontal relationships we have with one another (Exodus 20:12–17).

Putting Christ first in our lives will help us remember His faithfulness and His power. Relying on the presence of His Spirit within us will help us obey the greatest commandments: He will help us love.

CODE WORD: HINGE

Love is the hinge upon which the door of all God's commandments turn. Think of that when you open a door today. Love supremely stands alone.

Lord, as You live Your life through me today, help me to allow You to love others through me also. In Jesus' name, amen.

"Rise, let us be going. See, My betrayer is at hand."

MATTHEW 26:46

The night before the crucifixion, Jesus needed His disciples more than He ever had. There, in the garden of Gethsemane, Jesus asked them to wait and watch while He prayed. After agonized prayer, He returned to His disciples—to find them asleep. Asking them to wait with Him again, He returned to pray: "My soul is exceedingly sorrowful, even to death. . . . If it is possible, let this cup pass from Me; nevertheless, not as I will, but as You will" (Matthew 26:38–39).

Our Lord wrestled with His Father's will, finally coming to the place when He surrendered to the salvation plan: "Not as I will, but as You will."

Then, led by Judas the betrayer, the rabble arrived to arrest Jesus, and "all the disciples forsook Him and fled" (v. 56). They ran away into the darkness of the night.

In His hour of deepest need, Jesus was forsaken, abandoned, by some of His closest friends.

CODE WORD: SURRENDER

We often hear a challenge to "commit" ourselves to Christ. But the real secret is to "surrender" yourself unconditionally to Him.

Lord, all to You I surrender, all to You I freely give. You are Lord! In Jesus' name, amen.

Choose life . . . that you may love the LORD your God, that you may obey His voice, and that you may cling to Him.

DEUTERONOMY 30:19–20

An amazing aspect of God's love for us is the fact that He gives us choices. We are not His puppets. The Almighty is not some master puppeteer pulling our strings so that we play out our lives on stage exactly as He wants.

Instead, you are God's cherished creation, not a puppet. He loves you so much that He allows you to make choices in life. While most of these choices are small, some have the potential to be life-altering.

One of those life-altering choices is your decision about whether to love God. He wants you to know of His great love for you. He loves you so much that He demonstrated that love by sending His Son. You are deeply loved by the Lord, who both knit you together and died for your sins. How will you respond?

The love you voluntarily return to Him is indescribably valuable to Him.

CODE WORD: CHOICE

You are free to choose what you want to do. But, like all of us, you want to sin. It is in our nature. But God's love reaches you right now, wherever you are and whatever you have done. Choose life. Choose Christ.

Lord, I love You, but before I ever gave thought of You, You first loved me. In Jesus' name, amen.

"You are the salt of the earth; but if the salt loses its flavor, how shall it be seasoned? It is then good for nothing but to be thrown out and trampled underfoot by men."

MATTHEW 5:13

E ach of us called by Jesus' name needs to see ourselves as salt. Little does our world system realize that our presence is—by God's grace—preventing the final collapse of our civilization and the arrival of ultimate judgment. We are the only ones who can truly flavor the lives of those around us, sometimes even sting them a bit and wake them up, and make them thirsty for the Living Water that quenches our thirst forever! Yet some mainline Christian groups are choosing to be silent about such topics as the wrath of God, His judgment, the sole authority of Scripture, and the exclusivity of the gospel message.

As salt loses its flavor like that, the world cannot be seasoned. The lost need each of us to get out among them, to preserve, flavor, sting, and make them thirsty for Christ.

CODE WORD: THIRST

Have you ever tried to eat popcorn without a drink of some kind? Salt makes us thirsty. When we live as "the salt of the earth," it creates a thirst in others for Christ.

Lord, may my very life today bring a thirst in others to know You. In Jesus' name, amen.

He who looks into the perfect law of liberty and continues in it, and is not a forgetful hearer but a doer of the work, this one will be blessed in what he does.

JAMES 1:25

Have you looked at yourself in the mirror of the Bible lately? Oh, I don't mean a passing glance. Stand there in front of Psalm 51 or Psalm 139. Take a good look.

James talked about a man who does exactly that, who "looks into the perfect law of liberty and continues in it, and is not a forgetful hearer" (James 1:25). James spoke of one who—every day—opens the Word and learns it well enough to be guided along God's path by its teaching. This person is "blessed in what he does" (v. 25).

We come as we are before God's Word. We let it both change us and, in time, prompt us to act. Great blessings come with first being God's people and then being His hands and feet in this hurting, needy world.

CODE WORD: MIRROR

Each time you look in a mirror today, let it be a reminder that God's Word is a mirror revealing what is really in your heart. As you wash your face, let Him wash your soul with His Word.

Lord, how amazing is Your love and patience that You see me today as I really am, every wrinkle, every little blemish, and yet, You love and forgive. In Jesus' name, amen.

I believe that You are the Christ, the Son of God.

JOHN 11:27

Do you believe Jesus' claim about destiny? Jesus said that even though physical death is sure, we are going to live again. The body will die, but not the spirit: this part of you will one day be united with a glorified body and live with God for eternity. We have an eternal destiny either with God or apart from Him.

Do you believe Jesus' claim about deliverance? Jesus said, "Whoever lives and believes in Me shall never die" (John 11:26). The Lord was very clear: eternal salvation is through faith in Him alone, not through human effort, good works, or noble intentions.

Do you believe Jesus' claims about His deity and our own death and destiny? When Martha faced this question at Lazarus's death, she replied: "Yes, Lord, I believe that You are the Christ, the Son of God" (v. 27).

Will you join her?

CODE WORD: DESTINY

You have an eternal destiny. Your death is a beginning, not an end. A thousand years from this moment you will be alive . . . someplace.

Lord, I join Martha in her profession; I too believe that You are the Christ. In Jesus' name, amen.

*Trust in the L*ORD *with all your heart,*
And lean not on your own understanding;
In all your ways acknowledge Him,
And He shall direct your paths.

PROVERBS 3:5–6

I n this life, as we navigate this dark world, we absolutely need God to lead us. One reason is that our holy and loving God will never lead us to do wrong. And that leads me to make an important distinction between the temptations of life and the trials of life that come our way. Trials often come from God—or, perhaps better stated, God often allows trials—to teach us to stand in our faith and to trust Him whatever the circumstances of our life. Temptation, however, still passes through God's hands, but it comes from the devil, who wants us to stumble, if not fall away completely.

No wonder we need God's leadership and guidance every day.

CODE WORD: CONTRARY

God will never lead you to do anything that is contrary to what He has laid out for you in His Word. Make sure you run your plans through the filter of God's Word.

Lord, direct me, lead me today in the way You would have me
go. In Jesus' name, amen.

You are all sons of God through faith in Christ Jesus.

GALATIANS 3:26

When you pray, the reason you can say "Our Father" is that you have accepted our holy God's offer of forgiveness, made available by the death of His Son. No longer does your sin stand between you and your holy God, for you have been washed clean with the blood of Jesus. Being able to approach God as Father means having an effective prayer life: He hears, forgives you, and you hear the voice of your heavenly Father.

"Our Father." Say those words out loud, and marvel at their truth. We are not beggars cowering at a back door looking for a handout. We are the Almighty's children, seated at His table, making our requests known to Him, and able to go with boldness to His "throne of grace" (Hebrews 4:16).

What a privilege!

Code Word: FAMILY

We are not all God's children. We are all God's creation, but only those who have been born again in Christ are members of the family of God. "You are all sons of God through faith in Christ Jesus" (Galatians 3:26).

Lord, thank You for the privilege of addressing You as "Father" and knowing You in the intimacy of Father and child. In Jesus' name, amen.

*In his upper room, with his windows open toward Jerusalem,
[Daniel] knelt down on his knees three times that day, and
prayed and gave thanks before his God, as was his custom since
early days.*

DANIEL 6:10

According to the king's edict, for thirty days only the king himself was to be worshipped. Daniel did otherwise: he would obey God instead.

Too many people today assimilate into the culture simply because they do not know what the Bible says, or they have no real heart convictions.

We need to know God's commands, and we need to decide in advance of tough situations to live in obedience to the Word of God. When we, like Daniel, set our minds to doing the right thing, we honor God. Our task is to please God. It is not enough to say we believe Jesus is God's Son. Our lives need to reflect our faith.

CODE WORD: EVIDENCE

The evidence of your Christian character is not in what you say but in what you do. Decide now that when conflicts arise today you will obey God rather than man.

*Lord, help me put my feet to my faith today, my life to my lips,
my hands to my heart. Live through me to touch someone
today. In Jesus' name, amen.*

I said, "I will confess my transgressions to the LORD,"
And You forgave the iniquity of my sin.

PSALM 32:5

Many of God's promises are conditional on certain requirements being met by His children. The forgiveness talked about in 1 John 1:9 all hinges upon the "Big If": "if we confess our sins." The forgiveness of our sins is conditional upon the confession of our sins.

The word *confession* is a compound word in the Greek. It comes from one word meaning "to say" and another meaning "the same as." Confession, then, means that we say the same as God about our sin. Sin is not some little misstep we shrug off as not a big deal. Sin is not made okay if everyone is doing it. And sin is not just a mistake that isn't as bad as the sins other people commit. Sin is so serious that it necessitated the cross. Often, our own guilt is God's way of saying, "You have sinned." Confession, then, is our way of saying, "I agree with You, God. I have sinned."

CODE WORD: AGREE

Guilt is God's voice. It is His way of saying, "You have sinned." Confession simply means you agree with God. Your sin necessitated the cross. If you confess, He will forgive.

Lord, I agree with You. I am a sinner in need of a Savior. In Jesus' name, amen.

127

Do not remember the sins of my youth . . .
According to Your mercy remember me,
For Your goodness' sake, O Lord.

PSALM 25:7

Confession agrees with God about our sin. What we camouflage as concern, God calls the sin of worry. What we refer to as righteous indignation, God calls the sin of anger. What we say is just an admiring glance, God calls the sin of lust in our heart. Confession gets open and honest with God, and there is no forgiveness without it.

We cheat on a business deal, and God asks, "What happened?" We reply, "Oh, it was the pressure of the economy." Someone gets into an illicit affair, and God asks, "What happened?" We reply, "It started as a friendship, and it just happened." But confession says, "I cheated someone . . . I was greedy" or "I perpetrated the sin of passion . . . I am to blame . . . I take responsibility." Confession agrees with God on the matter. It confesses, "I have sinned."

The good news is that Jesus forgives.

CODE WORD: CAMOUFLAGE

Be cautious today that you not make feeble excuses to camouflage your own sin. You can't fool God. He knows you, loves you, and is ready to forgive and forget.

Lord, I have sinned by _____. I'm not excusing or minimizing it. Please forgive and cleanse me. In Jesus' name, amen.

Being confident of this very thing, that He who has begun a good work in you will complete it until the day of Jesus Christ.

PHILIPPIANS 1:6

M any personal salvation testimonies go something like this: "I heard the gospel of Jesus Christ; I decided to open my life to Him; I came to Jesus; I gave Him my heart; I received Him; I repented of my sins; I decided to follow Jesus." Note the continual use of the perpendicular pronoun "I" as if my salvation depended completely upon me. When we get to heaven, we will find out how little we actually had to do with our salvation and how true our verse today is—"He who has begun a good work in you."

Salvation is—from start to finish, from first to last—the work of God Himself in us. He sought us. He found us. He began the good work in us. He keeps us.

To God be the glory for our salvation!

CODE WORD: CONFIDENCE

Take confidence today in the fact that God is faithful to keep you from falling. No one can remove you from His strong hand. Lord, it is all about You from beginning to end . . . not I but Christ! In Jesus' name, amen.

Cleanse your hands, you sinners; and purify your hearts, you double-minded.

JAMES 4:8

We must admit our need for forgiveness and ask God for it. True sorrow for our sin is essential for repentance.

Cleansing our hands has to do with turning away from unwise actions. Purifying our hearts has to do with repenting of our ungodly attitudes. The actions of our hands are always a result of the attitudes of our hearts.

Clean hands and a pure heart are key to drawing near to God. That is why the psalmist asked, "Who may ascend into the hill of the LORD? . . . He who has clean hands and a pure heart" (Psalm 24:3–4). That hill is Mount Calvary, where Jesus was crucified. Who can ascend this hill of sacrifice and substitution? Only Jesus, for He is the only One in all history who lived a spotless life.

CODE WORD: CLEAN

The actions of your hands today will be in direct proportion to the attitude of your heart. Keep your heart clean.

Lord, my heart is fixed on You today. In Jesus' name, amen.

All Scripture is given by inspiration of God, and is profitable for doctrine, for reproof, for correction, for instruction in righteousness.

2 TIMOTHY 3:16

We do not have to defend the Bible. As preacher Charles Spurgeon said, "There is no need to defend a lion when he is being attacked. All we have to do is open the gate and let him out. He will defend himself."

The Bible will still be the Book of all books when all the other writings throughout the centuries have passed into obscurity. Let's open the gates. The Bible can defend itself.

Consider that the Bible is a library of sixty-six books written over a period of more than fourteen hundred years by at least forty different authors from all walks of life. Some were fishermen, and others were prophets, kings, shepherds, doctors, and rabbis. Yet this Book has come together with one theology, one plan of redemption, and one theme running throughout its pages, leaving no explanation for its unique nature outside of God Himself. It is "given" by God Himself.

CODE WORD: AGELESS

The Bible never grows old or out of date; it is ageless. Relevant to every passing generation, it has withstood the test of time and will still be the Book of all books when all the writings of men have passed into obscurity.

Lord, open my eyes to behold wonderful truth from Your Word today. In Jesus' name, amen.

Surely He has borne our griefs
And carried our sorrows.

ISAIAH 53:4

Think about where you are—and where you have been—on your life journey.

Maybe you've been tempted to give up—or maybe you're tempted right now. Maybe you are in a Gethsemane of your own, struggling to surrender your will to God's will. Your Savior has been there too. Let Jesus help you come to the point where you are able to relinquish your will to God's plan, just as Jesus Himself did.

And Jesus' bowing to the Father's plan meant being temporarily forsaken by His heavenly Father—after already being forsaken by family and friends—but only so we might never be forsaken. "Surely He has borne our griefs and carried our sorrows" (Isaiah 53:4). What a Savior!

Think, too, about the amazing truth that we never experience anything in this life that Jesus Himself—God in the flesh—did not experience before us and for us. Jesus knows what it is to be forsaken. Reach out to Him—your good and compassionate Shepherd—in prayer.

CODE WORD: EXPERIENCE

There is nothing, not a single thing, you will face today that Jesus didn't experience. Can you hear Him saying to you, "I understand . . . I have been there."

Lord, thank You for going before me today . . . and always. In Jesus' name, amen.

The disciples were filled with joy and with the Holy Spirit.

ACTS 13:52

Being "filled with the Spirit" (Ephesians 5:18) is a command. God does not present this as an option for the believer. But let's look at the verb *be filled*. Its number is plural: God issues the command to all believers. Its tense communicates present and continuous action. The voice is passive, which means the subject doesn't act; it is acted upon by some outside force. In this case, you and I are acted upon by God. So, properly translated, the Bible is saying, "All of us must always be *being filled* with the Holy Spirit."

How can we know that we are being filled with God's Spirit? Better still, how will others know?

For the disciples in today's verse, joy was evidence of the Spirit's presence.

CODE WORD: FILLED

God commands us, His people, to "be filled" with His Spirit. We are not filled by any effort to get more of Him (whatever that might mean!). We are filled by giving Him more of ourselves, by opening every inch of every room of our lives to Him.

Lord, I call You by that name, yet I don't open every inch of every room of my life to Your Spirit. Please forgive me for wanting to rule over certain aspects of my life. Spirit, help me open more of myself to You and the joy You bring. In Jesus' name, amen.

MAY

*Therefore humble
yourselves under the
mighty hand of God,
that He may exalt you in
due time, casting all your
care upon Him, for He
cares for you.*

1 PETER 5:6–7

*"'You shall love the L*ORD *your God with all your heart, with all your soul, with all your strength, and with all your mind.'"*

L<small>UKE</small> 10:27

W hat is your primary purpose in life? The primary purpose of an automobile is to transport us. The primary purpose of a pen is to write. And Jesus was very clear about our primary purpose as human beings: we are to "love the L<small>ORD</small> [our] God" with all that we are.

This commandment was Jesus' answer when a lawyer asked Him, "Which is the great commandment?" (Matthew 22:36). After this command to love God, Jesus offered the second most important commandment: "You shall love your neighbor as yourself'" (v. 39). Together, these commandments include all the Ten Commandments. The first four of "The Big Ten" have to do with our relationship with God (Exodus 20:2–11), and Jesus said, "You shall love the L<small>ORD</small> your God." The last six have to do with our relationship with one another (Exodus 20:12–17), corresponding to the Lord's call to love our neighbors.

C<small>ODE</small> W<small>ORD</small>: FIRST

The first and greatest commandment is to love God. Some think we love God by loving man. But Jesus puts it in proper order: the way to love man is to first love God.

Lord, You know that I love You. You are in first place in my life . . . in front of all others. In Jesus' name, amen.

*Hear, O Israel: The L*ORD *our God, the L*ORD *is one! You shall love the L*ORD *your God with all your heart, with all your soul, and with all your strength.*

DEUTERONOMY 6:4–5

The Lord Jesus referred to this, the first instruction Moses gave the Lord's people, as a commandment. It is neither an option nor a suggestion. Also note that this commandment is directed to people who know Christ in a personal way: it is the Lord *your* God. The emphasis here is on loving the One who first loved us and who gave His Son to die on the cross as payment for our sins.

So we are to love this gracious and generous God with all our heart, not merely giving our love lip service. We are to love God with our entire mind: a heart full of love is no excuse for an empty mind. As we love God with all of our strength and soul as well, we are to hold nothing back when we love God.

CODE WORD: PERSONAL

Do you see and sense Him as a personal Lord? Or, far off and removed, a creator and sustainer of all there is? You can know Him in the intimacy of Father and child. "You shall love the LORD *your* God."

Lord, You are my Lord! In Jesus' name, amen.

He who covers his sins will not prosper,
But whoever confesses and forsakes them will have
mercy.

PROVERBS 28:13

In Genesis 3, our holy and gracious God took the life of an innocent animal and used the skins of this sacrifice to cover the sin of Adam and Eve. God is still the Initiator in covering our sins today.

But before God covers our sins, we have to recognize those sins and confess them. In our natural condition, however, we are unresponsive to the gospel: we are "dead" in our sins (Ephesians 2:1). We are also unperceptive: the gospel is "veiled" to us, and the god of this world has "blinded" us (2 Corinthians 4:3–4). Without Christ, we are unteachable as well: not only can we not receive the things of God, but we also consider them foolish (1 Corinthians 2:14). Finally, we are unrighteous: we were actually shaped in iniquity and conceived in sin (Psalm 51:5). But God initiates our ability to recognize our sin, and He initiated our rescue.

CODE WORD: UNCOVER

Anything you attempt to cover today, God will eventually uncover. But the good news is everything you uncover He will cover with the blood of Jesus.

Lord, You know me, my every thought. Cover me today. In Jesus' name, amen.

[The Samaritan] went to [the beaten man] and bandaged his wounds, pouring on oil and wine; and he set him on his own animal, brought him to an inn, and took care of him.

LUKE 10:34

We are to love God first and foremost. When we do this, our actions toward others will issue out of our loving attitude for Him.

We can truly love our neighbor only if we love the Lord supremely. We cannot truly love God unless we really know Him, and we cannot know someone unless we spend time alone with Him.

When we love God, we will say yes to these questions: Do I like to spend time alone with Him? Do I value reading the Bible? Do I make talking to Him in prayer a priority?

When we love God, we are fulfilling the purpose for which we were created. When we seek to obey God by also loving our neighbors, they will know His love through our actions, just as the beaten man experienced when the Samaritan cared for him.

CODE WORD: ALONE

Love is often spelled T-I-M-E. I love my wife, Susie. I like to spend time with her . . . alone. The same is true with our love for the Lord. Jesus calls us to spend time with Him . . . alone.

Lord, I was that man on the Jericho road. Thank You for seeing my need . . . and meeting it. In Jesus' name, amen.

[Jesus] poured water into a basin and began to wash the disciples' feet, and to wipe them with the towel with which He was girded.

JOHN 13:5

For thirty-three years Jesus showed us what genuine love looks like: He was the very embodiment of love.

Jesus—God in flesh and blood—showed us by His life as well as by His sacrificial and excruciatingly painful death on the cross that genuine love is unlimited, unchanging, unselfish, and unconditional. The very natural self-love that all of us know all too well is the very antithesis of all those things.

On the night before He was crucified, Jesus gave us a "new commandment." Having just washed His disciples' feet, our Suffering Servant said, "A new commandment I give to you, that you love one another; as I have loved you, that you also love one another. By this all will know that you are My disciples, if you have love for one another" (John 13:34–35).

CODE WORD: RESET

Up until Jesus spoke this, the best we could do was live on the level of the old commandment of loving others as we love ourselves. But we have a reset commandment to love others as He loved us, unselfishly and unconditionally.

Lord, Your love has no boundaries known to man. Thank You for loving me unconditionally. In Jesus' name, amen.

Bless the L<small>ORD</small>, O my soul,
And forget not all His benefits . . .
Who redeems your life from destruction.

P<small>SALM</small> 103:2, 4

S ince being unresponsive, unperceptive, unteachable, and unrighteous is our natural state, something outside of us must intervene to enable us to become responsive to the gospel, perceptive of the things of God, teachable, and righteous before Him. Now, since we are indeed raised out of spiritual death (that is, born again) and since we are unable to perform this work on ourselves, then we must conclude it is God who initiates our salvation.

In other words, the origin of our salvation lies not within us but with God Himself. He takes the initiative. He convicts us of sin. He convinces us of our righteousness in Him. He calls us out of darkness into His marvelous light. He redeems us for His own.

What is the outcome of this marvelous salvation provided us in Christ? It means we are secure.

Just as we are not saved by performing good works, we are not kept by performing good works.

C<small>ODE</small> W<small>ORD</small>: SECURE

If faith is good enough to save you, it is good enough to live by and to keep you. You are eternally secure in Christ, now and forever.

Lord, help me live by faith today and not by what I see or sense. One day my faith will become sight and I will look upon Your face. In Jesus' name, amen.

"You shall love your neighbor as yourself: I am the LORD."

LEVITICUS 19:18

After the Last Supper, Jesus gave His disciples a new commandment. This call to love one another was not new in time—it dates back to the Old Testament—but the commandment was fresh in its expression.

The old commandment (above) called us to love our neighbor as we love ourselves. This self-love is a love with limits. It is often conditional on such matters as time or conduct, situations or social standing. It can also be changeable and fickle and selfish.

But this new commandment offers a different approach to real love. For thirty-three years Jesus gave us a picture of how real love was to be evidenced. In essence, Jesus said, "For over three decades now I have shown you real love. I am about to leave you, so before I go, a new commandment I am giving you. No longer are you to love one another as you love yourself, but as I have loved you."

CODE WORD: IMITATE

Paul said, "Imitate me, just as I also imitate Christ" (1 Corinthians 11:1). Since Jesus loves you unconditionally, imitate His love with someone who needs to be loved today.

Lord, often we need love when we deserve it the least. Thank You for loving me just as I am. In Jesus' name, amen.

"The Son of Man did not come to be served, but to serve, and to give His life a ransom for many."

We are totally incapable of loving people the way Jesus loved us.

As we've seen, Jesus' love is unlimited: nothing "shall be able to separate us from the love of God which is in Christ Jesus our Lord" (Romans 8:39).

Christ's love to us is unconditional. Jesus doesn't love us if we meet certain criteria or act certain ways. In fact, "God demonstrates His own love toward us, in that while we were still sinners, Christ died for us" (Romans 5:8).

Jesus' love is also unselfish, so much so that He willingly walked to the cross for your salvation and mine.

And Christ's love is also unchangeable: "Jesus Christ is the same yesterday, today, and forever" (Hebrews 13:8).

As the Spirit works to make us more like Him, we will be more able to love others with a love that is unlimited, unconditional, unselfish, and unchangeable, for that is how Jesus loves us.

CODE WORD: PERSPECTIVE

Christ's love didn't propel Him to the cross when you were worthy, but when you were a sinner. Keep this perspective in mind as you love someone today who may not deserve it.

Lord, I don't become more like You by getting more of You, but by giving You more of me. In Jesus' name, amen.

*Now as He drew near, He saw the city and wept over it, saying,
"If you had known . . . the things that make for your peace! But
now they are hidden from your eyes."*

LUKE 19:41–42

Most messages related to the Palm Sunday event have to do
with the crowds, the shouts of the hosannas, the parade. But
all that was a sham. And Jesus knew it. He knew that within a few
short days, the crowd would disappear, and their cheers would be
replaced by jeers.

Can you picture Jesus that day, entering Jerusalem on the back
of a donkey and welcomed with the people's praise? He was the
center of attention, celebrated by the cheering crowd. But "as He
drew near, He saw the city and wept over it" (Luke 19:41).

Hear Jesus speak through His tears as He says, "If you had
known . . . the things that make for your peace! But now they are
hidden from your eyes" (v. 42).

Jesus still weeps over our sins and is troubled by our blinded eyes.

CODE WORD: SIGHT

Make sure today that your eyes are not blinded to your own sin. Sin
is so serious that it necessitated the cross. Ask God for the kind of
sight that enables you to see yourself as He sees you today.

*Lord, help me to see myself through Your eyes today. In Jesus'
name, amen.*

MAY 10

*"I am the L*ORD *your God, who brought you out of the land of Egypt, out of the house of bondage. You shall have no other gods before Me."*

EXODUS 20:2–3

The Torah—the Jewish Scripture—is comprised of Genesis, Exodus, Leviticus, Numbers, and Deuteronomy. Those five books contain more than six hundred laws, but the Big Ten are found in Exodus 20.

These ten ancient laws are, in twenty-first-century America, experiencing an intense assault. Listings of and even references to them are being systematically removed from public view. Yet in our nation's capital the Ten Commandments are carved in granite on government buildings and in mahogany in public libraries. The commandments are also on the wall above where the Supreme Court justices sit and hold court. These public displays testify to our Founding Fathers' faith and to the principles that made this the greatest nation on earth.

The Ten Commandments have served as the building blocks of almost every civil society for more than three thousand years. Our American experiment in democracy is just one example.

CODE WORD: BOUNDARY

Football, basketball, and baseball are played within boundary lines. And so it is with life. God has set some boundaries for you (the Ten Commandments), and if you play within them, you will win at this game called life.

Lord, Your laws are a testimony of Your great love and concern for me. In Jesus' name, amen.

MAY 11

"Days will come upon you when your enemies will . . . surround you and close you in on every side, and level you, and your children within you, to the ground; and they will not leave in you one stone upon another, because you did not know the time of your visitation."

LUKE 19:43–44

J esus wept as He entered Jerusalem on Palm Sunday.

The Greek word that describes Jesus' weeping on Palm Sunday is not the same word used to describe His weeping at Bethany when His friend Lazarus had died. The Palm Sunday word for weeping refers to loud sobbing, groaning, and cries that could be heard a block away. Jesus poured out His heart over humanity's sin and spiritual neglect; He also knew what the future held for Jerusalem (Luke 19:43–44).

We in the Western church today do not seem to be weeping over the sins of those around us—or even our own sins—even though we know judgment awaits those who don't repent. Many of us have lost our tears, yet Jesus is still weeping.

CODE WORD: INDIFFERENCE

Search your own heart today to see if you may have joined others in their indifference to the sin around you in a crumbling culture.

Lord, put a burden on my own heart for the same things that caused You to weep. In Jesus' name, amen.

Whoever calls on the name of the Lord shall be saved.

ROMANS 10:13

W e are all different in many and varied ways. But we all have one thing in common: not a single one of us is perfect. We are all in need of rebuilding from within. When it comes to a personal knowledge of and faith in the Lord Jesus Christ, all of us need to receive the gift of salvation—of freedom from punishment for our sins—that Jesus offers us.

We can't rebuild ourselves, and we don't have to. That's one thing Jesus does when we choose to trust Him for our salvation. A personal faith means that you transfer your trust in yourself for your salvation over to trust in Christ alone. Know that our holy God has promised that "whoever calls on the name of the Lord shall be saved" (Romans 10:13).

Calling on Him will probably mean moving out of your comfort zone. Think of it as the beginning of an adventure, because that's exactly what it is.

Code Word: TRANSFER

Your salvation will become a reality when you transfer your faith from yourself and your own efforts to Christ alone. Make that transfer right now.

Lord, I want to begin the great adventure for which I was created. As an act of faith I now transfer my trust from myself to You alone. In Jesus' name, amen.

"Do you love Me? . . . Do you love Me? . . . Do you love Me?"

JOHN 21:15–17

I t happened after Peter had denied knowing Jesus three times . . . Jesus asked Peter, "Do you love Me?" and He used the word *agape*. That is, "Peter, do you love Me with this godly, sacrificial, unconditional kind of love?" Peter used a different word for "love" in his answer: "Yes, Lord; You know that I love You" (v. 16). Having failed to agape Jesus, Peter used *philos*, meaning "brotherly fondness."

Again Jesus asked about Peter's love, and again Jesus used *agape*. Grieved, Peter again used *philos*. Peter loved the Lord, but Peter knew his limitations: He knew he wasn't able to love the way Jesus loves.

Finally, Jesus asked Peter a third time, "Do you love Me?" But this time Jesus used *philos*: "Peter, as best you can, here and now, do you love Me?" And Peter replied, "Lord, You know all things; You know that I love You" (v. 17).

Only when we love Jesus are we able to love others as He commands us.

CODE WORD: CONDESCENSION

Jesus comes down to meet you at your level of love. What amazing condescension. He will meet you right where you are today.

Lord, You know all things; You know that I love You. In Jesus' name, amen.

I am Joseph your brother, whom you sold into Egypt. But now, do not therefore be grieved or angry with yourselves because you sold me here; for God sent me before you to preserve life.

P eople—even people who love God and are trying to love one another—encounter conflict. And, in a sense, the entire Bible is a textbook in the art of conflict resolution.

Consider Joseph. Jealousy, lying, plotting, and deception ripped his family apart, and motivated by burning jealousy, his brothers sold him into slavery. Joseph eventually found himself in Egypt. Through a miraculous set of events, Joseph became the equivalent of prime minister over Egypt.

Famine struck Israel, and Joseph's desperate brothers went to Egypt to try to buy grain. There—eventually—Joseph revealed his identity and reconciled with his startled and amazed brothers. In a very moving scene, Joseph and his brothers fell into each other's arms in a warm embrace of love and forgiveness.

Joseph didn't cut what he could untie. Good advice when we are trying to love one another.

CODE WORD: PROVIDENTIAL

God was behind all things good, and not so good, in Joseph's experience. And He is not removed from your life either. "All things work together for good" (Romans 8:28).

Lord, put before me today that someone to whom I need to show forgiveness. In Jesus' name, amen.

Nathan said to David, "You are the man!" . . . David said to Nathan, "I have sinned against the Lord."

2 Samuel 12:7, 13

One point about conflict resolution. Too few of us find the courage to confront the person with whom we have a conflict. Let's learn from Nathan, who had courage and wisdom to do—and do well—what we hesitate or avoid doing.

It's a well-known incident, King David's adulterous affair with Bathsheba and his murder of her husband. Like many people today, he was foolish enough to think he could cover it up with lies and deceit. He certainly didn't want his family or friends to find out about it.

But David was fortunate enough to have a trusted friend who refused to pretend it didn't happen. Nathan cared enough to confront the king, who was on a collision course with exposure and defeat. When Nathan spoke up boldly and with love, David came clean.

The confrontation hurt, but it also healed. It healed David's soul, David's relationship with God, and David's relationship with Nathan.

Code Word: CONFRONTATION

Many have a tendency to avoid this Code Word. But it is an essential element in relationships. Remember, it is never wrong to do right.

Lord, help me care enough to confront today in love as You lead. In Jesus' name, amen.

Do not be alarmed. You seek Jesus of Nazareth, who was crucified. He is risen! He is not here. See the place where they laid Him.

MARK 16:6

After the crucifixion, the women went to the tomb to anoint the Lord's body for burial. To their amazement, they found the tomb empty and, sitting inside, an angelic being who told them, "He is risen!" (Mark 16:6). The angel continued: "But go, tell His disciples—and Peter—that He is going before you into Galilee; there you will see Him, as He said to you" (v. 7). Did you notice "and Peter"?

Peter had denied knowing the Lord and greatly needed a word of encouragement, a new beginning, a second chance. Perhaps some of us have blown it. If so, the message of "and Peter" is for you, and it is the message of the second chance.

Easter means hope. It means a new life, a new start, a new beginning. Yes, a second chance is possible. "Go and tell the disciples—and Peter!"

What difference will that truth make in your life?

CODE WORD: HOPE

This is the word that can keep you going. The Bible is the story of men and women who got a second chance: Moses . . . David . . . Jonah . . . Mary Magdalene. One failure or setback does not make a flop. You get to bat again! Keep hope alive.

Lord, thank You for being the God of the second chance . . . and the third and the fourth, etc. My hope today is in You, Lord. In Jesus' name, amen.

MAY 17

*As bondservants of Christ, [do] the will of God from the heart,
with goodwill doing service, as to the Lord, and not to men.*

Ephesians 6:6–7

We can be God's light in this world by living with integrity. Rather than being "men-pleasers" (Ephesians 6:6), we Christ-followers who desire to influence our culture will not be governed by popular views or public opinion polls. Instead, our integrity emanates "from the heart," and we honor God when we live that way.

Further, God's people of integrity are aware that they are serving the Lord whether they are standing on an assembly line, working in a textile mill, sitting behind a computer, caring for people in a hospital, loving on kids in a day care, teaching at a public high school, or making decisions behind a big mahogany desk. Whatever their workplace, men and women of integrity are honest and honorable. God is honored as we serve people in His name and "as to the Lord," thereby shining His light into their lives.

Code Word: INSIDE

Remember to let your God-given decision making initiate from inside you, within your heart. Decisions made by popular views of public consensus (outside) are often in conflict with what you know to be right in your heart.

Lord, help me to follow my heart today. In Jesus' name, amen.

The LORD saw that the wickedness of man was great in the earth, and that every intent of the thoughts of his heart was only evil continually.

GENESIS 6:5

This is the first use of the word *heart* in the Bible. Here, it is associated with the thought process, the intellect. When the Bible speaks of the heart, it is not referring to the actual physical organ that pumps blood throughout our circulatory system, but to the thoughts that help shape our being. This is why we read, "As he thinks in his heart, so is he" (Proverbs 23:7). The heart is our intellect, the thinking part of our being.

When we read that the Lord looks upon our hearts, we understand that He is watching how we think; He is able to know whether our thoughts are pure or not. Man can observe outward appearances only, but the Lord looks into our hearts and knows what we really think. When the Scriptures speak of the heart, they are speaking about our intellect.

CODE WORD: THOUGHTS

You may think no one knows the thoughts you harbor within your own heart. But God does, all of them. Guard your heart today. He is watching.

Lord, I am what I think. Think through my mind today and love through my heart. In Jesus' name, amen.

[The Lord] was grieved in His heart.

GENESIS 6:6

The second time we see the word *heart* in Scripture, we learn that it refers to our emotions as well as to our intellect. Specifically, we read that when the Lord saw the rebellion of man, it "grieved [Him] in His heart." The heart is the seat of our emotions. It is not simply our intellect; it involves our feelings as well.

When the good Samaritan saw the beaten man on the road to Jericho, Jesus said that "he had compassion" upon him. Another translation says, "his heart went out to him" (Luke 10:33 THE MESSAGE). The night before the crucifixion, with His disciples in Gethsemane's garden, the Lord said, "My soul [heart] is exceedingly sorrowful, even to death" (Matthew 26:38). And we have Solomon's reminder that "a merry heart does good, like medicine" (Proverbs 17:22). Compassion, grief, sorrow, and happiness are all emotions that emanate from the heart. Clearly, when the Scriptures speak of the heart, they are speaking about our intellect *and* our emotions.

CODE WORD: GRIEVE

Did you know you can actually grieve the Holy Spirit (Ephesians 4:30)? It is easier to act your way into a new way of feeling than to feel your way into a new way of acting.

Lord, thank You that Your heart went out to me. My heart is open to You. In Jesus' name, amen.

*The L*ORD *said in His heart, "I will."*

GENESIS 8:21

T his appearance of the word *heart* refers to the essence of our own will, our volition. Often we find this volition entwined with the heart. The prodigal son was a long way from home when his heart was changed. He said, "I will arise and go to my father" (Luke 15:18). Then he got up and turned his heart—his intellect, his emotion, his volition—toward home.

At the point of our conversion, God Himself takes that old heart of ours and gives us one that is brand-new. That is what He promised to do: "I will give them a heart to know Me, that I am the LORD" (Jeremiah 24:7).

So, while man may look on the outward appearance, God is looking upon our hearts. He is mindful of our thoughts, our emotions, and our will. Today is a good time to "return to the LORD with all your hearts" (1 Samuel 7:3). And that is the real heart of the matter.

CODE WORD: RETURN

Are you in need of returning to the Lord? Then, from your heart, do it. You will find Him waiting for you with arms wide open.

Lord, You have given me a new heart. Use me to love others with it. In Jesus' name, amen.

"God did not send His Son into the world to condemn the world, but that the world through Him might be saved."

JOHN 3:17

I n His Great Commission—issued to every Christ-follower— Jesus told us to take the good news across our city, across our country, across our continent, and, yes, all around this big world. All of us are to be witnesses, and we are to go "to the end of the earth" (Acts 1:8).

Yet in thirty short years, those early believers fulfilled Acts 1:8. They witnessed about Jesus' saving grace in Jerusalem (Acts 1–8), in Judea and Samaria (Acts 9–12), and to the end of their world (Acts 13–28). They did not play leapfrog with this commission. They did not pass over hundreds of witnessing opportunities in their own city in order to go to the ends of the earth. They began at home, in Jerusalem.

And how were they able to accomplish so much? They were empowered by the Holy Spirit, and they worked with singleness of purpose in obedience to their risen Lord.

CODE WORD: 20/20

Some are nearsighted, seeing only the needs close around them. Others are farsighted, seeing only the needs far away on foreign fields. Make sure your spiritual vision is 20/20, seeing clearly those needs near and far.

Lord, in my concern for those who haven't heard abroad, help me not to look past next door. In Jesus' name, amen.

I can do all things through Christ who strengthens me.

PHILIPPIANS 4:13

C hrist's people are to share Christ's gospel all around this big world until every religion is confronted, every false belief is exposed, and everyone hears about Jesus' death for their sins. Yes, this is a huge task, but think about those early believers. Their assignment seemed geographically impossible (most people had no idea how truly big the world was); physically impossible (there was no air travel, radio, television, printing presses, Internet, or social media); legally impossible (government authorities forbade them to speak in Jesus' name); and socially impossible (who would listen to these scrubby Galileans, so void of culture and class?).

Yet people did listen . . . because these passionate Christ-followers were witnesses through the power of the Holy Spirit. They did so much with so little, yet we in the twenty-first century seem to do so little with so much. The modern church needs to get back to basics, follow the early believers' example, and fulfill Acts 1:8 in our lifetime as well.

CODE WORD: BASICS

In the midst of all our Christian sophistication, materials, and technological advances, it seems the early church had something basic we have lost along the way—power! We forget that we can do all things through Christ who strengthens us.

Lord, help me focus on the basics You have laid out for me . . . and do them. In Jesus' name, amen.

MAY 23

"Your kingdom come.
Your will be done
On earth as it is in heaven."

M ATTHEW 6:10

O n certain issues God's will is very clear. Jesus, for example, made this straightforward statement: "This is the will of Him who sent Me, that everyone who sees the Son and believes in Him may have everlasting life" (John 6:40). There is no doubt that those who believe in Christ will have everlasting life. The Father explicitly wills for us sinful human beings to recognize Jesus as God's Son and to believe in the efficacy of the cross.

But what about life's crossroads and decisions? How do we find out what is really God's will for us instead of what may simply be a selfish, personal desire? Getting to know God, His Spirit, and His Word will help us find God's will for our lives.

By the way, know that the Lord Jesus wants us to find His will for our lives. In fact, He may be more interested in our finding His will for our lives than we ourselves are.

C ODE W ORD: WILL

If you were a strong-willed child, chances are great you are a strong-willed adult. Are you prepared to put your own will aside and walk in His? His is always best.

Lord, Your kingdom come, Your will be done in me today. In Jesus' name, amen.

God our Savior . . . desires all men to be saved and to come to the knowledge of the truth.

1 TIMOTHY 2:3–4

I f we want to know God's will, we first have to come to know Him as our personal Savior. The acknowledgment of your sin, your confession of that sin, and your decision to name Jesus your Savior and Lord is the salvation that God desires for everyone. Without a saving knowledge of Christ and His Spirit living within, a person cannot discern the things of God. These things—including God's will—are "spiritually discerned" (1 Corinthians 2:14).

And the Holy Spirit who takes up residency within us gives us spiritual discernment in addition to empowering us for service. When we know Christ as our Savior and when we are being controlled by His Spirit, He becomes our Teacher, and Jesus promised that "He will guide [us] into all truth" (John 16:13). Being sensitive to the Spirit's leading in our lives is a key factor in our being able to discern God's will for us.

CODE WORD: IMPOSSIBLE

It is utterly impossible to find the will of God unless, in the words of Jesus, you have been "born again" (John 3:7). That is, unless He has come to live in your heart by your trusting in Him alone.

Lord, guide me today into Your truth at the very point of my own need. In Jesus' name, amen.

In the beginning God created the heavens and the earth.

GENESIS 1:1

E nglish doesn't capture the significance of the Hebrew word for *God* in Scripture's opening verse: "In the beginning God created."

The Hebrew word for *God* is the plural noun *Elohim*, implying that God is somehow plural—and He is: Father, Son, and Holy Spirit. Interestingly, the next word—the verb *created*—is singular. And it should be singular because our God is the great Three in One.

The doctrine of the Trinity is one of the great mysteries of the Christian faith. The mystery is often likened to water. We all know H_2O is a liquid. However, water can also be a solid (ice) or a vapor (steam). Yet, in all three manifestations, it is still the same in nature: H_2O. And so it is with God: Father, Son, and Spirit are the same in nature.

CODE WORD: MYSTERY

How God manifests Himself as three Persons in One is a mystery, a sacred secret. If, in fact, we could understand it all, there would not be much to it. Faith enables us to live with the majesty of this mystery, humbled and awed.

Father, thank You that this very evening the heavens will once again declare Your creative glory. . . . Jesus, thank You for laying aside Your glory and coming to us clothed in human flesh. . . . Holy Spirit, thank You for revealing Christ to us and empowering us to live in His power today. In Jesus' name, amen.

Thus says the LORD,
Who created the heavens,
Who is God,
Who formed the earth and made it . . .

ISAIAH 45:18

There is a huge difference between creating something and making something. Many of us have made things, but none of us has ever created something from nothing. A cabinetmaker may make a beautiful cabinet out of wood, but he is totally unable to create the wood itself. Yet the Hebrew word that we translate "created" suggests that something was indeed created out of nothing.

In fact, God spoke this physical universe into existence. On the fourth day of creation, He created the solar systems, the constellations, and the countless stars. Could their existence—or the clocklike precision with which they move through the infinite heavens—happen without a Master Creator and Designer?

The heavens do indeed declare the glory of God, and "the firmament shows His handiwork" (Psalm 19:1).

CODE WORD: PROOF

Do you really need proof that God is the Creator? How do millions of stars move in their orbits in clocklike precision? How can two tiny specks of protoplasm just happen to come together and result in all the intricacies of a nervous system? God is behind it all! Proof!

Lord, thank You for revealing Yourself in all creation and for making Yourself real to me today through Your Word and by Your Spirit. In Jesus' matchless name, amen.

The LORD God formed man of the dust of the ground, and breathed into his nostrils the breath of life; and man became a living being.

GENESIS 2:7

God created human beings differently than He did the rest of His creation. Before creating man, God simply spoke, and creation happened.

The Almighty changed His approach, though, when He created you and me. He did not just speak us into existence. He took existing material—the dust of the ground that He had made—and He formed man. And *formed* comes from the same Hebrew word used elsewhere in the Old Testament to describe a potter laboring over his clay, shaping and fashioning it into a beautiful vessel. The image is God the Artisan meticulously molding and making us. Then He animated us by breathing into us "the breath of life."

God spent time, He took great care, and He invested effort fueled by love when He created you.

CODE WORD: VALUABLE

Think about your DNA. It's uniquely yours unless you have an identical twin. And even if you do, there has never been and there never will be anyone just like you. You are truly one of a kind and indescribably valuable to God.

Lord, cause me to live today in the truth that You made me like no one else and You have assigned an "area of influence" to me . . . and me alone (2 Corinthians 10:13 ESV). Use me there today for Your glory. In Jesus' name, amen.

In everything give thanks; for this is the will of God in Christ Jesus for you.

1 Thessalonians 5:18

On Memorial Day each year, we Americans pause to remember those men and women who expressed what our Lord referred to as "greater love" (John 15:13) by laying down their lives for family, friends, and this nation.

As President Franklin D. Roosevelt said one week after the Pearl Harbor attack, "Those who long enjoy such privileges that we enjoy forget in time that others have died to win them." Freedom is never really free; it is almost always bought with blood that some individuals spilled for others.

The biggest battle Americans face today, however, is a battle for the very soul of a nation. We have today the immorality and turning from God that we tolerated yesterday. And we will inherit tomorrow what we tolerate today.

In honor of those who have died for our freedoms, may we as a nation repent and, rather than tolerate evil, stand for God's truth and shine as His light. God bless America!

Code Word: HONOR

History has its own way of repeating itself. Make sure you do not forget that others died on faraway fields so you could be free today. Remember this . . . and honor them.

Lord, the greatest freedom is what You bring today . . . freedom from sin and selfish ambitions. I stand today in the liberty whereby You have set me free. In Jesus' name, amen.

How can a young man keep his way pure?
By keeping it according to Your word.

PSALM 119:9 NASB

K nowing the Word will give you knowledge about God. As we walk in His ways—as we obey His commands—we gain knowledge of God. (There is a vast difference between the two!)

We must put the Word into practice. As Joshua said, we are "to do according to all that is written in it" (Joshua 1:8). You can never learn to play a musical instrument by simply memorizing the score and continually listening to your instructor play the instrument. The only way you can learn to play is to play it . . . over and over and over. It is better to do one Bible lesson than to hear a thousand of them.

So, in a culture where moral values continue to disintegrate, we must know God's Word because it contains the guidelines and commands that God established for our good. Once we know what Scripture says, then we must choose to do what it says.

CODE WORD: KNOWLEDGE

Knowledge is the accumulation of facts. You may know about God by reading the Bible. But you get to know Him by doing what it says.

Lord, help me to be a doer of Your Word and not a hearer only. In Jesus' name, amen.

I will instruct you and teach you in the way you should go;
I will guide you with My eye.

PSALM 32:8

It is virtually impossible for the Bible to impact our lives if we don't know much about what it says. This bestselling book of all time will do us little good if we don't know what's in it or how to apply its teachings to life.

First, be assured that "all Scripture is given by inspiration of God, and is profitable for doctrine, for reproof, for correction, for instruction in righteousness, that the man of God may be complete, thoroughly equipped for every good work" (2 Timothy 3:16–17). Investing time in Bible study is essential to living a life that pleases God.

We are to be "rightly dividing the word of truth" (2 Timothy 2:15). As we do so, God teaches us His ways and guides our steps through life. And that is only one of the blessings that comes when we obey God's command to study His Word.

CODE WORD: APPLY

Today seek for ways to apply to your life the Bible truths you have put in your heart and mind.

Lord, help me today to put into practice, to apply to my daily life, what I find in Your Word. In Jesus' name, amen.

Do not be conformed to this world, but be transformed by the renewing of your mind, that you may prove what is that good and acceptable and perfect will of God.

ROMANS 12:2

We who desire to see and to enter the kingdom of God must be born again.

The apostle Paul described this as being "transformed" (Romans 12:2). We get our English word *metamorphosis* from this single compound Greek word. The picture is of a caterpillar spinning a cocoon around itself and later emerging as a new creation, a beautiful butterfly. No longer doomed to crawl on its belly, no longer as limited in its perspective and location, this butterfly can now soar freely.

Similarly, we experience a new birth when we recognize our sin, repent of that sin, and trust in Christ alone to forgive us. At the point of this new birth, we can be sure that God's Spirit is at work within us, making us hungry for God's Word, passionate for His truth, and more like Jesus every day.

We are indeed new creations!

CODE WORD: TRANSFORM

There is a world of difference in being "conformed" outwardly to a new set of moral standards and being "transformed" inwardly by the Spirit of God. The Bible says it is like going from "darkness to light" (Acts 26:18) or from "death into life" (John 5:24).

Lord, it is all about You . . . not me. It is what You have done for me, not what I have done for You. In Jesus' name, amen.

JUNE

Now faith is the substance of things hoped for, the evidence of things not seen.

HEBREWS 11:1

JUNE 1

I know that my Redeemer lives.

JOB 19:25

Notice that Job did not say, "I think . . ." or "I hope. . . ." Job is rock-solid certain that he will live again.

And this confident proclamation comes from a man who has lost his wealth, his friends, most of his family, and his health. Yet his answer to his original question—"If a man dies, shall he live again?" (Job 14:14)—is an unwavering "Absolutely!"

Yes, there is life after death. God wants us to know that truth; He wants us to live with certainty that life continues after our earthly existence. The apostle John put it like this: "These things I have written to you who believe in the name of the Son of God, that you may know that you have eternal life" (1 John 5:13).

The Bible you often hold in your hands was written to you in order that you would have absolute assurance not only that there is life after your time on earth, but that you will spend it with Jesus.

CODE WORD: ASSURANCE

God doesn't want you to hope . . . but to know that you have eternal life. The reality is you are not really ready to live until you are ready to die and have that assurance.

Lord, thank You that I can know I have eternal life because Your Word says so! In Jesus' name, amen.

JUNE 2

In Him we have redemption through His blood, the forgiveness of sins, according to the riches of His grace.

EPHESIANS 1:7

Our Western culture has seen a systematic decline in traditional values over the past many decades. Ours is described as a postmodern culture, tolerance is valued to the *n*th degree, and truth is a personal matter.

By and large, the American church has awakened to the reality that at least two generations have been lost to the church. Sociologists, psychologists, and analysts of social trends have identified several common characteristics of these "lost generations."

As we look at each of five characteristics of these lost generations—they are searching for a meaningful relationship; seeking immediate gratification; wanting something for nothing; desiring guilt-free living; searching for prosperity—consider where these younger generations can find answers that meet their needs and desires. Only the church holds the answers and can meet all five needs of these lost generations. Look again at Ephesians 1:7 and spend a few minutes praying for these lost generations.

CODE WORD: TRUTH

In our world of tolerance, *truth* is a missing word. But truth will always win . . . in the end. It is what will set you free. "You shall know the truth, and the truth shall make you free" (John 8:32).

Lord, You are not just the way and the life . . . You are the truth. In Jesus' name, amen.

JUNE 3

Neither death nor life, nor angels nor principalities nor powers, nor things present nor things to come, nor height nor depth, nor any other created thing, shall be able to separate us from the love of God.

ROMANS 8:38–39

The number one quest of these lost generations is their search for a meaningful relationship. Many have never known one. They are the product of a culture of divorce, and they are crying out for a meaningful relationship.

What Christ has to offer is not about religion or ritual. It is about a relationship, a vibrant, personal relationship with Him. It is about unconditional, tough, and eternal love. The lost generations can find the very thing they are searching for in Christ and only in Him.

Furthermore, none of us will ever be properly related to others until we are properly related to ourselves. And that happens only when we discover Jesus' love and enter into a relationship with Him. Christ Himself is the answer for the very thing that compels our search for significance—a meaningful relationship in life.

CODE WORD: RELATIONSHIP

Think about it. You have the capacity to relate not only outwardly with others, but upwardly with God Himself. You can know Him in the intimacy of a Father and child . . . an awesome thought.

Lord, help me realize I will never be properly related to others until, first, I am properly related to You. In Jesus' name, amen.

[The jailer] said, "Sirs, what must I do to be saved?"
So [Paul and Silas] said, "Believe on the Lord Jesus
Christ, and you will be saved, you and your household."
Then they spoke the word of the Lord to him and to all
who were in his house. . . . And immediately he and all his
family were baptized.

ACTS 16:30–33

I n addition to a meaningful relationship, these lost generations seek immediate gratification. After all, they have grown up in an Internet world where everything is instant. They do not want to wait for anything.

What Christ has to offer is for right now. When Ephesians 1:7 says "we have redemption," the tense is present active indicative, meaning the event is occurring in actual time right now.

While they may think all Christ has to offer is for some future life in heaven, the reality is that He makes a difference right now. The moment we name Jesus our Lord, we are filled with His Spirit. Talk about immediate gratification! It is found only in knowing Jesus.

CODE WORD: INSTANTANEOUS

Salvation is an instantaneous act of God, bringing with it immediate gratification and taking place the very moment you repent of your sin and trust Christ as your Lord and Savior. Think back. When did it happen in you?

Lord, You are all I need today . . . and forever. In Jesus' name, amen.

Now abide faith, hope, love, these three; but the greatest of these is love.

1 CORINTHIANS 13:13

S lowly read through and answer these questions: Do I love others with God's love? Do others see in me—whatever my circumstances—the joy I have because of my salvation? Do people see peace in me regardless of what is going on in my life? Am I patient with people? Do I treat people with kindness? Is my lifestyle characterized by goodness and service? What evidence of my faithfulness to God do people see? Am I gentle with people? In what aspects of my life would more self-control be beneficial?

Allow Christ's love to rule in your life and shine through you today. In God's kingdom, being comes before doing, for what we do is always determined by who we are. And God's Spirit within us is at work, making us more like Jesus.

CODE WORD: THEME

Of all the themes of life, of music, of poetry, and of great literature, one stands supreme, and that is LOVE. May we make love the theme of our lives, our theme for eternity.

Lord, Your love has no limits; it knows no boundaries. Fill me afresh with Your love today, so that it overflows out of me to others for their good and for Your glory. In Jesus' name, amen.

The law of the LORD is perfect.

PSALM 19:7

Some people today say they believe only part of the Bible: "The Bible contains the word of God, but it is not necessarily the word of God."

But in 2 Timothy 3:16 the little three-letter word *all* means what it says: "All Scripture is given by inspiration of God." While there are different types of literature in the Bible, there are not different degrees of inspiration. The Sermon on the Mount (Matthew 5–7) teaches; the genealogy in Matthew 1 and the Old Testament accounts of the kings are historical; and we find poetry in the Psalms.

But every passage is just as inspired as every other: "All Scripture" is inspired. When Jesus broke forth from the obscurity of the Nazareth carpentry shop to begin His public ministry, He was immediately tempted by the devil. Jesus replied with the Scripture: "It is written, 'Man shall not live by bread alone, but by every word that proceeds from the mouth of God'" (Matthew 4:4). That's inspiration.

CODE WORD: ALL

This little three-letter word is the most inclusive in your vocabulary. It means every word of it, all of it. "Every word of God is pure." (Proverbs 30:5).

Lord, thank You for giving to me Your own Word, sufficient for all my needs today. In Jesus' name, amen.

[Peter] said to [Jesus], "Lord, I am ready to go with You, both to prison and to death."

LUKE 22:33

As Jesus stated in the Great Commandment, loving the Lord Jesus is our primary purpose in life (Matthew 22:37–38). And sometimes we fail.

Peter failed just as Jesus had said he would: Peter denied three times that he even knew Jesus. Consider what the resurrected Lord later said, as well as what He didn't say. Jesus didn't say to Peter, "Some friend you turned out to be. You are just all talk. You failed. You let Me down after boasting so loudly about how faithful you would be at the crisis hour." No, Jesus looked at Peter and simply asked, "Do you love Me?" (John 21:15).

Jesus' question to Peter is also the bottom-line question for us. It is not whether we love one another or love the lost and lonely. It is "Do you love Me?" Loving Jesus is our primary purpose, and doing so affects all other issues in life for our good and His glory.

CODE WORD: BOAST

Be careful not to boast to others about your own good works or commitment to things good. "Let him who thinks he stands take heed lest he fall" (1 Corinthians 10:12).

Lord, may I boast today, but only in You! In Jesus' name, amen.

"I am the way, the truth, and the life. No one comes to the Father except through Me."

T his is the most exclusive statement Jesus ever made. Jesus emphatically declared that He is the one and only way to eternal life, the door through which all must enter. Without Him there is no "way," there is no ultimate "truth," and there is no eternal "life" free of sadness and pain.

As if that declaration were not enough, Jesus also taught that there is no way for people to get to the Father unless we come through Him. In a world where pluralistic persuasions run rampant, the question arises: Is Jesus Christ really the only way, or is He simply one of many ways to life eternal?

One day Jesus got to the heart of His exclusive claim by asking His followers two very pertinent and penetrating questions: "Who do men say that I, the Son of Man, am?" and "Who do you say that I am?" (Matthew 16:13, 15). We all need to answer that second question.

CODE WORD: THE

Do you realize the heavy weight of this little definite article? Jesus is not "a" way. He is *the* one and only way, *the* only truth, and *the* only life.

Lord, You and You alone are the only hope for all mankind, and You are mine! In Jesus' name, amen.

JUNE 9

He is despised and rejected by men . . .
He was despised, and we did not esteem Him.

ISAIAH 53:3

For three years, Jesus gave and blessed, served and healed, taught and corrected, forgave and instructed. For three years, Jesus loved.

But did we love Him? We hated Him. We spit in His face. We beat Him with a leather strap until His back was a bloody pulp. We stripped Him naked and mocked Him. We put a scarlet robe on Him and smashed a crown of thorns on His brow. And then we laughed and laughed and laughed.

Finally, we took His hands—those same hands that once had calmed storms, stroked children's heads, multiplied the loaves and fishes, formed the spittle for the blind man's eyes, and clasped themselves in prayer in the garden—and we nailed them fast to a cross. Then we took those same feet that had walked miles to bring healing and truth, that had walked on the sea, and we nailed them to a cross.

CODE WORD: CULPABILITY

Do you sense any personal responsibility for the cross? Had you been the only one who ever lived who needed a Savior, we would still have the same story.

Lord, drops of grief can never repay the debt of love I owe to You. In Jesus' name, amen.

The woman . . . went her way into the city, and said . . . "Come, see a Man who told me all things that I ever did. Could this be the Christ?"

JOHN 4:28–29

W hat if Jesus were interviewed by one of today's talk-show hosts? And what if the topic were the breakdown of the American home?

Imagine the host's reaction if Jesus responded with an answer like the one He gave to the woman at the well. At one point of their conversation, Jesus said, "Go, call your husband, and come here." When she replied that she didn't have a husband, He remarked, "You have well said, 'I have no husband,' for you have had five husbands, and the one whom you now have is not your husband" (John 4:16–18).

The host's immediate reply might be, "And what is the problem here? The other relationships just didn't work out. Don't You want her to be happy? Besides, who do You think You are? You are completely intolerant!"

In fact, our culture has no moral absolutes; tolerance has become the only real absolute.

CODE WORD: ABSOLUTE

As we swim today in a sea of pluralistic thought all around us, are you holding fast to the moral and spiritual absolutes found in His Word?

Lord, You know all about me—everything I've ever done—and still You love me. In Jesus' name, amen.

"Go and sin no more."

JOHN 8:11

P erhaps our talk-show host would ask Jesus about the world's many religions. Imagine Jesus saying, "I am the way, the truth, and the life. No one comes to the Father except through Me" (John 14:6). That bold statement of exclusivity is the exact opposite of tolerance, the theme of our twenty-first-century world. Our modern culture is screaming that everyone's truth claims, values, lifestyles, and the like should be considered equal.

These screamers often cite Jesus' words to the woman taken in adultery: "Neither do I condemn you" (John 8:11). What a statement of tolerance! Yet—and this is often conveniently ignored—in the same breath Jesus added, "Go and sin no more." Jesus was not offering a suggestion. Its imperative mood and present tense indicate that our Lord forcefully said, "Stop your sinning right now! Stop it!"

Jesus knew this woman was stuck in a sinful lifestyle, but after meeting Him, she didn't stay there. Her life was changed because Jesus would not tolerate—or let her tolerate—a life of sin.

CODE WORD: STOP

When you come to a stoplight or stop sign today, think on this: It is one thing to hear God saying, "I do not condemn you," but let the stop sign remind you that He completes the sentence—"Go and sin no more." Just stop it!

Lord, convict me today of that about which You are saying to me, "Go and sin no more." In Jesus' name, amen.

Our God . . . is able to deliver us from the burning fiery furnace, and He will deliver us from your hand, O king. But if not, . . . we do not serve your gods, nor will we worship the gold image.

DANIEL 3:17–18

Shadrach, Meshach, and Abed-Nego refused to worship the golden image of King Nebuchadnezzar even though they knew the deadly consequences.

They also knew that God was able to deliver them from the fire. Shadrach and his two friends, however, placed their faith in God and God alone, not in what they could get from Him. God is always able to deliver us. The issue is His sovereign will.

Whether or not God delivers us from the furnace—the disease, the business failure—should never change our conviction that He is able. We all know people who have dropped out of the race because even though they said, "Our God whom we serve is able," they could not add those three little words *but if not*. Can you?

CODE WORD: ABLE

God's ability is never the issue. He is able, period, exclamation point! The issue is if you can complete the sentence "But if not . . ."

Lord, help me live in these three words today—but if not. In Jesus' name, amen.

JUNE 13

Be diligent to present yourself approved to God, a worker who does not need to be ashamed, rightly dividing the word of truth.

2 TIMOTHY 2:15

One of the great temptations of the busy believer is to stop studying the Bible. After all, over the years of our Christian lives, most of us have heard hundreds of sermons, attended many Bible classes, read a library of Christian books, and listened to Christian radio. Furthermore, in the twenty-first century, we have so many resources that we can easily spend most of our time reading about the Bible and less and less time actually studying God's Word.

Paul admonished young Timothy—and us—on this point: "Be diligent to present yourself approved to God, a worker who does not need to be ashamed, rightly dividing the word of truth." We are to be diligent and zealous about studying God's Word. The Bible is a miraculous book in which personal study never ends. Bible study is a lifetime endeavor for the committed believer. It is our assignment, our mandate from God.

CODE WORD: BEST

In the midst of all your Christian reading (even *The Believer's Code*), take great caution that you are not substituting the good for the best—the *Bible*.

Lord, Your very Word is the joy and rejoicing of my heart and life. Feed me with it. In Jesus' name, amen.

JUNE 14

The law of the LORD is perfect . . .
The statutes of the LORD are right.

PSALM 19:7–8

God's Word is the bread of our spiritual life. It nourishes and sustains us; it prompts growth; it fuels activity for the Lord. Another reason we believers spend a lifetime faithfully, regularly studying the Scriptures is so that when we stand before almighty God, we may know His approval. We are being good stewards of God's truth when we make time to study, memorize, and meditate on His Word. Don't you long to hear Him say, "Well done, good and faithful servant" (Matthew 25:21)?

What, then, is the manner by which we should go about our task of Bible study? We are to be diligent students, willing to work hard, to dig deep, to consult commentaries, and to use Bible dictionaries to confirm and correct our understanding of key terms. Yes, this is hard work, but this kind of Bible study equips us for "the work of ministry" (Ephesians 4:12).

Dedicated believers devote themselves to the wholehearted study of God's Word.

CODE WORD: BREAD

Think of your Bible as bread that can sustain you for the day. And remember, He taught us to pray for *daily* bread. You need to devour it day by day.

Lord, give me this day my daily bread. I wait for a fresh word from You. In Jesus' name, amen.

Always be ready to give a defense to everyone who asks you a reason for the hope that is in you.

1 PETER 3:15

God has called us to share the gospel truth, and that is another reason why we study His Word. We need to know well the message He has commanded us to share so that we are "ready to give a defense" of the gospel.

So may we approach the Bible with a deep reverence, even with a fear that we might mishandle or misrepresent God's truth. We are to be "rightly dividing the word of truth" (2 Timothy 2:15), and this is a serious assignment. Our message should always be centered in—and issue out of—God's holy Word.

What a high calling and awesome task, to "be diligent to present [ourselves] approved to God, [workers] who [do] not need to be ashamed, rightly dividing the word of truth." In the end, may we know God's approval rather than feel ashamed.

One more thing. Like all that God calls us to, this command to know His Word is for our good and His great glory.

CODE WORD: DILIGENT

Be diligent in your Bible reading. It is far better to take one verse and take time to meditate on it, letting its truth sink deep into your heart, than to speed-read ten chapters.

Lord, may Your Word dwell in me richly today. In Jesus' name, amen.

JUNE 16

Train up a child in the way he should go,
And when he is old he will not depart from it.

PROVERBS 22:6

How many parents have stood upon this verse during seasons of difficult dealings with wayward sons or daughters? There is no promise here that the child will never sow some wild oats. The promise is that the child will eventually return home to the truth upon which he or she was raised. Of course, the operative word in all of this is the very first word of the verse—*train*. This promise is not for all parents of prodigals. This promise is for parents who "train" their children "in the way [they] should go."

There is no more powerful example of this truth than Jesus' story of the prodigal son. Ironically, the story is not about the son—or his brother. The story is really about the father. The story begins, "A certain man had two sons" (Luke 15:11). The father stands center stage. Let's see what we can learn from him.

CODE WORD: TRAIN

We all need training. To train others in the ways of the Lord takes patience and perseverance . . . time and energy. But it is accompanied by a precious promise.

Lord, You are faithful and I hold to Your promises today, although I do not see the answer as yet. In Jesus' name, amen.

*"'Father, give me the portion of goods that falls to me.' . . . His
father saw him . . . and ran and fell on his neck and kissed
him."*

LUKE 15:12, 20

This wise father knew that the way to keep his child was to let
him go. He also knew that he had poured God's truth into
that boy since childhood, and this father trusted in those truths.
Some parents, however, hold their children so tightly that they lose
them. This dad knew that the time had come to open his hand and
let his son go.

When the boy "came to himself" and headed home, the father
saw him "when he was still a great way off" (Luke 15:17, 20) and
ran to him. No pointed fingers or "Where have you been?" or "How
could you do this to your mother?" Just open arms. The boy came
walking, but the father went running. Here was a truly repentant
son and a faithful father receiving him with open arms.

May we be wise about both letting go and receiving back.

CODE WORD: ENVIRONMENT

Like the prodigal, you may have removed yourself from the environment of God's love. But He hasn't moved and will never stop
loving you and waiting for you to come home.

*Lord, help me to let go of what I cannot control and focus
on abiding in the environment of Your love. In Jesus' name,
amen.*

JUNE 18

"Pray: Our Father in heaven."

MATTHEW 6:9

A notable characteristic of the prodigal son's father is his presence: he was there for his sons no matter what their complaints were. When the homecoming party was at its peak, where was Dad? Outside with the wounded older brother, assuring him of his love.

We parents need to be like this father, who had the wisdom to recognize when to open his hand and let his son go; to know to keep his arms open and ready to welcome him back; and to keep his heart ready to encourage and love.

The real message of Jesus' story is that our heavenly Father deals with us in the same way that this father dealt with his prodigal. God our Father has open hands: He gave us free will. God our Father meets us with open arms: they were opened wide on the cross. Finally, God shows us His open heart: He loves us with unconditional and never-ending love.

May God help us parents be the kind of parent He is.

CODE WORD: PRESENCE

You have a ministry of presence. Just being there for that someone, more often than not, speaks louder than any words that could escape your lips.

Lord, Your presence is always with me. Always. In Jesus' name, amen.

The serpent . . . said to the woman, "Has God indeed said, 'You shall not eat of every tree of the garden'?"

GENESIS 3:1

When they were first in the rich, lush garden God had created, Adam and Eve's fellowship with Him was sweet. But one day Satan approached Eve with a simple enough question: "Has God indeed said . . . ?" The enemy was subtly prompting her to doubt God and His promises. And Satan succeeded.

In the beginning, God placed man in paradise; Satan entered and sowed a seed of doubt; we fell. Then God drove our first parents out of Eden. The Bible records humanity's heartbreaking journey in search of what was lost, in search of what once satisfied our souls: intimate fellowship with God. Right now we are exiles from Eden. But God has made a way for us to get back into relationship with Him: Jesus Christ is the way.

What God says in His Word is absolutely true. We can trust Him to do what He says He will do. This week, when Satan tries to get you to doubt by asking, "Has God indeed said . . . ?" let your answer be a resounding yes. Doubt is deadly. God's trustworthiness is forever.

CODE WORD: DOUBT

How many times has doubt robbed us of potential victories we might have enjoyed? Today, when the devil casts a seed of doubt your way—and he will—choose to stand on God's promises.

Lord, You have left us Your Word, infallible and always applicable, for anything that may come my way today. I choose to believe You. In Jesus' name, amen.

[Eve] took of its fruit and ate. She also gave to her husband with her, and he ate. Then the eyes of both of them were opened, and they knew that they were naked.

Genesis 3:6–7

I n the beginning the world was without sin. But God had created human beings with free will, and the first humans chose to disobey.

In the beginning—before their disobedience—God had been the focus of their devotion, and Adam and Eve had not thought much about their nakedness. But when sin entered the picture, "they knew that they were naked" (Genesis 3:7). They were focused on themselves!

When God caught up with them, the buck-passing began. Adam blamed his sinful disobedience on Eve: "She gave me the fruit to eat." Adam even put some of the blame on God: "The woman whom *You* gave to be with me" (v. 12, emphasis added). Eve said, "The devil made me do it!"

Clearly, human nature hasn't changed much at all. The blame game continues, and the world, as well as every individual, suffers under the weight of sin.

Code Word: RESPONSIBILITY

You have a free will, free to do what you want to do. And that is the problem. Our sin nature wants to rebel against God. Take responsibility for your actions today.

Lord, it is never wrong to do right and never right to do wrong. Lead me today to do what is right. In Jesus' name, amen.

For Adam and his wife the LORD God made tunics of skin, and clothed them.

GENESIS 3:21

A fter Adam and Eve ate the fruit, they noticed their nakedness and "sewed fig leaves together and made themselves coverings" (Genesis 3:7). Very creative and resourceful, but not very effective. Fig leaves would never suffice.

So God, in His grace, intervened. Our Creator God, who is the Author of life, took an innocent animal and killed it. Then He covered Adam and Eve with its skin. When that little animal took its last breath, it became the first creature to experience the deadly toll that sin takes.

In its death, however, that animal did more than merely provide a covering for Adam and Eve. Its shed blood foreshadowed the Lamb of God: one day God's only Son, Jesus Himself, would experience the deadly toll of sin and, shedding His blood, die on the cross on our behalf.

Even when sin first entered the world—back in the very beginning—God was there with grace and an eternal plan for our salvation.

CODE WORD: COVERED

Have you ever had a friend say, "I will cover for you"? The truth is you have never had a friend like Jesus who has covered over your every sin.

Lord, whatever I cover You have a way of uncovering. But the good news is whatever I uncover You cover! Such love! In Jesus' name, amen.

About the ninth hour Jesus cried out with a loud voice, saying, "Eli, Eli, lama sabachthani?" that is, "My God, My God, why have You forsaken Me?"

MATTHEW 27:46

Was Jesus actually forsaken by the Father during His moments of agony?

As the battle between darkness and light raged, Satan tried to break Christ. At the cross the enemy sought to get Jesus to give up the spiritual battle and call legions of angels to set Him free. When His disciples deserted Him, Satan tempted Jesus to just give in: His soul was the battleground. And during Jesus' trials and beatings before the cross, the devil sought to get our Lord to give out under the pain of this physical battle.

Many today know the haunting feeling of being forsaken—by a spouse who had promised otherwise, by a mother or father for a reason a child could not conceive. Perhaps there is no more heart-breaking word in our English language than *forsaken*.

Jesus was forsaken when the holy Father turned away from Him who had become our sin.

CODE WORD: FORSAKEN

Think of it. Jesus was forsaken as He bore the weight of your sin on the cross in total darkness. Why? So that you might never be forsaken. Don't give in. Don't give up. Don't give out.

Lord, no one else ever loved me this much. Help me to love others today as You have loved me. In Jesus' name, amen.

And the king appointed for them a daily provision of the king's delicacies and of the wine which he drank.

DANIEL 1:5

D aniel lived in a crumbling culture much like ours, but he did not give in to its immorality and perversions. How? Because early on, back in Jerusalem, he had been trained "in the way he should go" (Proverbs 22:6). He was well grounded in God's truth, the truth that his faithful parents had taught him.

Daniel could not control the cultural influences of Babylon swirling around him, but he could control how he would react to them. The Bible says he "purposed in his heart that he would not defile himself with the portion of the king's delicacies" (Daniel 1:8). Daniel was learning a new language and reading a new literature, but he drew the line when it came to eating the king's meat. That act conflicted with his Hebrew faith. Daniel would not compromise when it came to the Word of God and His commands.

The Bible simply says, Daniel "purposed in his heart" not to turn from his God. And his parents would have been proud.

CODE WORD: REACTION

Jesus spoke the Sermon on the Mount to show us it is our reactions, not just our actions, that are so important (if slapped on the cheek, turn the other also [Matthew 5:39]). Watch how you react today to what may come your way.

Lord, fill me with such wisdom today that I may react to things around me in a way pleasing to You. In Jesus' name, amen.

JUNE 24

*"This Book of the Law shall not depart from your mouth, but
you shall meditate in it day and night, that you may observe to
do according to all that is written in it. For then you will make
your way prosperous, and then you will have good success."*

JOSHUA 1:8

Success as the world defines it is different from the way God defines it.

Nehemiah, the faithful layman, returned to Jerusalem to lead in the rebuilding of its broken walls, and Nehemiah had the promise, "The God of heaven will give [you] success" (Nehemiah 2:20 NIV). We read, "The LORD was with Joseph, and he was a successful man" (Genesis 39:2). And Joshua 1:8 says that if we keep the Word of God in our minds and in our mouths, day and night, and put it into practice, we will have "good success."

For the believer, success can be defined as the ability to find the will of God for your life and then doing it.

CODE WORD: SUCCESS

We all want to be successful at something. And all of us can be if we properly define the word *success* as the ability to find God's will for our lives and then to do it.

*Lord, finding and doing Your purpose for my life is where I
define my success. In Jesus' name, amen.*

[The righteous man's] delight is in the law of the Lord,
And in His law he meditates day and night.

Psalm 1:2

Like the psalmist, we are to meditate on God's Word, keeping it in our hearts and letting it permeate our very being, direct our thought processes, and guide our actions. We complete the purpose of hearing the Word when we put it into practice through personal obedience.

In fact, this is genuine success in life: staying in the Word of God until we find the will of God so that we can walk in the ways of God. The Word. The will. The walk. We read the Bible because it reveals God's general will for our lives. Godly success comes when—after that—we discern His more personal will for our lives and act on it. We "just do it"!

At the wedding feast in Cana, Mary, the mother of Jesus, gave us one of the most valuable lessons for life when she said, "Whatever [Jesus] says to you, do it" (John 2:5).

Code Word: DELIGHT

Do you find delight in the Word of God? The more you read it, the more you will delight in it. And the mystery is, the more you know, the less you seem to know.

Lord, may Your Word direct my thoughts and guide my actions today. In Jesus' name, amen.

JUNE 26

It displeased Jonah exceedingly, and he became angry.

JONAH 4:1

I t was God's decision to extend kindness and mercy to the people of Nineveh.

And Jonah's heart overflowed with anger. Earlier Jonah had refused to preach a message of repentance to Nineveh. Jonah ended up in the belly of a big fish for three days. . . . Then Jonah did obey and preach.

One would think that after all Jonah had been through, his heart would be softer and overflowing with praise when he learned that God had sent revival to the people of Nineveh. Instead, we see a sharp contrast between God's heart of grace and Jonah's heart of anger.

God's mercy "displeased Jonah exceedingly, and he became angry" (Jonah 4:1). The Greek word for *angry* means "to burn." Jonah was fuming; smoke was pouring out his ears. This is the first by-product of harboring resentment and anger: it takes away our own peace of heart and mind. Someone filled with God's Spirit has a heart of love, joy, and peace.

CODE WORD: ANGER

Anger is like a cancer. It doesn't affect the other person, it simply eats away at you. Don't allow anger to find a root in your heart. As soon as it appears, wave it goodbye.

Lord, fill me with Your love, joy, and peace so that there is no room for anything else. In Jesus' name, amen.

"Father, if it is Your will, take this cup away from Me;
nevertheless not My will, but Yours, be done."

LUKE 22:42

As the shadows fall upon Gethsemane, we find our Lord praying—and praying with such intensity and anguish that He began to sweat drops of blood. His passion was to accomplish the Father's will for His life. He had told His disciples exactly that: "I have come down from heaven, not to do My own will, but the will of Him who sent Me" (John 6:38).

Now, on the evening before He would hang on a Roman cross bearing the weight of the world's sins, Jesus was wrestling with that upcoming moment of ultimate submission to His Father's will. Having asked His Father if there was another way, Jesus nevertheless prayed, "Not My will, but Yours, be done."

God has a purpose and a plan for each of His children. We may struggle to know what His will is, and if we do know, we may struggle to yield our will to His. Jesus understands that struggle.

CODE WORD: UNVEIL

God does not veil His will from you. He longs for you to find it and walk in it. When you know the Savior, obey the Scripture, and trust the Spirit, you will be on your way to finding it.

Lord, being in and doing Your will for my life brings my greatest joy. In Jesus' name, amen.

He who testifies to these things says,
"Surely I am coming quickly."
Amen. Even so, come, Lord Jesus!

REVELATION 22:20

A person's final words can be poignant, significant, and intriguing. Consider the final recorded words of the resurrected, victorious Jesus—and John's prayer in response.

Jesus' five words comprise a straightforward statement of promise and hope: "Surely I am coming quickly." Each generation since the first century has been looking for Jesus' return to this planet, for "the blessed hope," for His "glorious appearing" (Titus 2:13).

The Bible speaks of three major comings. First, Jesus was born of a virgin in Bethlehem. He "dwelt among us" (John 1:14) and showed us how to love, yet many did not recognize Him as the Messiah.

The second major coming in God's Word is that of the Holy Spirit. When we come to know Christ, the Spirit comes to reside in us. On the day of Pentecost the Holy Spirit indwelled believers, yet many did not recognize Him and accused the disciples of being drunk.

The only major coming to be fulfilled is His return! And it could be today.

CODE WORD: RETURN

Jesus Christ will return to planet Earth. And in a moment when we least expect it.

Lord, I join John in praying, "Even so, come, Lord Jesus!" In Jesus' name, amen.

The disciples went and did as Jesus commanded them.

MATTHEW 21:6

W e come to know Jesus when we are in His presence. And when we quiet ourselves in His presence, we more easily hear His guiding voice, but will we honor Him with our obedience?

Remember when Jesus instructed two disciples to go into a nearby village, find a donkey, and bring it to Him? No doubt. No defiance. No delay. They just "went and did" in obedience to Jesus. (By the way, their act of obedience was key to the fulfillment of the Old Testament prophecy that "your King is coming to you . . . lowly and riding on a donkey" in Zechariah 9:9.)

Now these two followers could have decided that a white stallion would have been much more appropriate for their Master. But they didn't. They simply obeyed Jesus. Too many of us Christ-followers today, however, let our ideas of what ought to be take priority over His actual commands.

Jesus is still on His throne today, and we still honor Him by obeying Him.

CODE WORD: DELAY

If you sense God is speaking to you about a matter, don't doubt, defy, or delay. Take Him at His word and let it be said of you that you "went and did" according to the word of God.

Lord, I will act on Your word without delay now! In Jesus' name, amen.

Beginning at Moses and all the Prophets, He expounded to them in all the Scriptures the things concerning Himself.

LUKE 24:27

O ur knowledge of God's Word is evidence of the Spirit's work in our hearts and lives. The Bible is a sealed book until Jesus' Spirit opens it to us.

On the road to Emmaus, two disciples gained spiritual knowledge as the risen Jesus "expounded to them" the words of Moses and the prophets that pointed to Him. The word *expound* suggests translating a foreign language, and the Bible is like a foreign language to anyone who does not walk in the Spirit of Christ.

Later the two travelers realized that their hearts burned "while He talked with us" (Luke 24:32). Their hearts were set on fire when they stopped talking and started listening to Him, spirit to Spirit. We have a God who speaks to us by His Spirit.

Listen to Jesus' Spirit through His Scripture. And you, too, just might walk away with your heart burning.

CODE WORD: LISTEN

Focus today not so much on what you say to Him, but listen carefully to what He is saying to you through His Word and by His Spirit.

Speak, Lord. Before Your throne I wait. I believe the promise, and I will not let You go until I receive the blessing. In Jesus' name, amen.

JULY

"*Fear not, for I am with
you;
Be not dismayed, for I am
your God.
I will strengthen you,
Yes, I will help you,
I will uphold you with My
righteous right hand.*"

ISAIAH 41:10

Suddenly a light shone around him from heaven. Then he fell to the ground, and heard a voice saying to him, "Saul, Saul, why are you persecuting Me?"

And he said, "Who are You, Lord? . . . What do You want me to do?"

ACTS 9:3–6

Y ou may know this story: the murderous Saul, persecutor of Christians, became—by God's grace—the apostle Paul. Having found God's gospel truth and God's will for his life, Paul spent the rest of his days spreading the message and planting churches throughout the Mediterranean world.

How did Paul determine God's will? He asked God. In fact, Paul's question in Acts 9:6 is the question every one of us should ask: "Lord, what do You want me to do?"

Paul never stopped asking this Acts 9:6 question. Too many of God's people, however, say each morning, "Lord, here are my orders for today: bless me, take care of my family, meet this need, and straighten out that other person."

Let's begin our days with, "Lord, what do You want *me* to do today?"

CODE WORD: INQUIRY

This word has with it a sense of probing. Keep searching, inquiring of the Lord, as to what He would have you do through Him for others this very day. He will lead you to someone for something.

Lord, what do You want me *to do? In Jesus' name, amen.*

God, who is rich in mercy, because of His great love with which He loved us, even when we were dead in trespasses, made us alive together with Christ (by grace you have been saved).

EPHESIANS 2:4–5

T oday's young people often want something for nothing. People on both ends of the economic spectrum have an entitlement mentality. On one end, government programs have reinforced this compulsion. On the other end, wealthy parents have given their children every material need or want imaginable, and they have never had to work for anything.

What Christ has to offer is free, so He is the very thing for which these young adults are searching. Jesus is able to offer relationship for free because He paid the ultimate price: He died on the cross. By His blood Jesus purchased a way for us to be in relationship with the Father. That privilege is neither earned nor deserved, and it cannot be bought. It is provided freely to us through the sacrifice of Jesus' blood.

CODE WORD: FREE

We like that word! You can't earn your salvation. You don't deserve it. You can't purchase it. It is the *free* gift of God, which He already purchased for you with His own blood.

Lord, the most expensive gift I have ever received is eternal life through You. And You gave it to me as a free gift. May my life be my thank-You note. In Jesus' name, amen.

Repent therefore and be converted, that your sins may be blotted out, so that times of refreshing may come from the presence of the Lord.

ACTS 3:19

Many people are on a search for guilt-free living. At night, when they turn off the light, they still have a conscience that longs to live a certain moment over again and differently. This twinge in their conscience is the need for forgiveness.

Again, we who know Jesus are the only ones who hold the answer to their hearts' desires. Only through Christ can we find forgiveness for sins through our confession. Then, as the psalmist promises, "As far as the east is from the west, so far has He removed our transgressions from us" (Psalm 103:12).

And why "as far as the east is from the west" instead of the north from the south? Because the north and south have an end: the North Pole and the South Pole. However, the east and west know no end; they simply keep going. God removes our sin from us forever.

CODE WORD: CONSCIENCE

We all have one. And your conscience is nothing more than God's voice speaking to your heart of your need to turn from your sin. God put a conscience there—in you—as a check and balance.

Lord, when I sense a tinge of guilt rising in me, help me remember that is Your voice speaking to my heart. In Jesus' name, amen.

JULY 4

If My people who are called by My name will humble themselves, and pray and seek My face, and turn from their wicked ways, then I will . . . forgive their sin and heal their land.

2 CHRONICLES 7:14

In 1962 the Supreme Court prohibited this simple invocation in the classroom: "Almighty God, we acknowledge our dependency upon Thee and we beg Thy blessings upon us, our parents, our teachers, and our Country."

Ironically, the original colonies etched the gospel truth in their charters. Rhode Island proclaimed, "We submit ourselves, our lives, our estates unto the Lord Jesus Christ, the King of Kings, and the Lord of Lords, and to all those perfect and most absolute laws given in His Holy Word." Maryland was "formed by a pious zeal to extend the Christian gospel." The founders of Connecticut aimed to "preserve the purity of the Gospel of the Lord Jesus Christ."

We have fallen a long way since those charters were written, but I believe we could be on the threshold of another genuine spiritual awakening in our land. Don't give up on America. Keep praying!

CODE WORD: PATRIOT

A patriot is one who vigorously supports his country and is prepared to defend it against all enemies. Make sure your own highest loyalty is to the Lord and His kingdom as you go about your day.

Lord, I join Simon Peter today in saying, "We ought to obey God rather than men" (Acts 5:29). You hold my highest loyalty. In Jesus' name, amen.

"It is hard for a rich man to enter the kingdom of heaven. And again I say to you, it is easier for a camel to go through the eye of a needle than for a rich man to enter the kingdom of God."

MATTHEW 19:23–24

The youth of today are on a search for prosperity, but given the economic realities of twenty-first-century America, they have little hope of obtaining it. In fact, they will be the first generation in American history that, on the whole, will not raise their children in homes as nice as the ones in which they were raised.

But economic prosperity would not fully satisfy. Jesus is the real answer to their quest for prosperity. And our God has a rich supply of grace, and He is rich in His grace and mercy toward us. We are blessed to know "the grace of our Lord Jesus Christ, that though He was rich, for your sakes He became poor, that you through His poverty might become rich" (2 Corinthians 8:9). That's the gospel!

CODE WORD: RICHES

What is your own net worth? No matter what you have, someone has more. No matter how little you have, someone has less. True riches are deposited in your account in heaven and cannot be measured in bank accounts or stock certificates.

Lord, thank You that in You I am rich . . . in what money could never buy. In Jesus' name, amen.

"Whoever compels you to go one mile, go with him two."
MATTHEW 5:41

The Romans had conquered most of the Mediterranean world. In first-century Palestine, a Roman citizen or soldier could—by law—compel a subject in one of the conquered lands to carry his load for him for one mile, but one mile only.

But Jesus told His followers, "Whoever compels you to go one mile, go with him two" (Matthew 5:41). Can you imagine the reaction of the listening crowd—people who were living under Roman occupation—when it fell upon their ears? Jesus was calling on His hearers to do what was required of them—times two!

What is it that separates some from others in athletics, in education, in business, in the arts, in any endeavor? It is their drive—their willingness—to do more than is expected or required. When we who name Jesus our Savior and Lord go that extra mile, that act separates us out from the crowd, and we find ourselves shining Jesus' light by serving selflessly and with His love.

CODE WORD: EXCEED

Do you find satisfaction in just doing the minimum, that which is required of you? That is not enough. Decide now to exceed that, to do what is required of you and then some.

Lord, give me the servant heart of a second-miler today. In Jesus' name, amen.

Therefore, to him who knows to do good and does not do it, to him it is sin.

JAMES 4:17

Jesus taught about walking two miles carrying another person's burden, and that first mile is often ignored. I have never heard a sermon about the first mile, only about the second. The first mile is required, and that first mile can be tough. The second wind never kicks in on the first mile. Furthermore, it just is not as easy to enjoy the things we have to do as it is to enjoy the things we want to do.

It is tough to walk that the first mile. Ask any first-century Jew under Roman rule. When you are forced to carry an oppressor's load, the first mile interrupts your schedule.

Similarly, often the most difficult part of the Christian life—and of exercise programs and diets, for instance—is walking that first mile. Many want to play leapfrog: they want to enjoy the extras of the second mile, but they do not want to deal with the requirements of the first mile. That's not how it works!

CODE WORD: REQUIREMENT

There is something about us that resists this word. Don't resist. Find your joy today not simply in doing the things that you WANT to do, but, first, in the things you are required to do, those things you HAVE to do. Doing what is required paves the way to rich reward.

Lord, I can never get to the blessings of the second mile unless I walk the first mile . . . and do so with joy. In Jesus' name, amen.

JULY 8

Therefore comfort each other and edify one another, just as you also are doing.

1 Thessalonians 5:11

I magine a first-century boy working at his trade. A Roman soldier comes by, calls to him, and demands that he carry his backpack for the required mile. Yes, this command interrupts the lad's workday, but he has no choice.

This boy, however, is a second-miler. At the one-mile marker, instead of putting down the pack, spitting on the ground, and heading home, he volunteers to go an extra mile. Along the way, he asks the soldier about life in Rome. The soldier is baffled.

Individuals who travel that miracle mile lighten the load—figuratively as well as literally—of the people around them. One simply cannot travel the second mile without influencing others. It takes only one second-miler in a family, on a team, or in an office to lighten the mood and improve the environment.

This second mile is a miracle mile because it is motivated by and manifests the love of Christ.

Code Word: ATTITUDE

It is your attitude, not your aptitude, that will determine your altitude in life. Your attitude today is influencing all those around you for good or for bad.

Lord, let Your joy so fill me that it flows out from me to others today. In Jesus' name, amen.

He humbled Himself and became obedient to the point of death, even the death of the cross.

PHILIPPIANS 2:8

As you've probably figured out, the second mile is the mile our Lord Himself walked. He knows the road very well. It was love that took Him on the miracle mile to the cross.

Jesus journeyed that mandated first mile when He stepped out of heaven, into human flesh, and kept every detail of the law. But Jesus also went the second mile, motivated by His love for us. He who spoke the universe into existence, the One who formed and fashioned us with His own hands, said, "I love you, and I will walk with you." But we went our own way.

That's when Jesus said, "I will go the second mile." It took Him to the cross, where He bore the weight, not of a Roman soldier's backpack, but of our own sin.

Consider opportunities you have today to go the second mile. Doing so will brighten your road and lighten someone else's load.

CODE WORD: BLESSING

If it is great to get a blessing, it is much greater to be a blessing. Give by being a blessing to others, and you will receive the greater blessing.

Lord, it is more blessed to give than to receive. Lead me to someone whose load I might lighten today. In Jesus' name, amen.

JULY 10

May your whole spirit, soul, and body be preserved blameless at the coming of our Lord Jesus Christ.

1 THESSALONIANS 5:23

As he closes his letter to the church at Thessalonica, the apostle Paul described us human beings as a composite of "spirit, soul, and body" (1 Thessalonians 5:23). Our spirit is that part of us that will live as long as God lives. It is our spirit that connects with God's Spirit: our spirit bears witness with His Holy Spirit that we are His children.

You are a spirit—and I am a spirit—made in the very image of God. Our only means of truly knowing God is by our spirit. It is impossible to have a spiritual relationship with Him based on mere human knowledge. As Jesus said to the woman at the well, "God is Spirit, and those who worship Him must worship in spirit and truth" (John 4:24).

Without a relationship of spirit to Spirit, we can never know God because "the natural man does not receive the things of the Spirit of God" (1 Corinthians 2:14).

CODE WORD: ORDER

We are quick to say man is "body, soul, and spirit." But note the proper order: "spirit, soul, and body." You are a spirit-soul being. You just happen to live in a body.

Lord, help me today to be more spirit-conscious and less body-conscious. In Jesus' name, amen.

Whom He foreknew, He also predestined to be conformed to the image of His Son. . . . Whom He predestined, these He also called; whom He called, these He also justified; and whom He justified, these He also glorified.

ROMANS 8:29–30

T his God-choreographed series of events happens in the life of individuals who choose to follow Jesus. Those people—whom God foreknew—He predestined to be His followers. Those whom He predestined to follow Him, He called. Those He called—and who, by His Spirit, responded with faith—He justified: God accepted the shed blood of Jesus as the sacrifice that paid for our sins. And those individuals the Father justified, He also glorified. This blessed calling of God upon our hearts is a significant part of His total redemptive plan, wrapped as it is in the mystery of predestination and free will.

One day "every knee should bow . . . and . . . every tongue should confess that Jesus Christ is Lord" (Philippians 2:10–11). We are blessed to have been called to recognize that truth now and to walk through this life with Jesus.

CODE WORD: JUSTIFY

A court of law may acquit, it may pardon, but it cannot justify, make as if something never happened. But God can . . . and did . . . for you. It is one thing to be forgiven but quite another to be justified.

Lord, such knowledge is too wonderful—You took my sin and made it as if it never happened. In Jesus' name, amen.

JULY 12

*And the Spirit and the bride say, "Come!" And let him who
hears say, "Come!" And let him who thirsts come. Whoever
desires, let him take the water of life freely.*

REVELATION 22:17

We read in Revelation 22 that God's own Spirit joins with
the church in calling Jesus to return. That same Spirit also
called each of us to come to Christ.

At one point in your life, the Spirit issued an inward call to your
heart. I could beg you on my knees, with tears in my eyes, describing
the horrors of hell and the wonders of heaven, but you would
not have come to Christ unless the Spirit had drawn you.

When Peter made his pronouncement of faith, Jesus said, "Flesh
and blood has not revealed this to you, but My Father who is in
heaven" (Matthew 16:17). Peter wrote, "You are a chosen generation, a royal priesthood, a holy nation, His own special people, that
you may proclaim the praises of Him who called you out of darkness into His marvelous light" (1 Peter 2:9).

If you have embraced the gospel message, it is because the Spirit
spoke to your heart and said, "Come!"

CODE WORD: CALL

Most of us remember as children our mom calling us by name to
come to dinner. Jesus is calling you by name to come to Him.

*Lord, thank You that before I ever gave thought of You, You
called me to Yourself. In Jesus' name, amen.*

JULY 13

[Joseph] said to [his brothers], "Please hear this dream which I have dreamed: There we were, binding sheaves in the field. Then behold, my sheaf arose and also stood upright; and indeed your sheaves stood all around and bowed down to my sheaf."

GENESIS 37:6–7

I n this dream, God told young Joseph that he'd be the leader of a great people, but years later, as he—wrongly imprisoned—sat in his cell, its fulfillment was humanly impossible.

According to David, God was testing Joseph. In Psalm 105, David wrote that God "sent a man before [the people]—Joseph—who was sold as a slave . . . laid in irons. . . . The word of the LORD tested him" (Psalm 105:17–19). Could it be that when our own goals seem unreachable, God tests us to see if we are trusting Him or merely looking to Him to bless us?

So what did Joseph do? He simply held on to his God-given dream. He trusted God despite the discouraging circumstances.

Learn from Joseph. Make sure your dream is from God, and then keep following it.

CODE WORD: TENACITY

Don't let go. Have tenacity. When common sense may tell you the situation is hopeless, have the uncommon sense to believe that God can still make the impossible possible.

Lord, You have Your own ways of making my impossible situation possible. I believe. In Jesus' name, amen.

"I have put My words in your mouth."

JEREMIAH 1:9

All Scripture—*all Scripture*—is given to us by God. It originates with God, not with man. It is inspired. All of it.

Inspired literally means "God-breathed." God used men in the writing process—"Holy men of God spoke as they were moved by the Holy Spirit" (2 Peter 1:21)—but He did not breathe on them. Instead, He breathed out of them His Word.

Just as a skilled musical composer creates a score utilizing the flute, the trumpet, and other orchestra instruments, so God chose His own instruments. Some were as different from others as flutes are from trumpets. Yet God chose those instruments and breathed out His Word to us through them. He literally put His words in their mouths.

Inspiration means the words are God's words, and He gave them to man through man. The Bible does not originate with men; it originates with God. The writers' personalities and styles are unique to them, but it was God who—by His Spirit—moved them to write.

CODE WORD: INSPIRATION

Your Bible is a miracle book. It is unlike any other. It is the Word of God given to us through human hands divinely guided.

Lord, to know I have Your very Word, quickened in me by Your Spirit, is enough . . . enough for anything I might need today. In Jesus' name, amen.

Truly this Man was the Son of God!

MARK 15:39

Nailed to a Roman cross, in agonizing and excruciating pain, Jesus spoke seven times.

Jesus' first word was a prayer for His murderers: "Father, forgive them, for they do not know what they do" (Luke 23:34).

Next came a promise for the penitent thief hanging next to Him: "Today you will be with Me in Paradise" (v. 43).

Then came a pronouncement: "Woman, behold your son!" (John 19:26). Jesus commended His mother, Mary, into John's care. Significantly, He referred to her as "woman," for He would no longer be her son; now He would be her Savior.

Then came the darkness that, after three hours, was pierced with the haunting words of an ancient prophecy: "My God, My God, why have You forsaken Me?" (Psalm 22:1).

And after the darkness, a plea: "I thirst!" (John 19:28). Then, the proclamation: "It is finished!" (v. 30). Jesus paid our sin debt in full. Finally, a profession: "Father, 'into Your hands I commit My spirit'" (Luke 23:46).

And Jesus died.

CODE WORD: FORGIVE

How long has it been since you have tasted the forgiveness of God? Don't rush past that question . . . think about it. How much more do you need to forgive someone else today?

Lord, if You forgive me, how can I not forgive others? Help me let go and forgive that someone today. In Jesus' name, amen.

You are of purer eyes than to behold evil,
And cannot look on wickedness.

HABAKKUK 1:13

During the crucifixion, sinless Jesus took our sin in His own body, suffering shame, hurt, humiliation, pain, agony, separation from God, and death—the consequences that we deserved. Our holy God is not able to even look upon sin, however. He could not look upon the sin His Son was bearing, so He turned away. Darkness enveloped the earth as Jesus fought our battle with Satan.

Jesus was willing to endure this separation so that absolutely no one who comes to Him—who names Him Savior and Lord—will ever have to be separated from God. No one will ever experience the pain of being forsaken by their heavenly Father.

Furthermore, Jesus paid in full our sin debt. He died our death so we could live His life. He took our sin so we could take on His righteousness. Jesus was forsaken so we might never be forsaken.

To quote the apostle Paul, "Thanks be to God for His indescribable gift!" (2 Corinthians 9:15).

CODE WORD: FORSAKEN

There is no sadder word in our English language than to be "forsaken" by someone we thought cared for us. Let this sink in—Jesus was literally forsaken so that you might never be forsaken.

Lord, such love for me is too difficult to understand. Thank You for dying my death so I can live Your life today. In Jesus' name, amen.

Entreat me not to leave you,
Or to turn back from following after you.

RUTH 1:16

T he words of our text today have become immortal. First, the backstory.

When famine came to Bethlehem, Naomi, her husband, and their two sons moved to Moab. In due time, her sons married Moabite women. Later, Naomi's husband died, as did her sons.

When the grieving Naomi heard there was again bread in Bethlehem, she encouraged her two daughters-in-law to go back to their people and to their gods. Orpah kissed Naomi and went back. The other, Ruth, clung to Naomi as she spoke the words recorded in today's passage.

These now familiar words offer us an example of how to respond to new things—and may we cling to Christ just as Ruth clung to Naomi. After all, He is the One who speaks from the throne of heaven, "Behold, I make all things new" (Revelation 21:5).

CODE WORD: CLING

Have you ever clung to someone or had someone grab you and not let go? Cling to Christ. And don't let go. He will never let go of you.

Lord, I will not let You go . . . no matter what. In Jesus' name, amen.

For wherever you go, I will go;
And wherever you lodge, I will lodge.

RUTH 1:16

Are you like Ruth? Do you see a change—in home, in job—as a time for personal change and renewal? Ruth seized the opportunity to go to Bethlehem and, with heartfelt determination, clung to Naomi. Her mother-in-law made sure Ruth knew the way would be hard: she would be a pagan Moabite in Bethlehem. Yet Ruth was determined to follow Naomi.

And Ruth's determination meant that she was choosing a new direction for her life. When Ruth said, "Wherever you go, I will go," she was saying, "This will be my life's direction." And that direction was taking her where she had never been.

In spiritual terms, the choice of a new direction is always evidence of genuine spiritual renewal. We come to care more about what Jesus cares about, and we are determined to follow Jesus wherever He takes us. And He will make all things new—He will make us new—when we say to Him, "Wherever You go, I will go."

CODE WORD: DIRECTION

What direction are you headed in life? You will never reach your destination if you don't know where you are headed and how to get there. Make sure your life's road map is the Bible and you are headed in the right direction.

Lord, where You go, I will go . . . all I have to do is follow. In Jesus' name, amen.

Your people shall be my people,
and your God, my God.

RUTH 1:16

As widowed mother-in-law and widowed daughter-in-law walked toward Bethlehem, they were walking with a greater dependence on God.

When Ruth declared, "Wherever you lodge, I will lodge" (Ruth 1:16), she was saying she would trust Naomi to meet her basic needs. Ruth's determination to go with Naomi and forge together a new life in Bethlehem instilled in Naomi a new dependence on God.

Later Ruth instilled in her children and grandchildren this faith in God. Yes, Ruth became a wife and a mother. She met and married Boaz. They had a son named Obed, who had a son named Jesse, who had a son named David—the shepherd, the psalmist, the warrior, the king of Israel, a man after God's own heart.

When personal renewal comes, it is accompanied by a new degree of trusting the Lord to meet our basic needs. And faith-filled Ruth believed that home was in the middle of God's will.

CODE WORD: DETERMINATION

Be determined that you will trust the Lord to meet your needs. He will never forsake you. He has a plan and a purpose designed specifically for you.

Lord, I trust you with every detail of my life and am determined to follow Your way and Your will. In Jesus' name, amen.

Where you die, I will die, and there will I be buried.

RUTH 1:17

Having declared her commitment to Naomi—and to the new direction of her life, the new dependence on God, the new people who would be her family, her new faith—Ruth then said that not even death would separate Naomi and her. Ruth would not return to Moab even if life in Bethlehem did not work out. What a picture of dedication!

So Ruth went to Bethlehem with Naomi, married wealthy Boaz, and became great-grandmother to King David. Yes, Ruth the Moabite has a place in Jesus' (earthly) family tree.

May we yield our lives to God the same way Ruth yielded her life first to Naomi, then to Boaz, then to God Himself. And may we boldly say to Christ what Ruth said to Naomi: "Wherever you go, I will go; and wherever you lodge, I will lodge; . . . your people shall be my people, and your God, my God" (Ruth 1:16). He does indeed make "all things new" (Revelation 21:5).

CODE WORD: DEDICATION

If certain things in your own life are not working out in just the way you think they should, rest in this promise: He has not abdicated His throne, and He is still in control. Dedicate yourself to this truth.

Lord, nothing, not even death, can separate me from You. You are with me now and forever. In Jesus' name, amen.

"The Lord does not see as man sees; for man looks at the outward appearance, but the Lord looks at the heart."

1 SAMUEL 16:7

W hen the prophet Samuel went to Bethlehem to anoint the future king of Israel, he sought out a son of Jesse. The proud father lined up six strong and strapping, hardened and handsome sons. None were God's choice, so Samuel asked if there was not another son. Indeed there was. A shepherd boy named David was out tending his father's sheep. The rest is history, and the incident reminds us that "man looks at the outward appearance, but the Lord looks at the heart" (1 Samuel 16:7). The Lord looks where? At the heart.

What is it, exactly, that the Bible refers to when it mentions "the heart"? The word appears over eight hundred times in the King James Version, referring not to that critical muscle that pumps blood throughout our bodies. Instead, the Bible refers to our thoughts, emotions, and will. Are you honoring God with your thoughts? Your emotions? Your will?

CODE WORD: HEART

Remember, God is not looking at your outward appearance but at what is inside you. He knows what is in your heart.

Lord, search my heart and see if there is any wicked thing in me. In Jesus' name, amen.

Pray without ceasing . . . for this is the will of God in Christ Jesus for you.

1 Thessalonians 5:17–18

W hat is prayer? First, what prayer is not—prayer is not saying ancient words by rote or the same old words by ritual.

What is prayer? Prayer is two-way communication. God communicates to us through His Word. Burning hearts come when we hear from the Lord, and we hear from Him when He opens the Scriptures to us.

Prayer is the talking part of a relationship. To have a positive and productive relationship with our wives, husbands, children, parents, or whomever else, there must be verbal communication. Yet some Christians think they can go for days, or even weeks, without communicating with God. Prayer is, likewise, the talking part of our relationship with the Lord. No wonder He wants us to "pray without ceasing"!

CODE WORD: TALK

Prayer is simply talking to God as you would talk to a close friend. Leave all the high and lofty verbiage behind. He wants to hear your heart speak.

Lord, what a privilege to have Your promise that You hear me right now. In Jesus' name, amen.

All we like sheep have gone astray;
We have turned, every one, to his own way;
And the LORD has laid on Him the iniquity of us all.

ISAIAH 53:6

In Genesis 3, God sacrificed an innocent animal and used its skin to cover the nakedness of Adam and Eve. The first Old Testament shadow of the cross appeared.

Among these shadows is God's command to Abraham to sacrifice his son Isaac. Here is a picture of the coming death of Christ: the father was willing to sacrifice his beloved son. Also, just as the ram God provided took Isaac's place on the altar, Jesus died in our place. Jesus willingly took the punishment for our sin. His act of self-sacrifice meant our forgiveness.

Another shadow is found in the Isaiah 53:6 phrase "All we like sheep." We humans resemble these woolly creatures, so dependent upon their shepherd for their survival.

And in a holy paradox of our faith, our Good Shepherd is also the sacrificial Lamb of God.

CODE WORD: SURROGATE

Just think of this: Christ took your place. He was your Surrogate. He died the death you deserved so you can live the forgiven life you don't deserve. As John the Baptist said, "Behold! The Lamb of God who takes away the sin of the world!" (John 1:29).

Lord Jesus, I thank You for being my substitutionary sacrifice.
Thank You for coming to earth and dying in my place, so I may
live in heaven with You for eternity. In Jesus' name, amen.

Our citizenship is in heaven, from which we also eagerly wait for the Savior, the Lord Jesus Christ.

PHILIPPIANS 3:20

An increasing number of people today do not believe in an eternal hell, a place of everlasting punishment. Disputing its existence, they frequently ask, "How could a loving God allow anyone to go to hell?" The theological answer is that God is letting them have for eternity what they chose in life—and they chose to have nothing to do with Him.

I have no problem believing in hell. But how could there be such a wonderful place like heaven? How could the love and grace of God be so awesome as to make it possible for a sinner like me to spend eternity in such a glorious place?

From the lonely island of exile called Patmos, John saw "a door standing open in heaven" (Revelation 4:1). God has given us a few open doors in Scripture through which we can catch a glimpse of the heaven that awaits us, the place that Jesus has prepared for us.

CODE WORD: OPEN

When you open a door today, let it remind you that God is opening the door to heaven for you to enter by faith in Him.

Lord, I'm overcome with this amazing reality. I'm really going to heaven! In Jesus' name, amen.

There is none righteous, no, not one . . .
There is none who seeks after God.
They have all turned aside; . . .
There is none who does good, no, not one.

ROMANS 3:10–12

T he prophet Isaiah preached this gospel truth well: "All we like sheep have gone astray; we have turned, every one, to his own way; and the LORD has laid on Him the iniquity of us all" (Isaiah 53:6). Every sin you ever committed—every bad thing you have done and every good thing you chose not to do—Christ took in His own body and suffered the punishment you deserved. He took on your sin, so you can take on His righteousness. He died your death, so you can live His life. He took on Himself the wrath of God you deserved, so you could receive the very grace of God that none of us deserves.

As Paul put it, "If you confess with your mouth the Lord Jesus and believe in your heart that God has raised Him from the dead, you will be saved" (Romans 10:9).

CODE WORD: WRATH

Wrath is another of those lost words in modern Christian vocabulary. God is a God of love, but the same Bible says He is also a God of wrath. And His wrath against your sin was poured out on Christ, in your place, as He hung on the cross.

Lord, how You suffered. A simple thank-You seems so inadequate in light of Your receiving the wrath for sin I so deserved. In Jesus' name, amen.

"Follow Me, and I will make you become fishers of men."
MARK 1:17 NASB

Follow Me.

Whenever Jesus spoke those two words, they always proved life-changing to those who heard and followed.

Jesus came upon a group of fishermen hard at work in their lifetime fishing business. Looking them squarely in the eyes, Jesus called them to put away their nets and follow Him.

In Capernaum, Jesus saw a traitorous Jew collecting tax money from his fellow Jews for the Roman oppressors—and his own pocket. Again, Jesus spoke those two simple words, and Matthew put down his money pouch and followed after Him.

Jesus continues to call people to follow Him today. When we heed His call today and become His followers, we will find ourselves becoming interested in what Jesus is interested in. And Jesus was clear about His top priority: "The Son of Man has come to seek and to save that which was lost" (Luke 19:10).

So, if we are genuinely following Jesus, we are also fishing.

CODE WORD: FOLLOW

How simple. All you have to do is follow. As you follow Him you will find yourself becoming increasingly interested in the things He is interested in.

Lord, I hear Your voice saying, "Follow Me." I am staying close today. In Jesus' name, amen.

*Know this day, and consider it in your heart, that the L*ORD *Himself is God in heaven above and on the earth beneath; there is no other.*

DEUTERONOMY 4:39

God has implanted within the soul of man a longing for heaven. All primitive people believed in an afterlife. The ancient Egyptians, for instance, buried their pharaohs with supplies, eating utensils, weapons, and even servants in preparation for life beyond this one. Every human being desires more than what we have on earth, more than what this world offers.

This longing continues today. We long for a world that is free of pain and disease, a world without poverty and homelessness, a world that is pristine and unharmed, and a world without war and conflict. The God-created human soul needs heaven, and heaven is real. We pray to "our Father in heaven" and ask that His "will be done on earth as it is in heaven" (Matthew 6:9–10). Heaven is the place Jesus was referring to when He said, "I go to prepare a place for you" (John 14:2).

CODE WORD: PERFECT

Think of it. Heaven is a perfect place. Whatever takes away the joy of life will be gone, and gone forever.

Lord, to me, heaven is far more than a place. It is a person— You! In Jesus' name, amen.

Now in the morning, having risen a long while before daylight, He went out and departed to a solitary place; and there He prayed.

MARK 1:35

A mong the many good reasons we should pray is that the Lord knows better than we do what we really need.

Prayer makes God real to us.

Just as the Bible gives our prayer direction, prayer brings a new dynamic to our Bible reading: God speaks to us through His Word, and we speak to Him through prayer. Prayer is like a symphony: the Bible is the score, the Holy Spirit is the conductor, and we are the instruments. As we read God's Word, the Holy Spirit leads us in our prayer life, and we actually begin to pray the Scriptures for ourselves and for others.

Another reason we should pray is because Jesus prayed. If He who never sinned saw the need to pray so often, how much more do we, sinful as we are, need to call upon Him?

Prayer has a way of setting us free.

CODE WORD: NECESSITY

We are a needy people, and one of our greatest necessities is to pray. Since we find Christ Himself praying so frequently and fervently, how much more do we need to do likewise?

Lord, as I read Your Word today, put people and needs into my mind for whom and which I need to pray. In Jesus' name, amen.

"You shall receive power when the Holy Spirit has come upon you; and you shall be witnesses to Me in Jerusalem, and in all Judea and Samaria, and to the end of the earth."

ACTS 1:8

B efore the resurrected Christ returned to heaven, He left His disciples—and us—with a challenge to be His witnesses not only at home but also to the very ends of the earth. First, He issued the Great Commission: we are to make disciples by leading people to Christ. We are to baptize these new disciples. And then we are to mature them by "teaching them to observe" all those things Christ commanded (Matthew 28:20).

Immediately before His ascension, Jesus restated His Great Commission to take His good news to entire nations, to the whole world. This command is a basic tenet of the Christian faith: each of us is to be His witness to the lost and dying world around us. This call to evangelism—to share the good news of Christ—is one of Jesus' most basic callings to every believer.

CODE WORD: WITNESS

A witness is one who gives verbal testimony to what he or she has personally experienced. Ask God to give you courage to be a verbal witness to His saving grace today.

Lord, give me the spirit of Simon Peter so that I cannot help but speak the things I have seen and heard. In Jesus' name, amen.

These who have turned the world upside down have come here too.

ACTS 17:6

"Y ou shall be witnesses to Me" (Acts 1:8). This commission to take the gospel to the world is one Jesus gives to all of us. None of us is exempt from this basic element of Christian living, that is, to share the good news of our resurrected Lord.

And God gives us power to do what Jesus has called us to do. We all need power, first, to live the Christian life and, second, to share the news of God's saving love with others. The word Jesus used for power is the root of our word *dynamite*. We need this power to be His witnesses.

The book of Acts is the story of a group of men and women just like you and me who—despite the brutal Roman oppressors—went out and told the story of Jesus. They "turned the world upside down" (Acts 17:6) because they had received dynamite power from on high.

CODE WORD: BOLDNESS

Someone you know needs to know the Lord. Boldness comes not by getting more of Jesus but by giving Him more of you.

Lord, I have the power to be Your witness . . . give me boldness to use it. In Jesus' name, amen.

It came to pass in those days that He went out to the mountain to pray, and continued all night in prayer to God.

LUKE 6:12

W hen should we pray? As we've seen, the Bible encourages us to "pray without ceasing" (1 Thessalonians 5:17). We should live our lives in a constant state of communion with God as we go about our days.

Jesus Himself also shows us when to pray.

Our Lord prayed "a long while before daylight" (Mark 1:35). On occasion, He spent whole nights in prayer (Luke 6:12).

Jesus prayed before each great work He performed. Remember His prayer as He stood outside the tomb of Lazarus? And Jesus prayed before He fed the multitudes on the Galilean hillside with a few rolls and a handful of fish.

Gethsemane shows us how Jesus prayed when submitting to His Father's will would cost Him physical, emotional, and spiritual pain beyond imagining.

And—a final example to us—the busier our Lord's life became, the more He gave priority to His own prayer life.

CODE WORD: EXAMPLE

Jesus prayed before dawn and on occasion all night. He prayed before great undertakings and after them. He is Your constant example to "pray without ceasing."

Lord, the busier I get today, may it be a reminder of the more I need to pray. In Jesus' name, amen.

AUGUST

"Take My yoke upon you and learn from Me, for I am gentle and lowly in heart, and you will find rest for your souls."

MATTHEW 11:29

My brethren, take the prophets, who spoke in the name of the Lord, as an example of suffering and patience. Indeed we count them blessed who endure.

JAMES 5:10–11

After the martyrdom of Stephen in Acts 7, the Christians in Jerusalem came under increasing persecution from the Roman Empire. They refused the Romans' demand to confess "Caesar is Lord." Instead, these Spirit-empowered believers insisted there was only one Lord, the Lord Jesus Christ. Thus, the Bible informs us, "They were all scattered . . . except the apostles" (Acts 8:1).

And James was writing to those believers who had to leave their homes, their jobs, their properties—everything. Talk about stress! Yet God permitted these early believers to experience the scattering and the resulting stress for a purpose. Had these believers stayed in Jerusalem, chances are the gospel would not have spread so completely through the known world. Everywhere these early followers of Jesus were scattered, they shared the good news of Christ's redemptive work, and in just one generation the gospel spread throughout the Roman Empire.

CODE WORD: CIRCUMSTANCE

Often the circumstances that come your way—which on the surface appear so detrimental—are the hand of God behind it all, moving with purpose and power on your behalf.

Lord, nothing takes You by surprise. Help me see Your hand in my life today. In Jesus' name, amen.

The wages of sin is death, but the gift of God is eternal life in Christ Jesus our Lord.

ROMANS 6:23

Through the years, pop culture has popularized good news/ bad news jokes.

For example, there is the one about the pastor who stood up on Sunday and declared, "The good news is we have enough money here this morning to pay off the church debt and to build our new building." He continued, "But the bad news is, it is still in your pockets!"

Or there is the one where the church moderator said, "The good news is the deacons have voted to send a get-well card to our ill pastor. However, the bad news is the vote was 31 to 30!"

When we come to Romans 6:23, one of the most informative and inspirational verses in the Bible, we find some good news and some bad news. The bad news is that "the wages of sin is death." But the good news is that "the gift of God is eternal life in Christ Jesus our Lord."

CODE WORD: NEWS

When you read the news in the paper today or watch the news on television, remember there is good news in Christ always.

Lord, You have given me the promise of eternal life. I have very good news. In Jesus' name, amen.

I have gone astray like a lost sheep.

PSALM 119:176

Have you ever been to a circus? If so, you probably saw an array of trained animals. Huge elephants can be trained to stand on their back legs atop tiny stools. Monkeys can be trained to ride bicycles. Lions can be trained to jump through rings of fire. But have you ever seen a trained sheep? No. Why? Because sheep are not that smart. Sheep cannot be trained to do anything. They tend to just wander around. Focused as they are on the ground—on food—they walk with their heads down and frequently get lost.

No wonder the prophet says, "All we like sheep have gone astray" (Isaiah 53:6). Focused on our appetites for status, money, power, the perfect family or body or spouse or car, we can walk through life with our heads down, and we can get lost. Our being lost— our straying from our Shepherd and Savior—can have eternal consequences.

CODE WORD: TRAIN

If training up a child in God's ways (Proverbs 22:6) is good advice for parents, it is good advice for all of us as God's children. You and I are not past the point of needing spiritual training and discipline— and we never will be.

Lord, I open Your Word today because from it I will receive training in the way You would have me go and—more importantly—training in the person You would have me be. In Jesus' name, amen.

AUGUST 4

"The Son of Man has come to save that which was lost."
MATTHEW 18:11

S heep tend to simply wander and meander aimlessly along the hillsides. Unlike other animals, sheep have no sense of direction.

One day when I was a boy, my dog Penny followed several neighborhood boys as they rode their bicycles to a lake over ten miles away. Late in the afternoon they returned . . . without her.

More than three weeks later, I heard a familiar scratching on the back door. When I opened the door, I was surprised to see my little dog home at last. Many animals—dogs among them—have an instinct that enables them to find their way home even from great distances. But not sheep. They are directionless.

Yes, "all we like sheep have gone astray" (Isaiah 53:6). But Matthew tell us "the Son of Man has come to save that which was lost" (18:11). Many men and women go through life without any real sense of direction, without any perceived purpose. These people merely exist: like sheep, they don't have a sense of direction in life. Do you?

CODE WORD: AIMLESS

So many go through life aimless, with no real direction. These people simply wander around with their heads down like sheep moving from one patch of grass to another. Before they know it, they are alone in the wilderness. Take care to keep your aim in life on Him.

Lord, You are my Shepherd, so I ask You to guide me. Lead me. Protect me. And help me follow You wherever You go. In Jesus' name, amen.

How then can I do this great wickedness, and sin against God?

GENESIS 39:9

Potipher's wife burned with lust and passion for the young Hebrew, Joseph, and the timing seemed perfect for her to approach him. Potipher was away from home. Nobody would know about the rendezvous. She certainly wouldn't tell! Most young men would have been flattered by the attention, but Joseph fled. Saying, "How then can I do this great wickedness, and sin against God?" he ran the opposite direction. Joseph knew that all sin is primarily against God; Joseph would not only be sinning against her husband.

"How then can I do this great wickedness, and sin against God?" It would be a much better world if each of us asked ourselves this question when we encounter temptation and need to decide which way to turn.

The most tragic thing about our sin is that it is not simply against ourselves or someone else; when we sin, we sin against God. And sin is so serious that it necessitated Christ's death on the cross.

CODE WORD: RUN

When temptation comes knocking on your door today (and it will), don't try and fight it . . . don't try and faith it, and don't flirt with it. Flee it. Run. Get out of there.

Lord, give me the wisdom and the power to say no, from the very beginning when I am tempted. In Jesus' name, amen.

AUGUST 6

Keep back Your servant also from presumptuous sins;
Let them not have dominion over me.

PSALM 19:13

When King David faced temptation, he chose differently than Joseph did.

First, David saw Bathsheba, and this is not sin. Neither is it a sin to have thoughts pass through our minds. The problem comes when we don't allow those thoughts to pass through but instead grab them.

Next, David coveted. He inquired as to who she was—and whose she was. Then, even though she was the wife of one of his valiant soldiers, David took her. After committing adultery with her, David tried to hide his adultery, even to the extent of arranging for her faithful husband, Uriah, to be killed in battle.

It makes no difference whether it is David, or Adam and Eve, or you or me. The course of sin is the same: we see . . . then we covet . . . we take . . . and we try to hide, hoping against hope we will not be found out.

Code Word: PROGRESSION

When you fall into sin, there is a downward progression. We see—covet—take—and hide. Do you find yourself at one of these stops today?

Lord, guard my mind so that I do not allow sin to have a room in my heart. In Jesus' name, amen.

If [my people] break My statutes
And do not keep My commandments,
Then I will punish their transgression.

PSALM 89:31–32

King David tried to hide his sin with treachery, lies, and the death of Bathsheba's husband. This is the curse of sin: once we indulge, it begins to dominate our thinking and can start to control our actions. We find ourselves constantly looking over our shoulder, wondering if we will be found out. One lie is necessary to cover another, and then another lie covers that one, and on it goes.

David actually thought he could sin and win. He thought he could get away with adultery, lies, and murder. But he was wrong. David learned that the pleasures of sin are fleeting. We deceive ourselves when we think we can satisfy our desires outside God's will without suffering any consequences. Sin's momentary pleasures are never worth the pain sin brings.

Bathsheba conceived as a result of her encounter with David, but their little boy died as an infant. What had begun in pleasure ended in pain and loss.

CODE WORD: EFFECT

You can never sin and get away with it. There is a cause and effect. Be sure it will find you out. Sin always brings unexpected consequences.

Lord, help me remember today that nowhere I go and noth-
ing I do will be hidden from Your eyes. In Jesus' name, amen.

I have been crucified with Christ.

GALATIANS 2:20

In this bold statement of Paul's, the verb tense is perfect: the action was completed in the past but it has continuing results. The voice is passive: the subject is the recipient of the salvation action of Christ; we cannot crucify ourselves. We might get a hand or a foot nailed to our cross, but we cannot crucify ourselves. And the mood is indicative: it is a straightforward statement of fact.

The crowd gathered on Calvary saw only one man on that center cross. But God the Father saw hanging there not just Christ, but you and all others throughout history who would put their faith in Him. When we come to Christ, God takes our old life from us. We are "crucified with Christ." We are to live like dead men and women today, dead to our old life and alive to a new life in Christ. And open to the revival God longs to send.

CODE WORD: CROSS

If you lived in the first-century world and saw a man carrying a cross, it meant one thing—he was on his way to die. You were crucified with Christ. Live like a dead person today—dead to your own sinful and selfish passions.

Lord, I take up my own cross today and follow You. In Jesus' name, amen.

"Unless a grain of wheat falls into the ground and dies, it remains alone; but if it dies, it produces much grain."

JOHN 12:24

I magine dropping a grain of wheat into the earth and covering it with soil. That little grain dies—and only then does it release its life germ. After a while a tiny blade pushes its way through the soil and eventually becomes a full-grown plant that produces hundreds of little seeds, just like the one you planted.

During His time on earth, Jesus produced no one like Him. In fact, not long before His death, the disciples—hardly reflecting Jesus' servant heart—argued among themselves about who would be the greatest in His kingdom.

So Jesus died, and He was planted in the earth only to burst forth on the third day! His resurrection has indeed produced much grain: by God's grace, two thousand years after Jesus walked this earth, His followers love with His love.

Eternal life came after Jesus' death and resurrection, and His life germ exists in His people as a result.

CODE WORD: LIFE

The world teaches us that death comes from life. But the converse is true; it is just the opposite. Life comes from death. There is another life awaiting us all . . . beautiful and eternal.

Lord, reproduce Your life in me so that I might bring forth good fruit to honor You. In Jesus' name, amen.

Then He taught, saying to them, "Is it not written, 'My house shall be called a house of prayer for all nations'? But you have made it a 'den of thieves.'"

MARK 11:17

Before it is to be called a house of Bible teaching, a house of evangelism, a house of discipleship, or a house of social action, Jesus said His house is to be called a "house of prayer."

It is interesting to note that the disciples asked Jesus, "Lord, teach us to pray" (Luke 11:1). They never asked Him to teach them to preach or to evangelize or to organize or to mobilize. According to the gospel records, the only thing these faithful followers requested was that Jesus teach them to pray. They observed Him for three years. They saw the intensity and frequency of His own personal prayer life. They knew that if they could capture the essence of prayer, they would be well on their way to preaching or doing any of the other ministries their Lord called them to do.

CODE WORD: PRECEDENCE

Let prayer take precedence today and make it your priority and not a sort of tagged-on afterthought to the business of the day.

Lord, teach me to pray and to make it a priority in my life. In Jesus' name, amen.

I said to the king, "If it pleases the king . . . I ask that you send me to Judah, to the city of my fathers' tombs, that I may rebuild it."

NEHEMIAH 2:5

Pursuing a new beginning and following God's leading can often mean moving out of our comfort zones. That is exactly what Jesus did when He laid aside His glory in heaven: Jesus left His comfort zone, encased Himself in human flesh, and walked among us. Not asking people to do anything He Himself hadn't done, Jesus constantly calls men and women to leave their comfort zones and follow Him.

Listen to Nehemiah: "I was the king's cupbearer" (Nehemiah 1:11). That was Nehemiah's job and comfort zone, but God had a special assignment for him. Rebuilding the walls of Jerusalem—that was the assignment—meant Nehemiah would leave his comfort zone, take a risk, return to Jerusalem, and be vulnerable to hostile people and unknown challenges. But the result would be rewarding. Nehemiah was the agent of an incredible rebuilding process that brought much good to others and much glory to his God.

CODE WORD: RISK

God's kingdom moves forward when His people take risks. Jesus risked the cross, confident that the Father would raise Him on the third day. Move out of your comfort zone today when God calls.

Lord, give me the courage to be a risk taker with You. In Jesus' name, amen.

What man can live and not see death?
Can he deliver his life from the power of the grave?

PSALM 89:48

Death is sure. It is certain. We deal with death in many ways. Some attempt to flee from it. Some go to the extreme of cryonics, freezing their bodies in hopes that future medical break-throughs will be able to bring them back to life at some later date. Some try to forget death. They simply ignore the subject—as if it will somehow go away! Others fear death: they have no hope for what happens after death and no security in Christ. Then there are people, like David, who realize that their days are numbered and accept death as a natural part of life.

Yet we who know the Lord need not fear the inevitable. Instead—whether we are grieving the loss of a friend to that universal enemy or we are facing death ourselves—we can be assured that God is with us. We can declare like the psalmist, "You are with me" (Psalm 23:4).

CODE WORD: RELEASE

You are never ready to live until you are ready to die. Only Christ can bring the peace, the release that passes understanding and takes away the fear of death.

Lord, the world cannot take away the peace that You give to me. In Jesus' name, amen.

Yea, though I walk through the valley of the shadow of death, I will fear no evil; for You are with me; Your rod and Your staff, they comfort me.

PSALM 23:4

A lot of voices tell us how to live, and self-help books flood the marketplace. But only one Book tells us how to die. And no verse in that Book of books is more relevant to the subject than the verse above.

Tradition tells us that David penned these words about the "valley of the shadow of death" while sitting in the Judean wilderness between Jerusalem and Jericho. The spot—known today as Wadi Kelt—is a long valley about four and a half miles long, and its canyons run as much as fifteen hundred feet in depth. The sun casts a shadow over the canyon and on the sheep trails across the way, which snake their way up, down, and through the rugged terrain.

Aware of how deep the valleys around him were, David knew he would walk with his Lord through the deepest "valley of the shadow of death."

CODE WORD: SHADOW

When you see a shadow, let it always remind you that you will never walk through the valley of death. Jesus did that for you. You will walk only through the valley of the "shadow" of death.

Lord, a shadow might frighten me, but it can never hurt me, and You are with me. In Jesus' name, amen.

AUGUST 14

He will swallow up death forever,
And the Lord God will wipe away tears from all faces.

ISAIAH 25:8

In Psalm 23, David spoke of walking through the valley of the shadow of death. That valley was not his final destination. David knew that we enter this valley from time to time as we journey through life, but we don't stay there. When we lose a loved one, our Good Shepherd walks us through those days of darkness and grief, and He brings us out the other side. Isaiah says he will "swallow up death forever."

When it is our own death, our Good Shepherd walks us through the valley to the glories of heaven, a resurrected body, and a place free of crying and pain.

Consider a caterpillar's transformation. It was buried in a shroud called a cocoon. By and by, the grave burst open, and from it emerged a magnificent creature so different from its former self, a creature gifted now with delicate butterfly wings of freedom.

We understand the caterpillar/cocoon metamorphosis. Do we know as much about our own destinies?

CODE WORD: THROUGH

You do not walk "in" the valley . . . you walk "through" the valley. You don't stay there. If there were no valleys, there would be no mountaintops.

Lord, I hold to Your promise that You are with me always. In Jesus' name, amen.

"I am the light of the world. He who follows Me shall not walk in darkness, but have the light of life."

JOHN 8:12

Note carefully what David said in Psalm 23:4: followers of Christ never walk through the valley of death, only through the valley of the *shadow* of death.

The Lord Jesus Himself, however, walked through the valley of death. For three days and nights He walked that valley—and then emerged from the empty tomb and said, "Behold . . . I have the keys of death and of Hades" (Revelation 1:18 NASB).

So the believer walks through the valley of the shadow of death. A shadow may horrify, but it cannot harm. And David walked "through the valley of the shadow of death" because that is what we do with a shadow: we simply walk through it.

Also, the only way you can have a shadow is to have a great light shining. Jesus said, "I am the light of the world" (John 8:12). We believers therefore deal with only the shadow of death.

CODE WORD: LIGHT

The light of the whole world is Jesus. If you are walking through a shadow experience right now, it simply means He is near . . . very near.

Lord, surprise me today with Your presence as I seek to walk in Your light. In Jesus' name, amen.

We are His workmanship, created in Christ Jesus for good works, which God prepared beforehand that we should walk in them.

EPHESIANS 2:10

D id you see that? You are God's "workmanship." (We get our English word *poem* from the Greek word translated "workmanship.") You are God's special creation, a work of art He Himself crafted.

God created you not only for His delight but also "for good works." He gave you a one-of-a-kind combination of gifts and talents, and He has planned opportunities for you to use them. Doing those good works will mean joy and fulfillment as you shine God's light and share His love.

It's all God's amazing grace. When we come to Him by faith, we begin the great adventure of doing the good works He has prepared for us to do.

CODE WORD: WORKS

Our eternal salvation is not dependent upon faith and works, but our salvation will be evidenced in a faith that works. Somewhere there is something for you to do that no one else can do quite like you can. That work is what God created you for.

Lord, I know that my works are not a requirement for my salvation, but are instead evidence of it. As I work where You have placed me, help me remember I am Your "workmanship," created for good works. In Jesus' name, amen.

There shall be no night there: They need no lamp nor light of the sun, for the Lord God gives them light.

REVELATION 22:5

G od loves beauty.
Look around at our sin-cursed earth. Think about Yosemite and Zion and the Grand Canyon. Think of the oceans and the stars, flowers and sunsets. Now imagine the beauty of a place created by God but untarnished by sin. You are imagining heaven.

John got a glimpse of heaven's beauty one day and tried to express it in words: "Its wall was of jasper; and the city was pure gold, like clear glass" (Revelation 21:18). The apostle Paul knew that heaven is beyond description and even beyond imagination: "Eye has not seen, nor ear heard, nor have entered into the heart of man the things which God has prepared for those who love Him" (1 Corinthians 2:9).

Heaven is a place of unparalleled beauty and radiance. The book of Revelation offers glimpses of its glory. Our limited human vocabulary permits us only to attempt to describe its radiance.

CODE WORD: INDESCRIBABLE

There are certain realities where words are useless to describe things. At the top of this list is a place called heaven.

Lord, thank You for giving us a glimpse of what awaits us for eternity! In Jesus' name, amen.

For prophecy never came by the will of man, but holy men of God spoke as they were moved by the Holy Spirit.

2 PETER 1:21

Peter chose an interesting word when he wrote "holy men of God spoke as they were moved by the Holy Spirit." The Greek word translated here as "moved" appears in the account of Paul's shipwreck recorded in Acts 27.

There had been a fierce storm, and the sailors onboard were unable to guide the ship because of the strong winds. At one point they simply let the winds take the ship wherever they blew it. Oh, the sailors remained active on the ship as the storm raged around them, but they had relinquished control over where it would go. So it was with the Bible writers. In a very real sense, the writings were not the writers' own. God Himself put His own words in their hearts and minds, allowing His truth to be recorded and thus preserved for us forever.

CODE WORD: ANALOGY

What a vivid analogy. Just as sailors working feverishly in the storm with no control over where the wind took the ship, so the Bible writers had pen in hand as God Himself directed the very words they wrote.

Lord, Your Word is my lamp today. Light the way for me. In Jesus' name, amen.

AUGUST 19

"I am He who lives, and was dead, and behold, I am alive forevermore."

REVELATION 1:18

As David wrote in Psalm 23, we will fear no evil. Why? Because the Lord has conquered death, hell, and the grave and because He is with us when our life journey takes us through that shadow.

The apostle John got a glimpse of Jesus' resurrection glory that we will see in heaven. On the lonely island called Patmos where he was exiled, John saw a vision of the exalted Christ: "When I saw Him, I fell at His feet as dead. But He laid His right hand on me, saying to me, 'Do not be afraid; I am the First and the Last. I am He who lives, and was dead, and behold, I am alive forevermore. Amen. And I have the keys of Hades and of Death'" (Revelation 1:17–18).

That is why David—and you and I—will walk through the valley of merely the shadow of death. And we need not fear evil because our resurrected Lord—our Good Shepherd—walks with us.

CODE WORD: KEYS

When you hold your keys today, let them remind you that Jesus holds the keys to death. One day He will open the door to heaven to you and to me. We can trust Him. He is always right on time.

Lord, You are from beginning to end. Lead the way for me today, and I will follow. In Jesus' name, amen.

And about the ninth hour Jesus cried out with a loud voice, saying ... "My God, My God, why have You forsaken Me?"

MATTHEW 27:46

God the Father is holy, and He cannot even look upon sin. This truth is why, on the cross, "the LORD has laid on Him [Christ] the iniquity of us all" (Isaiah 53:6).

On the cross, Jesus took our sin in His own body, and He willingly suffered the shame, hurt, humiliation, pain, agony, and death—the consequences of our sins—that we deserved. God the Father could not look upon the sin His Son was bearing, so He turned away, prompting Jesus to cry out, "My God, My God, why have You forsaken Me?" (Matthew 27:46; originally Psalm 22:1). Jesus was saying with His actions, "I will endure this separation so that people who come to Me will never have to be separated from God, so that they will never experience the pain of being forsaken by their heavenly Father." What a Savior.

CODE WORD: SEPARATION

Christ's greatest agony on the cross was not His physical pain. It came during those hours of darkness when the Father looked away as Jesus, separated from the Father, bore the weight of your sin in His own body. He suffered separation from all that was holy so you might never be separated from the love of God.

Lord Jesus, no one—at any time or in any place—has ever loved me or could ever love me as much as You love me. Thank You for Your willingness to be forsaken by God Almighty so that I never will be. In Jesus' name, amen.

AUGUST 21

As the body without the spirit is dead, so faith without works is dead also.

JAMES 2:26

So are we saved by works? Or are we saved by faith? People in the early church—and even through the centuries until today—tend to gravitate toward one or the other. One view overemphasizes faith while underemphasizing works; the other overemphasizes works while underemphasizing faith. The former is referred to as "easy believism": proponents think one can say a simple "sinner's prayer" without making any change of lifestyle, without spending time in prayer or Bible study, and still be saved. The other option is referred to as a "works salvation": proponents think one can earn salvation through good works.

In his epistle, James addressed this conflict head-on. He wrote in no uncertain terms that "faith without works is dead" (James 2:26). Scripture clearly teaches that salvation is wholly by grace through faith in Christ Jesus alone and "not of works, lest anyone should boast" (Ephesians 2:9). But Scripture also teaches that true saving faith is always accompanied by good works.

CODE WORD: THAT

It is not about faith *and* works, or faith *or* works. The Christian character is about a faith *that* works!

Lord, it is faith alone that saves, but faith that saves is never alone. In Jesus' name, amen.

[T]here shall be no more death, nor sorrow, nor crying. There shall be no more pain, for the former things have passed away.

REVELATION 21:4

L ife on this earth makes us exhausted—emotionally, mentally, and physically.

But in heaven we will never see a hospital, a counseling center, a nursing home, or a funeral home: there will be no more sickness, depression, mental illness, aging, or death. We will never see a police station or courthouse: there will be no more crime. We will never hear the shrill sound of an ambulance siren: there will be no more accidents. We will never have to lock our doors: there will be no more fear.

Consider again the "no mores" of heaven. No more death. No more tears. No more mourning. No more crying. No more pain. No more farewells. No more separation. No more sorrow. No more sin. Whatever that robs you of the joy in this world will be gone—and gone forever.

Heaven is a place of peace. Heaven is a place of rest.

CODE WORD: POLICE

When you see a police officer today, let it remind you that in heaven there will be no need whatsoever for the men and women in blue!

Lord, what a place You have prepared for us! In Jesus' name, amen.

We ought to obey God rather than men.

ACTS 5:29

I t happens sometimes. More often in some governments than others. I'm talking about a direct conflict between man's law and God's law.

As believers, we have the biblical responsibility to submit to and support governmental authority. After all, its authority issues forth from God Himself. Our observance of the law is a positive public testimony of our faith. Obedience is the right thing to do, unless civil law directly contradicts God's law. Then we should "obey God rather than men" and face the consequences.

In this world that is increasingly advocating tolerance of everything except Christianity, we must learn to live with pressure and be guided by the truths we find in God's Word, the Bible. There may come a time when obeying God's law means disobeying our nation's laws. May we be willing to suffer the consequences of our civil disobedience just as generations of believers have done and just as brothers and sisters in the Lord around the world today are doing.

CODE WORD: COURAGE

It takes courage to stand for what is right in our world today. Be strong and have the courage not to condone nor compromise what is clearly opposed in Scripture.

Lord, why should I expect a life of ease while others fought to win the prize and sailed through bloody seas? In Jesus' name, amen.

AUGUST 24

Faith comes by hearing, and hearing by the word of God.

ROMANS 10:17

God uses His Word to bring people to salvation. As Paul clearly stated, "Faith comes by hearing, and hearing by the word of God" (Romans 10:17). No one has ever been converted apart from God's Word.

Conviction always precedes conversion in a Christian's life, and the Word of God reveals to us that we are sinners in need of salvation. Yet Romans 5:8 says this: "God demonstrates His own love toward us, in that while we were still sinners, Christ died for us." God's Word also makes plain to us the way to eternal life: "Believe on the Lord Jesus Christ, and you will be saved" (Acts 16:31).

The Word of God teaches us about salvation and, as the Holy Spirit works in our hearts, prepares us to receive that gift. True faith involves knowing Christ as Savior and Lord, and we arrive at that point—at least in part—because of the truth God sets forth in His written Word.

CODE WORD: INVITATION

Most of us receive dozens of invitations to attend various events throughout the year. And we are not invited to certain events we wish we were. Here is an invitation that beats them all: "Whosoever will may come."

Lord, thank You for knocking at my own heart's door and inviting me to the greatest place of all—heaven. In Jesus' name, amen.

Jesus wept.

JOHN 11:35

These two words offer incredible insight into the heart of our Lord. What powerful evidence of the humanity of our Savior, the God-man.

Scripture reports two times when our Lord actually wept, and both of them take place on the Mount of Olives opposite Jerusalem. On the eastern slope of the mountain, in the small village of Bethany, we find Jesus weeping over our sorrows at the grave of Lazarus (John 11:35). On the western slope of the mountain, we find Him on Palm Sunday weeping over our sins (Luke 19:41).

Is Jesus is still weeping today? Chances are, He is. Even though He has proved victorious over death and sin by His resurrection, both death and sin continue around the world, around the clock. He surely cries with those—even those believers—who grieve the loss of a loved one. And He who cried over the sins of Jerusalem undoubtedly cries over our sins.

Tears have a language all their own, and Jesus' tears here speak of love and compassion.

CODE WORD: TEARS

Think about this word today . . . *tears.* They have a language all their own. They can speak words that can't be uttered. Your tears are a telescope through which you can peer into God's own heart.

Lord, as You wept over Jerusalem, give me tears to weep over that for which You wept. In Jesus' name, amen.

[The Lord] is gracious, and full of compassion, and righteous.

PSALM 112:4

With poignant brevity, John simply stated in his gospel account of the incident, "Jesus wept" (11:35). The event was the funeral of His close friend Lazarus. Jesus did not weep because Lazarus was dead. He knew that in a moment He would restore life to him—and He did!

Jesus wept when He saw Lazarus's sisters crying. Tears touch the heart of our God. Mary's heart was broken. Her brother was dead, and that wouldn't have happened if Jesus had come sooner. Mary was hurting and inconsolable, weeping with deep sobs and wails. When Jesus saw her, He wept with her. Our great God is touched by our own hurts and broken hearts. The psalmist said that our God is compassionate (Psalm 112:4) and that He keeps our tears in a bottle (Psalm 56:8). Truly, we serve a Lord who weeps with us over our sorrows and who is touched by our broken hearts.

Tears truly have a language all their own. They often speak of compassion and love more clearly than words can.

CODE WORD: COMPASSION

The same God who stood by Mary is your God. He stands by you right now and is touched by your own hurts and heartaches.

Lord, thank You that You are not far off and removed, but very near . . . right now. In Jesus' name, amen.

Faith was working together with his works, and by works faith was made perfect.

JAMES 2:22

S alvation does not and cannot result from any human effort or good works. Salvation begins with God, not with us. We don't initiate it; God does. We didn't originate it; He did. Had God not chosen us, we never would have chosen Him.

Our eternal salvation rests entirely on God's grace and is appropriated through our faith in the finished work of Christ. Salvation is the free gift of God to everyone who will receive it. The Bible also says that true, saving faith will always result in good works. After all, how could the living Christ take up residency in your life, be alive in you, and not make any difference in the way you think and act?

Our part is to receive salvation, understanding that it has its origin in God, not in us, that we learn about salvation through God's Word, and that our salvation results in good works.

CODE WORD: ORIGIN

Everything we know has an origin, a place of beginning. Your salvation originates with God, not with you or me. He is the origin of everything.

Lord, You who began this good work in me are faithful to complete it. In Jesus' name, amen.

AUGUST 28

Pure and undefiled religion before God and the Father is this:
to visit orphans and widows in their trouble.

JAMES 1:27

I n the first century there were no life insurance policies or Social Security benefits, no orphanages or retirement homes. If the breadwinner died, orphaned children became residents of the street, often abused and traded by slave owners. Widows had no social standing, and some turned to immorality to provide for themselves. As Christians, we are to show mercy and kindness to people in such great need, especially those who can never reciprocate.

James's command to visit those in need uses the Greek word meaning, literally, "to care for" these individuals. The word means much more than paying a simple visit to these people from time to time. After all, a true sign of Christian character is a genuine concern for anyone in need.

But James wasn't suggesting we can be saved by good works prompted by that Christlike character. Salvation never results *from* good works, but it always results *in* good works.

CODE WORD: J-O-Y

Look around you at others today. Joy comes by putting Jesus first, others second, and yourself third. J-O-Y!

Lord, help me to esteem others I see today as better than myself. In Jesus' name, amen.

With my whole heart I have sought You;
oh, let me not wander from Your commandments!
PSALM 119:10

H ow can a young man cleanse his way?" the psalmist asked. And then he answered his own question: "Your word I have hidden in my heart, that I might not sin against You" (Psalm 119:9, 11).

It is not enough to know the truths and teachings of God's Word in our head; we need to stow God's Word in our hearts. When we memorize and meditate on God's Word, we are able to take the Bible with us in all the traffic patterns of life without actually carrying it. Dwight L. Moody, founder of the Moody Bible Institute, wrote these words in the flyleaf of his Bible: "The Bible will keep me from sin, or sin will keep me from the Bible."

How can we cleanse our ways and keep our ways pure? We must know God's Word in our heads and stow that holy Word in our hearts through memorization and meditation.

CODE WORD: MEMORIZE

How long has it been since you memorized a verse of Scripture? Think about it seriously. Set out today to memorize a verse a week for the rest of the year.

Lord, it is hard to not "wander from Your commandments" if
I have not stored them up in my heart. Help me to memorize
Your Word this week. In Jesus' name, amen.

My hands also I will lift up to Your commandments,
Which I love,
And I will meditate on Your statutes.

PSALM 119:48

Joshua was the first person the Lord instructed to meditate on the Word of God day and night. Abraham didn't get his marching orders in writing. Joseph received God's revelation through God-given dreams. Moses heard God speak through a burning bush (Genesis 12:1, 4; 37:5–10; Exodus 3:2, respectively).

Joshua had been named Moses' successor, and Moses had left Joshua the Books of the Law—Genesis, Exodus, Leviticus, Numbers, and Deuteronomy—that he had received from God. Joshua could learn God's truth in the same way we do: from words that had been written down. Joshua was to keep it in his mouth and in his mind. The emphasis for Joshua—and for us—is upon making Bible study and meditation a constant practice. We are to go over and over and over God's truth in our minds to deepen its impression on us and to set it in our hearts so it permeates our thinking processes.

CODE WORD: MEDITATION

Don't allow this word so identified with Eastern religions to rob you of a needed spiritual discipline—meditating on His Word.

Lord, help me to be still . . . and know that You are God. Be that song whose melody stays with me all day. In Jesus' name, amen.

Obey all these words which I command you, that it may go well with you and your children after you forever.

DEUTERONOMY 12:28

W hy does God tell us to "obey all these words which I command you, that it may go well with you and your children" (Deuteronomy 12:28)? By keeping God's Word in our minds and speaking it with our mouths, we will be mindful of what it says and therefore able to apply it to our lives and obey.

Reading the Bible gives us knowledge about God and His ways, and that knowledge serves as a strong foundation for a life of faith. But we need to live out what we learn. Many of us, however, seem to pick and choose what we will obey and what we will ignore. But God's call to us is to do "all that is written" (Joshua 1:8) in Scripture.

Our purpose is to move beyond studying the Bible to obeying the commands and putting into practice the principles we read there.

CODE WORD: PRACTICE

Note that mere observation is not the issue here. You are to *do—to put into practice*—according to what is written in the Word. It is your obedience—not your observation—that is the key to blessing.

Lord, whatever You say today I will obey. In Jesus' name, amen.

SEPTEMBER

"These things I have spoken to you, that in Me you may have peace. In the world you will have tribulation; but be of good cheer, I have overcome the world."

JOHN 16:33

As far as the east is from the west,
So far has He removed our transgressions from us.

PSALM 103:12

A good starting point for prayer is confession, and *confess* means to agree with God about our sin. We aren't to minimize our sin because it isn't as bad as someone else's. Nor are we to excuse our sin because everyone else is doing it. Sin is so serious it necessitated Jesus' death on the cross.

So we confess our sinful words, sinful actions, and sinful thoughts. We also confess sins of omission, things we knew were right but didn't do. And "if we confess our sins, [God] is faithful and just to forgive us our sins and to cleanse us from all unrighteousness" (1 John 1:9). He actually removes our transgressions from us.

As we thank God for His forgiveness, we move to prayers of thanksgiving. We thank God for people, material blessings, and spiritual blessings. Thanksgiving has a liberating effect. In fact, when Jonah prayed "with the voice of thanksgiving," the Lord delivered him from the belly of the fish (Jonah 2:9).

CODE WORD: SEPARATED

When you confess your sin, God separates it from you as "far as the east is from the west." Not "north to south." There are ends there, a north pole and a south pole. But there is no end to the east and the west.

Lord, thank You for separating my sin from me and depositing it in the sea of Your own forgetfulness. In Jesus' name, amen.

SEPTEMBER 2

God demonstrates His own love toward us, in that while we were still sinners, Christ died for us.

ROMANS 5:8

It was a bitter cold winter afternoon. Snow and ice covered the windswept cemetery as I stood with a young couple at the open grave of their newborn baby. We wept and prayed, I read Scripture, I said a few words, and we left.

At home that evening, I could not get that brokenhearted mother and father out of my mind. I went into our firstborn daughter's room, picked her up, and sat down in the den. I wondered how I would have felt if God had taken my child. She was just a few days old and didn't know me any more than she knew the man next door. If I had lost her, she never would have known just how much her father loved her and was willing to give himself for her.

And that is one tragic thing about living without Christ. Those who do not know Christ can never know how much the Father loves them.

CODE WORD: DEPTH

Paul prayed you would know the width, length, depth, and height of God's love (Ephesians 3:18). Down He came from heaven to earth to prove the depth of His love for you.

Lord, how deep is Your love for me . . . how vast beyond all measure. In Jesus' name, amen.

SEPTEMBER 3

Certainly every man at his best state is but vapor.
PSALM 39:5

L ife is only a vapor. In the context of eternity, we are on this small planet in this vast universe for a short period of time.

One day someone will look at your tombstone and note the year of your birth or the year of your death. But what matters most will be hidden in the dash between those years, specifically, what your response to Jesus was when you walked this earth.

Make sure the years represented by your dash are characterized by your focus on your relationship with Jesus. After all, as James wrote, "What is your life? It is even a vapor that appears for a little time and then vanishes away" (James 4:14). Trust in Christ so that when your appointed time comes, you have the rock-solid assurance that, rather than leaving home, you are actually going home.

All that matters in this life and in the next is our response to the Lord Jesus Christ.

CODE WORD: STEAM

Think of the steam rising from a tea kettle and vanishing into thin air. Such is your life. It is here now for a little while but is vanishing away.

Lord, help me make every day I have count for You . . . beginning today. In Jesus' name, amen.

SEPTEMBER 4

He who looks into the perfect law . . . and is not a forgetful hearer but a doer of the work, this one will be blessed in what he does.

JAMES 1:25

The vibrant Sea of Galilee is a beautiful blue and, in many places, as clear as crystal. The appropriately named Dead Sea is stagnant water with no life and a nauseating sulfur smell.

What makes these two bodies of water so different? First, the Sea of Galilee has an inlet: the Jordan River flows into it from the north. On its southern shore, the Sea of Galilee also has an outlet: water flows into the Jordan and on through the Great Rift Valley. Like the Sea of Galilee, the Dead Sea has an inlet: the Jordan flows into it. But the Dead Sea has no outlet: it takes in, but it does not give out.

Vibrant believers not only take in, but they also give out. They put into action the Word they receive. May our focus be steady and our commitment, sure; may we be "doers of the word, and not hearers only" (James 1:22).

CODE WORD: SEA

Remember these two bodies of water throughout your day. There is a world of difference between the Sea of Galilee and the Dead Sea. Make sure you are not just taking in . . . but giving out today as well.

Lord, make me a channel of Your blessing to someone today. In Jesus' name, amen.

We must all appear before the judgment seat of Christ, that each one may receive the things done in the body, according to what he has done, whether good or bad.

2 CORINTHIANS 5:10

Perhaps there is no other subject more often relegated to the back of our minds than the fact that each of us will one day stand before the supreme Judge of all the earth. In His court there are no mistrials, no appeals, no probations, no adjudicated sentences, and no hung juries. It is the one court where ultimate and perfect justice will prevail. The Lord's judgment means one of two options: "everlasting punishment, but the righteous into eternal life" (Matthew 25:46).

The subject of judgment can be one of the most confusing ones in all Scripture. But we can be sure of this truth: "[The Lord] is coming to judge the earth. He shall judge the world with righteousness, and the peoples with His truth" (Psalm 96:13).

CODE WORD: APPOINTMENT

We all have an appointment at the Judgement Seat of Christ. And this is an appointment where you will be on time . . . God's time!

Lord, thank You that Christ has taken the judgment of my sin. In Jesus' name, amen.

When the fullness of the time had come, God sent forth His Son, born of a woman, born under the law.

GALATIANS 4:4

A nd that is how God proved His love toward us. He did not proclaim His love by shouting from the heavens or writing flaming letters across the sky. God demonstrated His love for us by sending His Son to die on the cross for our sins.

And Jesus was not some sort of remedial action, a last-minute splint for a broken world when everything else had failed. The preparation God had done was staggering. He had raised up the Hebrew nation through which He would send the Messiah. He had raised up a Greek nation that took the Greek language across the known world so the gospel could spread without a language barrier. He raised up a Roman empire that built a road system of fifty thousand miles across the known world so people could more easily move from country to country and take the gospel with them.

Yes, Christ came in the "fullness of the time" (Galatians 4:4).

CODE WORD: TIME

Each time you look at the time today, let it remind you that God is always right on time, never early and never late.

Lord, Your timing is always perfect. Help me to wait on You when necessary. In Jesus' name, amen.

O Lord, how long shall I cry,
And You will not hear?

HABAKKUK 1:2

I f there really is a God who is all good and all powerful, why doesn't He always answer our prayers for good and right things? Why does He allow evil and suffering?

The true test of our Christian character may well be how we respond when we don't see an immediate or—in our eyes—acceptable answer to our prayers.

Sometimes we pray and immediately see God's answer. Sometimes we have to wait for God's response. At other times He answers in a way we didn't expect, so we don't recognize it. And then sometimes God denies our request. But God does always answer. Always.

We need to be sure we are always praying according to God's Word and His will.

And on occasion I have asked Him time and again for certain things He had no intention of giving me because He had something far better in mind.

You see, in the kingdom of God, we live by promises, not by explanations.

CODE WORD: CONFIDENCE

You can trust the Lord today. In fact, when you are not able to trace His hand in your circumstance, you can always trust His heart. You can have confidence that He is with you.

Lord, thank You that You not only hear my prayers, You answer them. In Jesus' name, amen.

SEPTEMBER 8

No temptation has overtaken you except such as is common to man; but God is faithful, who will not allow you to be tempted beyond what you are able, but with the temptation will also make the way of escape, that you may be able to bear it.

1 CORINTHIANS 10:13

I t is not a sin to be tempted—and we will be tempted. One should not confuse temptations with trials. Most often, trials are allowed—or even sent—by God to strengthen the Christian. Temptations, however, are sent from the devil to cause the Christian to stumble.

Arriving in a variety of shapes and sizes, temptation is a reality that is not going to go away. But our minds are like a hotel. The manager cannot keep someone from entering the lobby, but he can certainly keep that person from getting a room. Likewise, when a temptation passes through our mind, we haven't sinned. We sin when we give that thought a room in our mind and let it dwell there.

CODE WORD: GUARD

Guard your heart and mind today as temptation comes knocking on your door. Don't give it a room.

Lord, put a guard over my mind and keep watch over the door of my thoughts. In Jesus' name, amen.

Being found in appearance as a man, He humbled Himself and became obedient to the point of death, even the death of the cross.

One phenomenal thing about the love of God is that He most clearly revealed it to us "while we were still sinners." In fact, "scarcely for a righteous man will one die; yet perhaps for a good man someone would even dare to die. But God demonstrates His own love toward us, in that *while we were still sinners*, Christ died for us" (Romans 5:7–8, emphasis added). Those two little words—BUT GOD—make all the difference.

Jesus came and clothed Himself in human flesh. He came to where we are so that one day we could go to where He is. In other words, He came to earth so we could go to heaven. He was forsaken so that we might never be forsaken. As someone said, "The Son of God became the Son of Man in order that the sons of men could become the sons of God."

CODE WORD: BUT

Most people have an aversion to this conjunction. It sometimes denotes an unpleasant reversal. But I love it. It can change everything for the good when one word is added—"But God"!

Lord, how many times when my situation appeared hopeless did those two words come into play—"But God"? In Jesus' name, amen.

You have dishonored the poor man.

JAMES 2:6

As people who love God and are called to love others, we should guard against dishonoring anyone, especially those whose dignity is about all that they have.

Like our Lord, we are to show no partiality to anyone, rich or poor. When Jesus went to Jerusalem, He spent time with an invalid at the Pool of Bethesda as well as with Nicodemus, a ruler of the Jews. When Jesus journeyed through Jericho, He called out to rich Zacchaeus, who was perched in a tree, and He healed blind Bartimaeus, who was begging by the roadside. Jesus made a place for Nicodemus, a ruler of the Jews, as well as the woman at the well of Sychar who was formerly a woman of ill repute. The early church made room for Onesimus, the former slave, at the same table as Philemon, the wealthy landowner and his former master.

The gospel gives everyone, everywhere a place of dignity at Christ's table because "God is love" (1 John 4:16).

CODE WORD: LEVEL

All ground is level at the cross. Remember this. Make sure your love is not limited to those who live where you live, look like you look, or act like you act.

Lord, help me look through Your eyes today and see dignity in every face I see. In Jesus' name, amen.

"A new commandment I give to you, that you love one another; as I have loved you, that you also love one another."

JOHN 13:34

My high school chemistry teacher always talked about the "acid test." He was referring to the surefire way to identify a substance.

The Bible reveals that the acid test of the Christian life is love. Love is not simply a virtue of the Christian life; it *is* the Christian life. It is—as I've said—the oxygen of the kingdom. There simply is no life—no Christian fellowship, no life that reflects Jesus—without love.

Furthermore, everything—the spiritual gifts, prophecy, knowledge, wisdom—will come to an end, but love knows no end. It goes right on through the portal of death and beyond, into eternity.

We aren't to love just with words; we are to love with our actions. But those actions—our ministries, our service, the sacrifices we make for the Lord—are to be motivated by love, just as every one of Jesus' actions was.

CODE WORD: MOTIVATION

What motivates you to keep going today? Love, first for God, then for others, should be your highest motivation. Fuel your life with His love today, and let it show.

Lord, You are in me, and You are the personification of love. Keep love in the forefront of my actions today. In Jesus' name, amen.

So it was, when I heard these words, that I sat down and wept, and mourned for many days; I was fasting and praying before the God of heaven.

NEHEMIAH 1:4

What was the news that moved Nehemiah to tears? This cupbearer to King Artaxerxes of Persia had learned that people in the province of his beloved Jerusalem were suffering and that the wall around Jerusalem had been destroyed and its gates burned.

This terrible news prompted Nehemiah to fast and pray. For this faithful man of God, prayer was warfare. And as he persisted in prayer, Nehemiah soon realized that God was calling him to be very much involved in the rebuilding project.

So he agonized over the possibility, he wept, he fasted, and he mourned for days. Is it any wonder that God chose Nehemiah to initiate and oversee the rebuilding of God's own holy city? Commissioned by God during his time of prayer—during his asking, seeking, and knocking—Nehemiah truly felt an urgency about getting the project done—and done for God's glory.

CODE WORD: DESPERATION

Isn't this one of our problems today? Too few of us are desperate to really see God move in us and through us. If you can do without personal revival—you will!

Lord, give me this heart of Nehemiah that my own heart might be broken over the sins of my loved ones and the broken walls and burned gates around my own life. In Jesus' name, amen.

"Enter by the narrow gate; for wide is the gate and broad is the way that leads to destruction, and there are many who go in by it. Because narrow is the gate and difficult is the way which leads to life, and there are few who find it."

MATTHEW 7:13–14

Truth is narrow.

Mathematical truth is narrow: 2 plus 2 always equals 4, not 3 or 5. Scientific truth is narrow: water freezes at 32 degrees Fahrenheit, not 35 degrees. Geographical truth is narrow: I live in Texas, and we are bordered to the north by the Red River, not the Sabine River. Historical truth is narrow: Neil Armstrong set foot on the moon on July 20, 1969, not December 20.

So why should we be surprised that theological truth is narrow? All truth is narrow.

Jesus is the only way to relationship with the Father, the only way to the Father's eternal home. Indeed, Jesus is "the way, the truth, and the life" (John 14:6). And no one comes to the Father's house unless they come through Jesus!

CODE WORD: NARROW

This is the very nature of all truth—it is narrow. Jesus is not "a" way, He is the only way. And narrow is the gate that leads to life.

Lord, while many go on the broad road, lead me by the narrow way. I am following. In Jesus' name, amen.

He was wounded for our transgressions,
He was bruised for our iniquities. . . .
He poured out His soul unto death.

ISAIAH 53:5, 12

The price Jesus paid to demonstrate His love for sinners was indescribably high. In fact, every lash of the whip that tore at His flesh, every sound of the hammer that drove nails into His body, was the voice of God saying, "I love sinners."

I remember holding my baby daughter and thinking I'd give the world to her if I could. Then it occurred to me that God had said just the opposite to straying, rebellious, and sinful mankind. He had said, "I'll give My Son to the world." Even the songwriter of old marveled at that gift: "Oh, the love that drew salvation's plan. Oh, the grace that brought it down to man. Oh, the mighty gulf that God did span . . . at Calvary."

It truly is incredible—"the breadth and length and height and depth" of God's love for you and me (Ephesians 3:18 NASB).

CODE WORD: VALUE

The value of any item is ultimately determined by the price one pays for it. How much God must value you! He paid a high price to purchase your salvation.

Lord, love so amazing, so divine, demands my soul, my life, my all. In Jesus' name, amen.

"By this all will know that you are My disciples, if you have love for one another."

JOHN 13:35

W hat results when Jesus' followers love others the way He loves us?

Jesus answered that question: "By this all will know that you are My disciples, if you have love for one another" (John 13:35).

Yes, love is the Christian life. It is the oxygen of the kingdom. It is the acid test of our own discipleship. God did not write in the sky or send a tract in order to reveal His love toward us. He sent His Son. Love did that. That is the one way God demonstrated His love for us.

The Bible paints a picture of real love for us by showing us—especially in the four gospel accounts of His life—the way Jesus loved people in everything He said and did. Our challenge is now to obey the "new commandment" (v. 34) by loving others unconditionally and unselfishly . . . the way Jesus loves us.

CODE WORD: TEST

The true test of discipleship is love. "By this all will know . . . if you have love." Keep this Code Word in mind today as you go about your work and witness.

Lord, test me today to see if love is truly a priority in my life. In Jesus' name, amen.

Let no one say when he is tempted, "I am tempted by God"; for God cannot be tempted by evil, nor does He Himself tempt anyone.

JAMES 1:13

S ome people live with the erroneous concept that the longer we walk the Christian path and the deeper we go with God, the less we will be tempted. But none of us will ever arrive at the place when temptation will not be a reality in our lives. Some great heroes of the Bible faced their greatest temptations near the end of their pilgrimage. This was certainly true of Moses, Elijah, and David.

Temptation is "common to man . . . but God is faithful" (1 Corinthians 10:13). As James reminded us, "Every good gift and every perfect gift is from above, and comes down from the Father of lights, with whom there is no variation or shadow of turning" (James 1:17).

Difficulties in life are never caused by God's turning or changing. We can rest in the reality that even though we may be tempted, we have a Lord who is faithful.

CODE WORD: PRESUME

Don't presume today that because you are a believer you are immune to any or all types of temptation. Stay alert.

Lord, the longer I walk with You, the more I see the need to become utterly dependent upon You. In Jesus' name, amen.

*I said to the king, "If it pleases the king, . . . I ask that you send
me to Judah . . . that I may rebuild it."*

NEHEMIAH 2:5

After much focused and impassioned prayer, Nehemiah knew that God wanted him to lead the Jewish people in rebuilding the wall around Jerusalem. Summoning up the courage, Nehemiah asked King Artaxerxes for a leave of absence and permission to undertake the project. Many people, however, never get started on their rebuilding projects because they keep waiting for God to open a door for them.

In my own experience, I have found that opportunity doesn't usually come knocking at my door out of nowhere. More often than not, opportunity opens the door when I am doing the knocking in my prayers and with my actions! I think of what Knute Rockne, the revered Notre Dame football coach, once said: "I've found that prayers work best when you have big [football] players."

Again, opportunities often come our way when we are knocking on the door in our prayers as well as with our actions.

CODE WORD: INITIATIVE

Stop waiting for God to open your doors. Get up and take initiative. You will find more doors of opportunity in life will open when you get up and get on the move with God.

Lord, open my eyes today to a specific opportunity You place before me, and I will take the initiative to put my hand on the doorknob as You open it for me. In Jesus' name, amen.

Who is so great a God as our God?
You are the God who does wonders.

PSALM 77:13–14

In His Word, God has revealed to us patterns in human history. We who have named Jesus our Savior and Lord don't have to wonder about the ultimate outcome, and we can be sure we are on God's winning team. Kingdoms of this world rise up and bark for a while, but they are only temporary. The Babylonian Empire, for instance, died and never rose again.

Our Lord died also—but He did rise again, and He is coming back to rule and reign. In fact, it was this second coming and not the first that hymn writer Isaac Watts actually had in mind when he wrote what we sing during the Christmas season each year: "Joy to the world! The Lord is come. Let earth receive her King." And he concluded the song saying, "He rules the world with truth and grace, and makes the nations prove the glories of His righteousness and wonders of His love!"

CODE WORD: WONDER

There is a difference in being childish and childlike. Never lose your childlike wonder in the work of Christian service.

Lord, You are the God of wonders . . . and wonder of wonders—You love me. In Jesus' name, amen.

Daniel purposed in his heart that he would not defile himself with the portion of the king's delicacies, nor with the wine which he drank.

DANIEL 1:8

I t's a pressure you may be all too familiar with. It's the pressure to fit in, to live according to the status quo, to quietly go along with the culture.

An exile in a foreign land, Daniel knew this pressure to conform to the culture and the ways of Babylon, yet he was ready to stand up to that pressure. Of course life would be so much easier if he let himself just fit in—and who would know? After all, he was a long way from home. No one would really know if he, for instance, changed his diet.

Yet Daniel chose to not give in. He went along with nonessentials like learning the language and reading Babylon's history. Daniel, however, refused to do anything that was diametrically opposed to his God's commands.

The Lord helped Daniel make some tough decisions and stand by them. Daniel's God is your God.

CODE WORD: DARE

Have the courage today to stand alone if necessary. Dare to be a Daniel. Dare to stand alone, dare to have a firm purpose, and dare to make it known.

Lord, help me draw the line today along the boundaries of the clear teaching of Your Word. In Jesus' name, amen.

You, through Your commandments, make me wiser than
my enemies;
For they are ever with me.
I have more understanding than all my teachers,
For Your testimonies are my meditation.

PSALM 119:98–99

The psalmist valued Scripture for the same reasons Paul did: it is indeed "profitable for doctrine, for reproof, for correction, for instruction in righteousness" (2 Timothy 3:16). In fact, the Bible is like a road map.

First, there is doctrine: we begin our journey with proper teaching that shows us God's plan of salvation and sanctification. But what happens if something causes us to veer off the road? The Bible is then profitable for reproof: it shows us our wrong turn. However, the Bible does not leave us in our reproof. Next, the Bible is profitable for correction: it corrects our mistakes and gets us on the road again. Finally, Scripture is profitable for instruction in righteousness: the Word teaches us how to stay on a road that honors God and blesses us.

God's Word does indeed make us wise and give us understanding.

CODE WORD: MAP

Think of your Bible as your road map guiding your journey. It starts with doctrine. If you get off the road it will reprove you and correct your path. Then it will instruct you in the way to your destination.

Lord, direct me today in the way You have mapped out for me. In Jesus' name, amen.

"A prophet is not without honor except in his own country and in his own house."

MATTHEW 13:57

Jesus' own brothers and sisters distanced themselves from Him when He began His public ministry. Hearing some of the statements He made, they thought for a while that He was mentally imbalanced. No wonder Jesus commented that He had no honor "in His own house": He was forsaken by His family.

But when those who knew Him best forsook Him, Jesus knew to turn to His faithful heavenly Father in prayer: "He went up on the mountain by Himself to pray" (Matthew 14:23). When Jesus was forsaken by His own family, He did not give up. All alone, He reached up to His heavenly Father.

This is an option for all of us who know what it is to be forsaken. Instead of giving up, we can turn to the Lord in prayer. He can truly identify with your feelings and needs. He offers comfort and compassion, for He, too, knows what it is to be forsaken.

Code Word: FORWARD

Keep moving forward . . . even if those who know you best are disappointing you and don't believe in you. God does.

Lord, help me look beyond my own needs and keep my eyes on You today. In Jesus' name, amen.

And do not be drunk with wine, in which is dissipation; but be filled with the Spirit.

EPHESIANS 5:18

The Christian life is not a changed life, but an exchanged life. It is not that we simply take on a few new sets of moral standards and attempt to change our attitudes and our activities. Instead, at the moment of conversion, we give God our old life, He puts it away, and He comes to live in us in the Person of the Holy Spirit. God's promise to us is that He will abide within us, filling us with His presence and empowering us for service.

Today's verse begins with, "Do not be drunk with wine, in which is dissipation." Paul was contrasting being "drunk with wine" and being "filled with the Spirit." The former causes one to be out of control; the other enables one to be in control. One is counterproductive; the other is productive. One makes one powerless; the other empowers. One often brings sorrow; the other brings joy.

Be filled with the Holy Spirit.

CODE WORD: PERSON

The Holy Spirit is not a substance; the Holy Spirit is a Person. God exists as three Persons: God the Father, God the Son, and God the Spirit. When you place your trust in Jesus, His very Spirit takes up residency in you!

Holy Spirit, awaken afresh in me the amazing reality that You are truly alive in me right now! May I let that truth make a difference in my life—in all I think, say, and do. In Jesus' name, amen.

Then all the disciples forsook Him and fled.

MATTHEW 26:56

The night before the crucifixion, Jesus needed His friends and followers more than He ever had. After Jesus had agonized in prayer, sweating drops of blood, He found His disciples asleep. After the crowd arrived to arrest Him, "all the disciples forsook Him and fled" (Matthew 26:56). They ran away into the darkness of the night. In His hour of deepest need, Jesus was forsaken, abandoned, by some of His closest friends.

But after His disciples deserted Him, instead of giving in . . . Jesus reached in. Hear Him from under the olive trees of Gethsemane: "My soul is exceedingly sorrowful, even to death. . . . If it is possible, let this cup pass from Me; nevertheless, not as I will, but as You will" (vv. 38–39). Our Lord did not give in to the circumstances that swirled around Him. Instead He reached in—into the depths of His own being to find His solace, not in His own will, but in the will of the One who sent Him. Have you reached in lately? That is, have you come to the place in your own experience where you join Jesus in praying, "Not as I will, but as You will"?

CODE WORD: CUP

Each time you pick up a cup to drink today let it remind you of the bitter cup Jesus drank as He remained faithful to the Father's will.

Lord, help me run to Your will today and not from it. You-in-me is my hope. In Jesus' name, amen.

[God] made [Jesus] who knew no sin to be sin for us, that we might become the righteousness of God in Him.

2 CORINTHIANS 5:21

J esus had been hanging on the cross for hours. At noon, darkness covered the land. Jesus' cry penetrated the darkness: "My God, My God, why have You forsaken Me?" (Matthew 27:46).

Does a loving God forsake His own? The Almighty did not forsake Daniel in the lions' den (Daniel 6). He did not forsake the three Hebrews in the fiery furnace of Babylon (Daniel 3). But did the sovereign God forsake His own Son?

Our holy God cannot look upon sin (Habakkuk 1:13). On the cross, Jesus was bearing your sin and mine in His own body, suffering the punishment for our sins as though they were His own, and the Light turned away. There, on the cross, bearing our sin, Jesus was temporarily forsaken in order that we might never be forsaken.

When this happened, our Lord was tempted by the devil to give out, to cry, "Enough! I quit!" But instead of giving out . . . He reached out. Hear Jesus from the cross as He reached out and said, "Father, forgive them, for they do not know what they do" (Luke 23:34). Hear Him reaching out to the dying thief alongside Him: "Today you will be with Me in Paradise" (v. 43). Jesus did not give out; He reached out.

CODE WORD: ARMS

Jesus' arms are still outstretched today in welcome to you. Whoever will (that is you) may come.

Lord, You said, "Come unto me" (Matthew 11:28 KJV). Jesus, I rush today into Your strong arms. In Jesus' name, amen.

Each one is tempted when he is drawn away by his own desires and enticed.

JAMES 1:14

Earlier in this letter, James wrote, "count it all joy when you fall into various trials" (v. 2), and then he moved to temptations. There are key differences between trials and temptations.

Trials come from God to strengthen the Christian's ability to stand; temptations come from the devil to cause the Christian to stumble. None of us can avoid trials. In fact, no matter who we are or how long we have journeyed in the Christian faith, we will experience trials that God uses to grow our faith.

Temptation to sin is a very personal matter: what tempts one person may not tempt the next person. No one is immune to sinful desires, and we cannot blame God, the devil, or circumstances. If there were no evil desire in our heart, we would experience no temptation to sin. Yet this internal source causes us to want to play outside of God's boundaries.

Thankfully God strengthens us in both trials and temptations.

CODE WORD: SOURCE

Remember today that the source of temptation comes from within your own heart. Don't allow a sinful desire within to +draw you away from God's best for you today.

Lord, search my heart right now and see if there is any wicked way in me. Lead me. In Jesus' name, amen.

The entirety of Your word is truth,
And every one of Your righteous judgments endures
forever.

PSALM 119:160

An effective ministry of God's Word will balance teaching doctrine, reproving sin, correcting false paths, and instructing in godly living. Some believers overemphasize doctrine: they are doctrinally sound, but living without power. Others focus too much on reproof or correction, apparently thinking it is their calling to reprove and correct everyone else. Still others concentrate on "instruction in righteousness" (2 Timothy 3:16) to the exclusion of teaching doctrine, and thus they have no direction in life. An effective Christian life is a balanced life, and God's Word helps give balance to a ministry and to a person's life.

In fact, as Paul taught, the desired end of knowing Scripture is that "the man of God may be complete, thoroughly equipped for every good work" (v. 17). So when you study the Bible, do not judge it; it judges you. God's Word has withstood the test of time and will still be the Book of all books when all others have passed into obscurity.

CODE WORD: BALANCE

The longer you journey along the Christian life, the more you understand the importance of balancing the Christian life. Keep balanced with doctrine-reproof-correction-instruction in righteousness and don't go to seed on any single one of them.

Lord, keep me in balance today as I desire others to see You in me. In Jesus' name, amen.

Be doers of the word, and not hearers only.

JAMES 1:22

J ames talked about a person who "looks into the perfect law of liberty and continues in it, and is not a forgetful hearer but a doer of the work" (James 1:25). James spoke of a person who— every day—opens the Word and looks intently into it. As a result, this person stays on the Lord's course and is "blessed in what he does" (v. 25).

You see, God's blessings are just beginning when we hear the Bible's truth. Greater blessing comes with doing it, with actually putting into practice what we read. We are blessed, for instance, not by studying what the Bible teaches about tithing, but in doing it.

When we humbly receive God's Word in our hearts, it has a supernatural way of leading us to "be doers of the word, and not hearers only." True faith involves not just knowing Christ, but also developing and maintaining consistency between what we read and our conduct, our words, and our thoughts.

CODE WORD: DO

As a pastor for many years I would rather have my people "do" one sermon than "hear" a hundred of them. You are blessed in what you *do* . . . just do it!

Lord, help me to be a doer of what You say, not simply a hearer. In Jesus' name, amen.

Do you see that faith was working together with his works, and by works faith was made perfect?

JAMES 2:22

Again, are we saved by works? Or are we saved by faith? Even on the surface Paul and James seem to disagree. For example, James asked, "Was not Abraham our father justified by works when he offered Isaac his son on the altar?" (James 2:21). Paul, however, wrote, "If Abraham was justified by works, he has something to boast about, but not before God. For what does the Scripture say? 'Abraham believed [that God would give him as many descendants as there were stars in the sky], and it was accounted to him for righteousness'" (Romans 4:2–3).

In reality, these two perspectives on Abraham do not contradict each other. Yes, Abraham's faith in God—faith that God would give him descendants as numerous as the stars—was accounted to him as righteousness (see Genesis 15:5–6), and that faith was evident when he willingly laid his son Isaac on the altar as a sacrificial offering to God.

CODE WORD: COMPLEMENT

Faith and works are not contradictory to each other. In fact, in Scripture we find them complementing each other. The next time you see two things working well together—like chocolate and vanilla ice cream—let it remind you that faith and works are "working together."

Lord, good works are never the proof of my salvation, but they are the fruit of it. In Jesus' name, amen.

Ask in faith, with no doubting.

JAMES 1:6

J esus asked in faith that the cup of the crucifixion be taken from Him, and His Father said no. Jesus surrendered His will to His Father's.

Similarly, when we ask God for something, we must be willing to surrender our will to His. Every prayer of faith must always be offered according to God's will and His Word. But until we are parents, the concept of God saying no may be harder to understand. When Susie and I were raising our daughters, we didn't always give them everything they asked for. Just like our heavenly Father knows what is best for us, we knew what was best for them when they didn't.

Looking back over my life, I am extremely grateful God didn't give me everything I've asked Him for. At times, my own personal preferences and prejudices clouded my thinking and definitely took precedence over His will for my life. When He did say no, I saw—time and again—that He had something better for me in mind.

CODE WORD: NO

NO is not a four-letter word. If God has not given you that for which you have asked, it is because He knows best and has something better for you. Trust Him.

Lord, help me to accept Your no as a token of Your love for me. In Jesus' name, amen.

Being in agony, [Jesus] prayed more earnestly. Then His sweat became like great drops of blood falling down to the ground.

LUKE 22:44

I'm pretty sure you've never been under such stress that your sweat was "like great drops of blood." But I'm very sure that you are familiar with stress. It's the human condition in this fallen world. Stress is a matter of when, not if. Ignored, stress can be physically, emotionally, and spiritually destructive.

But consider that stress provides us an incredible opportunity to identify with Christ. Jesus knew family stress: His own brothers disowned Him for a while and accused Him of being deranged. He knew the stress of having His friends desert Him in His time of greatest need. Then came the stress of the cross, when He was forsaken by the Father (Matthew 27:46) so we might never be forsaken.

Jesus was constantly misunderstood, falsely accused, cruelly beaten, and ultimately executed, only to return from the grave, the living Lord victorious over sin and death. Stress may be inevitable, but it can also be profitable.

CODE WORD: STRESS

Stress is not necessarily your foe. It can be your friend . . . leading you to trust totally in Christ. It is often God's voice saying, "Rest in Me."

Lord, nothing I will face today can top what You endured . . . for me. Give me strength for the day. In Jesus' name, amen.

OCTOBER

*For God has not given
us a spirit of fear, but of
power and of love and of
a sound mind.*

2 Timothy 1:7

OCTOBER 1

[The believers] were all filled with the Holy Spirit, and they spoke the word of God with boldness. . . . With great power the apostles gave witness to the resurrection of the Lord Jesus.

ACTS 4:31, 33

The resurrected Christ met Peter and some of the disciples on the north shore of the Sea of Galilee. There Jesus provided Peter with three opportunities to reaffirm his love for Him. Peter never turned back. Restored, he became the rock for the church's greatest days of expansion (Matthew 16:18).

Peter went from that seaside meeting with Christ to become the powerful preacher of Pentecost, and his message brought about the birth of the church. We find Peter over and over in the book of Acts being imprisoned and beaten yet saying, "We cannot but speak the things which we have seen and heard" (4:20). Tradition tells us he met a martyr's death by crucifixion. But telling his executioners that he was unworthy to die in the same manner as his Savior, Peter requested to be crucified upside down. And so he was.

CODE WORD: VALOR

The early believers "turned the world upside down" (Acts 17:6) because of their boldness. They knew Christ was real. Your boldness comes from Jesus Christ, who is alive in you. Let Him out.

Lord, grant me the boldness today to speak up for You and not be a silent witness. In Jesus' name, amen.

"Who do men say that I, the Son of Man, am?"
MATTHEW 16:13

J esus' disciples had just come from several days in Galilee, where they had been with huge crowds. Jesus asked, "Those people you were spending time with—who do they think I am?" The disciples had been among the people and had undoubtedly taken an informal poll.

When our Lord asked this question, the answers flew back in rapid succession: "Some say You're John the Baptist, others say Elijah, still others think You are Jeremiah, and others suggest You are just another one of the many prophets who have come our way" (from Matthew 16:14).

Many people today are also interested in what people say about Jesus. Today people talk about Him as being a wise prophet or a good teacher. We still live in a world that seems more interested in what men say about Jesus than in what God says about Jesus or what Jesus says to us.

CODE WORD: CONSENSUS

Beware of consensus promoters. Public consensus is not always right. Make sure you are more geared today to personal conviction, to what God says rather than what people say.

Lord, I have Your all-sufficient Word. Speak that Your purpose be fulfilled in me. In Jesus' name, amen.

"But who do you say that I am?"

MATTHEW 16:15

W ho do you say that I am?" Our answer to this question has eternal ramifications. Is Jesus who He said He was—the way, the truth, the life? Is He really the only way to the Father and to eternal life?

In response to this question, inspired by the Spirit, and without hesitating, Peter declared, "You are the Christ, the Son of the living God" (Matthew 16:16). And Peter was absolutely right.

Later Peter died his own martyr's death: he was crucified upside down because—as he told his executioners—he was not worthy to be crucified in the same manner as his Master.

What motivated Peter to accept martyrdom? Did he give his life for pluralism, for the idea that there are many roads to heaven? Did Peter give his life for inclusivism, the idea that everyone is eventually covered by the Atonement? No! A thousand times, no! Peter gave his life because he insisted that Christ is the only way to eternal life.

CODE WORD: QUESTION

Jesus was always asking questions. And this one is intensely personal. Jesus is still asking today, right now: "Who do *you* say that I am?"

Lord, whatever questions may come my way, You are always the answer. In Jesus' name, amen.

When [the rulers, elders, and scribes] saw the boldness of Peter and John, and perceived that they were uneducated and untrained men, they marveled. And they realized that they had been with Jesus.

ACTS 4:13

I t has always puzzled me. Maybe it has puzzled you too . . .
When it came time for Jesus to pick His team—when He chose the men He would train and then send out with a commission to share the gospel with entire nations—Jesus picked a motley crew. He started, for instance, with rough, callus-handed men who had spent their lives in the fishing business.

Jesus did not go to institutions of higher learning looking for the best and the brightest. He did not go to the halls of government looking for those with persuasive powers and organizational skills. Nor did Jesus go to the yeshivas and pick students most knowledgeable in the Torah. Instead, Jesus went to Galilee, to a bunch of ragtag fishermen, and called them to follow Him. He promised that He would make them "fishers of men" (Matthew 4:19).

And they followed.

Code Word: CONFOUND

Jesus still has a way of confounding the wise. His ways are not always our ways, nor His thoughts ours. But His ways are always the best.

Lord, if You could use these semi-literate, callus-handed fisherman who followed You, You can use me. All I have to do is follow. In Jesus' name, amen.

We are ambassadors for Christ, as though God were pleading through us: we implore you on Christ's behalf, be reconciled to God.

2 CORINTHIANS 5:20

As believers, we are to be ambassadors for the King of kings. That sounds important, but what exactly is an ambassador? An ambassador is a representative. For instance, our president will appoint an ambassador to represent the interests of our country in a particular nation somewhere in the world. Since the leader of our nation cannot be everywhere, he sends ambassadors to live in each of the various countries to represent the United States.

So when Paul wrote, "We are ambassadors for Christ," he was acknowledging that this earth is not our home, that instead we have been sent from heaven into this foreign land called Earth to be Jesus' representatives. And we are to be Christ's ambassadors on our block, in our school, at our office, wherever we go. By God's grace, we will represent our Lord with honor, with integrity, and with a winsomeness that attracts others to Him.

CODE WORD: REPRESENTATIVE

You may be the only Christian someone will ever know. As Christ's own appointed ambassador, make sure you are a faithful representative of Christ, the King, with others today.

Lord, mine is a huge assignment . . . to represent You to whomever I meet and wherever I go today. In Jesus' name, amen.

"[My followers] are not of the world, just as I am not of the world."

JOHN 17:16

To be a United States ambassador to a foreign nation, I must be a citizen of America. No noncitizen can represent our nation in a distant country. None of us would expect our government to, for instance, send someone from Syria to represent the United States in Egypt.

Similarly, a true ambassador of Christ is one whose "citizenship is in heaven" (Philippians 3:20). Those who are truly Christ's ambassadors have passed from darkness into light by trusting in Christ alone by faith for their salvation.

The apostle John understood his citizenship: "I . . . was on the island that is called Patmos. . . . I was in the Spirit on the Lord's Day" (Revelation 1:9–10). John knew it was not where he was but whose he was that mattered most as he represented his Lord.

God's ambassadors reside in the world, but they are not "of the world" (John 17:16). They—we!—belong to another kingdom.

CODE WORD: CITIZENSHIP

Remember today that your highest loyalty is to Christ and His kingdom above all others. Your true citizenship has a passport with "heaven" stamped on it.

Lord, it is not what I am today, but whose I am, that matters most. In Jesus' name, amen.

OCTOBER 7

"When they bring you to the . . . authorities, do not worry about . . . what you should say. For the Holy Spirit will teach you in that very hour what you ought to say."

LUKE 12:11–12

Effective U.S. ambassadors have mastered the art of communication. They are in constant, daily communication with the State Department, and they regularly communicate with leaders of the nation where they serve. In most situations, ambassadors are bilingual, speaking both the language of home and the native language of the country where they are serving. And these effective communicators know not only how to word their thoughts carefully but also how to listen to what is being said—and not said.

Now, if we are to be effective ambassadors for Christ, we ourselves must be in constant, daily communication with our King and Lord: we must speak as well as listen to Him. Then we must communicate His will, His instructions, and His commands to those among whom we live.

If we aren't effective communicators for our Lord, we have fallen short of our calling and our task.

CODE WORD: CONTACT

Are you staying in close, constant contact with headquarters? Check in with God from time to time throughout the day.

Lord, speak in Your still small voice to my heart today. I am listening closely. In Jesus' name, amen.

OCTOBER 8

Let your gentleness be known to all men.

PHILIPPIANS 4:5

A mbassadors need to be people of tact, wisdom, and diplomacy—and Webster's defines *diplomacy* as "the art and practice of conducting negotiations; skill in handling affairs without arousing hostility." Ambassadors do this most effectively when they are winsome as they go about their work. (Abrasive, annoying people do not make effective ambassadors!)

How much more should we, as Christ's ambassadors, be winsome as we go about our own work and witness? We should be the most appealing and welcoming people found anywhere. In fact, the Bible says we are to be "the fragrance of Christ" to those around us (2 Corinthians 2:15).

As Christ's ambassadors, we have a single purpose: to "implore [others] on Christ's behalf; [to] be reconciled to God" (2 Corinthians 5:20 NIV). This is our assignment, and we can do well as—by God's grace—we take on the characteristics of an ambassador for Jesus. Appointed by our King and empowered by His Spirit, we can represent our Lord in a manner worthy of this calling.

CODE WORD: SCENT

You are the "fragrance of Christ." Think about that. When you leave the presence of others, what scent is left lingering?

Lord, may the sweet smell of Your own fragrance linger in my life today and be left with others. In Jesus' name, amen.

What must I do to be saved?

ACTS 16:30

S alvation is not spelled "d-o," but "d-o-n-e."
Many people, however, think their own good works are the pathway to eternal life, so they do this or don't do that in order to earn salvation. But our salvation has already been purchased by Christ's blood. Our part is to believe in its sufficiency.

When the Philippian jailer asked the apostle Paul the question above, Paul replied, "Believe on the Lord Jesus Christ, and you will be saved" (Acts 16:31). But believing means more than simply giving intellectual assent to Jesus' claims. It means choosing to trust Him alone for our salvation.

I believe *in* George Washington, but not *on* him: I don't trust my life to him. I believe in Jesus. I also believe on Him: I trust my life and life eternal to His death on the cross and His resurrection from the grave.

CODE WORD: CONDITION

God loves you and offers you eternal life, but it comes with a condition: only those who believe can receive it. So some miss heaven by eighteen inches—that's the distance between your head and your heart. We can know in our heads much about Jesus. It is "with the heart [that] one believes unto righteousness" and salvation (Romans 10:10).

Lord, take Your rightful place on the throne of my heart today and rule. You are my Lord! In Jesus' name, amen.

OCTOBER 10

Beloved, now we are children of God; and it has not yet been revealed what we shall be, but we know that when He is revealed, we shall be like Him, for we shall see Him as He is.

1 JOHN 3:2

We will know one another in heaven. In fact, the Bible says we will be known as we are known (1 Corinthians 13:12).

When Peter, James, and John stood with Jesus on the Mount of Transfiguration, Moses and Elijah appeared before them in their glorified forms, and both of them were recognizable (Matthew 17).

No one, then, will have to introduce me to Paul or Peter or anyone else who loves the Lord—and these heroes of the faith will know you and me. It is one thing for us to know who the president of the United States is, but it is something quite different for him to know us, to call us by name. In heaven we will know and be known. We will be home.

CODE WORD: INTRODUCTION

In heaven there will be no need for any introductions. We will be "like Him," and He knows us all and loves us all equally.

Lord, what joy to know I will see family and friends again . . . but even more to know that one day I will look upon Your face! In Jesus' name, amen.

Be filled with the Spirit, . . . singing and making melody in your heart to the Lord.

EPHESIANS 5:18–19

In Ephesians 5, the first evidence that we are being filled with and led by God's Spirit is that we will have a song in our heart. Buddhists may have their impressive temples, but they do not have a song in their hearts. Hindus may have their mantras, but there is no song in their hearts either.

Notice that the Bible says we are not making rhythm in our hearts. Rhythm generally appeals to the flesh. Nor does it say we are making harmony, which appeals to our emotions. It is the melody that gives us the song. Like Paul and Silas in a Philippian jail at midnight, we can have a song in our hearts regardless of our circumstances.

And our choice to sing, even in the darkness, is evidence of the Holy Spirit within us.

CODE WORD: SING

Our choice to sing is evidence of God's Spirit being within us— but notice that Paul wrote of singing that is "in your heart." That is a good thing for those of us without a singing voice. We may be completely unable to carry a tune with our voices, but we can still have a song in our hearts, a melody even at midnight.

Holy Spirit, thank You for giving me a song, even in the night! Thank You for the melody You give to my life. In Jesus' name, amen.

"You are worthy, O Lord,
To receive glory and honor and power;
For You created all things,
And by Your will they exist and were created."

REVELATION 4:11

The Bible speaks of certain crowns that believers will receive as rewards in heaven. The crown of righteousness, for instance, is given to those who live godly lives and "all who have loved His appearing" (2 Timothy 4:8). The incorruptible crown goes to those who run the good race of faith and finish strong (1 Corinthians 9:24–27 KJV). The crown of life (Revelation 2:10), or martyr's crown, is for believers who undergo severe trials and even die on Christ's behalf and in His service. The crown of rejoicing—known as the soul winner's crown (1 Thessalonians 2:19–20)—is given to people instrumental in leading others to faith in Christ. Finally, the crown of glory recognizes faithful pastors and teachers who share God's Word (1 Peter 5:4).

Whatever crowns we receive, may we—like the twenty-four elders—cast them before the throne and sing with them the song of Revelation 4:11.

CODE WORD: CROWN

A crown is a symbol of authority, often celebrating the triumphant conclusion of a life well lived.

Lord, You alone are worthy of any and all crowns of life. I long to gladly join the redeemed in laying all crowns at Your feet. In Jesus' name, amen.

*You do not know what will happen tomorrow. . . . You ought to
say, "If the Lord wills, we shall live and do this or that."*

JAMES 4:14–15

Many people—even believers—seem to have the idea that
heaven is a long way off. But it really isn't. James asked his
readers, "What is your life?" Then he answered his own question
by saying that life is really just "a vapor that appears for a little time
and then vanishes away" (James 4:14).

Heaven is actually only one heartbeat away. One of these days
your heart will stop, and so will mine. At that moment we will
begin eternity . . . somewhere. Ten thousand years from today you
will be alive . . . somewhere. Heaven awaits all who have come to
God by faith in Christ—and only by faith, only in Christ. Jesus is
the way—the only way—to the Father's house.

As the old spiritual proclaims, "This world is not my home,
I'm just a-passing through" on your way to your forever home of
heaven.

CODE WORD: HEARTBEAT

Put your hand on your heart. Feel it beat. Today it will beat 115,200
times. Every heartbeat is God's gift to you.

*Lord, everything I am is in Your hands, and all I'm promised
is today. Help me use it for Your glory. In Jesus' name, amen.*

You ought to say, "If the Lord wills, we shall live and do this or that."

JAMES 4:15

We are to meditate on God's Word so it can transform our hearts. We are to ask God what His will for us is and then listen for His answer and direction. Once we hear it, we are to obey.

In order to best determine God's will, be sure you know the Savior, be sure you know the Spirit, and be sure you know the Scripture. Trusting in Christ alone and knowing His gracious pardoning of your sin is the essential starting line for knowing the Lord's will for your life. Then allow His Spirit within you to lead you according to His Word. God will never lead us to do anything contrary to what we find in Scripture. Also, as you meditate upon Scripture, you will often find His will for you. Remember, success is finding God's will for you and doing it.

CODE WORD: GUIDE

We all need spiritual guidance. Your Bible is your guide. Do you see it as such? God will never lead you to do something that is contrary to its teaching.

Lord, thank You that You are still speaking to me today and always by Your Spirit and through Your Word. In Jesus' name, amen.

OCTOBER 15

He who walks with integrity walks securely,
But he who perverts his ways will become known.

PROVERBS 10:9

What is the single most important trait of a person who wants to make a difference in our world today? Some would say it is intellect. After all, knowledge is power in many ways. Others contend it is intensity, that spirit of conquest accompanied by a passion that becomes contagious. Still others suggest it is insight, good old common sense, along with the ability to clearly see certain issues. However, I contend the most important trait is integrity.

According to Webster's, *integrity* is "firm adherence to a code of especially moral or artistic values: incorruptibility; the quality or state of being complete or undivided: completeness." We think of integrity as being characterized by honesty and fairness; by careful evaluation of a situation; and by selfless decision making.

No wonder "he who walks with integrity walks securely." And no wonder—in this day of defining our own morality—integrity is rarer than in earlier generations and therefore of even greater value.

CODE WORD: INTEGRITY

Be cautious not to pride yourself on your own intellect or intensity or insight. You can have all that, but if you lack integrity, you will have no influence in life.

Lord, may I so get out of Your way that others will see You in my life today. That is integrity. In Jesus' name, amen.

O LORD, You have searched me and known me.
You know my sitting down and my rising up;
You understand my thought afar off.

PSALM 139:1–2

Each of us lives in four distinct spheres. First, you have a private world. There is a part of you no one really knows. Not even the people closest to any of us know all our private thoughts. Alone in your private world are you . . . and God.

You also live in a personal world. You share this with a small circle of immediate family members and perhaps a few friends who really know you intimately.

Next comes your professional world: you know dozens or even scores of men and women in a business relationship and a professional setting.

Finally, you live in a public world: people have never met you personally or dealt with you professionally, but they have formed an opinion about you.

These four aspects of life raise an important question: How does one live with integrity in all four spheres simultaneously?

CODE WORD: WORLD

Remember today that in reality you are living in four different worlds. Make sure you root your integrity in the private world, alone with God.

Lord, the most effective way I can have a productive personal life is to have a private life alone with You. Help me get my priorities in order. In Jesus' name, amen.

My lips will not speak wickedness,
Nor my tongue utter deceit. . . .
Till I die I will not put away my integrity from me.

JOB 27:4–5

O nce integrity is rooted in our private life, it begins to be reflected in our relationships with those people closest to us. Family members and friends who know us best know whether we walk in private what we say in public. They can see any hypocrisy and two-faced ways. (If you want to know whether I have integrity, ask my wife or my daughters!) By the same token, these family members and friends will also see us stand up for our convictions and stand strong in our faith despite painful opposition.

In addition to seeing us live with integrity, these close family members and friends can—by their own commitment to live with integrity—help us stand strong even in unpopular but God-honoring situations. Integrity does not find its roots in the personal world. However, it is certainly reflected there, and it can be reinforced by like-minded people.

CODE WORD: REFLECTION

Your relationship with those who know you the best and who love you the most is a reflection of who you are in private. You can't fool those closest. The best way to restore a personal relationship is to have a solid relationship with Christ.

Lord, thank You for those close to me who encourage me. We need each other . . . and we need You. In Jesus' name, amen.

But as for me, I will walk in my integrity;
Redeem me and be merciful to me.

PSALM 26:11

O nce we are thrust into the public arena, it may be too late to develop integrity as our default approach to life. If we do not already possess integrity, we face quite the challenge in our private world as well as in our marketplace relationships and public interactions.

Oh, some of us will spin our personal promotion in an effort to convince others that we are people of integrity. But integrity is not rooted in spin; it is rooted in our private world where we nurture our relationship with Jesus. Solomon's words ring true today: "He who walks with integrity walks securely, but he who perverts his ways will become known" (Proverbs 10:9).

When integrity is rooted in our private world, people in our public world will see it, and the God whom we love and serve will be glorified.

May we therefore keep as a priority our hidden life, our time alone with God.

CODE WORD: REVEAL

Warning: your integrity or lack thereof will be ultimately publicly revealed.

Lord, keep me true. There is a race I must run and a victory to be won. In Jesus' name, amen.

"They will see the Son of Man coming in the clouds with great power and glory. . . . But of that day and hour no one knows, not even the angels in heaven, nor the Son, but only the Father."

MARK 13:26, 32

The only major coming spoken of in Scripture and yet to be fulfilled is Jesus Christ's return to this earth. He is coming for His bride, the church, and when He reappears, the event will hardly be hidden: "He is coming with clouds, and every eye will see Him, even they who pierced Him" (Revelation 1:7). All people will recognize Him as the almighty King: "every knee should bow . . . and . . . every tongue should confess that Jesus Christ is Lord" (Philippians 2:10–11).

The promise of Revelation 22:20—yet to be fulfilled—marks the climax of history. Jesus said, "Surely I am coming quickly." Yet no one knows the day or the hour when our Lord will return. The fulfillment of this promise is one of the most anticipated events in all of human history. Are you ready?

CODE WORD: CLIMAX

The climax is the most exciting and important part of a book or movie, most often occurring at the end. And thus we await . . . the greatest climax of all human history.

Lord, help me live today as if this were my last day of life in this world. In Jesus' name, amen.

OCTOBER 20

In the multitude of words sin is not lacking,
But he who restrains his lips is wise.

PROVERBS 10:19

Words have power. They can bless or break; they can help or hurt.

Too many children have heard a frustrated parent say, "You are worthless and will never amount to anything." And the children believed it, allowing those words to shape their self-image and determine their self-worth.

Other children had parents affirm them: "You are important, and God has something for you to do that no one can do quite like you can." These children believed that message and ultimately acted on it.

Jesus said when rebuking the Pharisees: "For every idle word men may speak, they will give account of it in the day of judgment. For by your words you will be justified, and by your words you will be condemned" (Matthew 12:36–37).

May we parents rely on the Spirit to help us control our tongues.

CODE WORD: RESTRAINT

Remember this important truth: you never have to take back what you do not say. Show some restraint . . . and you will be glad you did.

Lord, put a guard over my mouth; keep watch over the door of my lips (see Psalm 141:3). In Jesus' name, amen.

Wisdom is the principal thing;
Therefore get wisdom.

PROVERBS 4:7

All parents need wisdom for training their children in the way they should go.

In his epistle, James noted that the world's wisdom is rooted in the secular, the sensual, even the satanic. Worldly wisdom has contributed to much of what is wrong with our culture: the drug epidemic, the abortion holocaust, and a national debt of astronomic proportions are only three examples.

Never have we needed wisdom more than we do today. But the wisdom we need is the wisdom of the Word, not the wisdom of the world. "The wisdom that is from above," wrote James, "is first pure, then peaceable, gentle, willing to yield, full of mercy and good fruits, without partiality and without hypocrisy" (James 3:17). This kind of wisdom is the God-given ability to perceive the true nature of circumstances in order to apply His will to matters.

And God makes wisdom available to us parents as we train up the children He has entrusted to our care. We just need to ask.

CODE WORD: WISDOM

There is a difference between knowledge and wisdom. Knowledge is the accumulation of facts. Stay in the library long enough, and you can have knowledge. Wisdom is what we need. It is the ability to discern and use those facts wisely. We get wisdom from God.

Lord, I need the pure wisdom of Your Word today and not the pseudo-wisdom of this world. In Jesus' name, amen.

Be filled with the Spirit, . . . giving thanks always for all things to God.

Ephesians 5:18, 20

An attitude of gratitude to God is evidence that we are filled with the Holy Spirit. Our looking upward with thanksgiving no matter our circumstances is something we are able to do because of the Holy Spirit's presence within us.

If we are allowing ourselves to be filled with the Spirit, we will find ourselves living with a spirit of heartfelt thanks. A Holy Spirit–filled person is always giving thanks and, at the same time, is thankful for all things. A Holy Spirit–filled person finds reasons to give thanks in the darkest of nights and driest of deserts. After all, our God is with us always, and that is a great reason to always give thanks!

So, the inward evidence of a song in our hearts gives us confidence that we are being filled with the Spirit. Then, our continual attitude of thanksgiving to God for all things is upward evidence of the Spirit's presence in us.

Code Word: THANKSGIVING

God calls us to give thanks when? "Always." God calls us to be thankful for what? "All things." We can't be filled with the Spirit and not give thanks.

Lord, please keep my eyes open today to the many things around me that I can thank You for! In Jesus' name, amen.

There is born to you this day in the city of David a Savior, who is Christ the Lord.

LUKE 2:11

J esus was born!

He lived out His thirty-three years in this world. He was the unique God-man. As God, He walked on water, calmed the storm, healed the sick, and rose from the dead. As man, He got thirsty and tired; He felt sorrow and pain.

Jesus did not cling to the brightness of His glory, nor did He shun us for our sinful condition. Instead, He humbled Himself to become a servant and to clothe Himself in flesh. That's why Jesus understands every emotion, temptation, and pain we experience.

And Jesus came not as a full-grown man, but as a helpless, tiny seed planted in the womb of a young Jewish virgin. Later, Jesus was born, not in a clean and sterile hospital, but in the dung and filth of a Bethlehem stable. This is amazing condescension: in Jesus, God Himself took on the garment of human flesh.

CODE WORD: UNIQUE

That is Christ. He was not God and man. He was the one and only, unique, God-man. There has never been anyone like Him.

Lord, nothing I could face today is foreign to You. Lead me. In Jesus' name, amen.

"Father, forgive them, for they do not know what they do."
LUKE 23:34

I n the incarnation, we see God's amazing grace: God "dwelt among us . . . full of grace and truth" (John 1:14). The word translated *dwelt* means "to take up temporary residence as though one lived in a tent." Jesus took on human flesh in order to pay the penalty for our sin, that He might bring us to the Father.

John 1:14 also tells us that Jesus was "full of grace." From the cross He prayed for the forgiveness of those who were killing Him, and that is grace. That is unmerited favor.

In addition to being "full of grace," our Lord was "full of . . . truth." We are truly free only when God's grace leads us to know the truth that we are sinners in need of a Savior and Jesus is that Savior. Jesus came not to talk to us about God, but to show us what God was like so that children might know the Father as intimately as theologians can.

CODE WORD: UNDESERVED

Grace is getting what you do not deserve. Mercy is not getting what you do deserve. And God is rich in both of them. They are the gifts of His grace to you.

Lord, when I did not deserve it, Your grace reached down to me where I was and found me. Such unmerited favor! In Jesus' name, amen.

A stone was cut out without hands, which struck the image on its feet of iron and clay, and broke them in pieces.

DANIEL 2:34

Complete fellowship with our Lord will come when He returns—an event the prophet Daniel saw foretold in King Nebuchadnezzar's dream. The image of gold, silver, bronze, iron, and clay in the dream represents empires rising and falling. Then a stone comes out of heaven and strikes the statue at its feet. The statue crumbles, indicating the virtual end of the world as we know it. Then the stone grows into a great mountain and fills the earth, representing the coming eternal kingdom of our Lord.

The stone represents Jesus. This stone was "cut out without hands" (Daniel 2:34), meaning it was supernatural in its origin. We New Testament believers know that Jesus existed before "the beginning" (John 1:1–2, 14) and that when He came to earth, He clothed Himself in human flesh, miraculously born of a virgin. This stone in the king's dream is the Lord Jesus—and He is the only hope of all of human history.

CODE WORD: STATUE

When you see a statue, let it remind you today of this Bible prophecy. This world will come to an end. Jesus, who came first as a suffering Servant, is coming back as King of all kings and will usher in eternity.

Lord, it may be at morn, it may be at midday, it may be that the blackness of midnight will burst into light in the blaze of Your glory when You return to planet Earth. Come, Lord Jesus. In Jesus' name, amen.

Men of Galilee, why do you stand gazing up into heaven? This same Jesus, who was taken up from you into heaven, will so come in like manner as you saw Him go into heaven.

ACTS 1:11

N o one knows the hour Jesus will return, but signs that the time is coming can help us stay alert and ready.

We are, for instance, to watch for a polluted pulpit. As Paul said, "The time will come when [believers] will not endure sound doctrine . . . and they will turn their ears away from the truth" (2 Timothy 4:3–4). We live in such a day: denominations are dying, and in many pulpits Jesus is no longer preached as "the way, the truth, and the life" (John 14:6).

The Bible also says that before Christ returns, Israel will become a major player on the world stage, and our generation has seen the nation's miraculous rebirth after twenty-five hundred years. For the first time since Nebuchadnezzar and the Babylonian captivity, the children of Israel are ruling their country from Jerusalem.

CODE WORD: THE

When you write or read this definite article today, let it remind you that Jesus is *the* only way to eternal life.

Lord, You are not "a" Lord, but "the" Lord . . . and You are "my Lord"! In Jesus' name, amen.

He chose to give us birth through the word of truth, that we might be a kind of firstfruits of all he created.

JAMES 1:18 NIV

Paul consistently emphasized that no one enters God's kingdom except by faith—and by faith alone. Absolutely agreeing with Paul, James began his letter saying, "[God] chose to give us birth through the word of truth" (James 1:18 NIV). In his next chapter, James was simply reinforcing the point that good works—fruits— are the natural response of true and saving faith. He was not saying that works are the requirement for salvation, but that they are the result of our salvation.

"As the body without the spirit is dead, so faith without works is dead" (James 2:26). It is not a faith with works at issue here, but a faith that works. Paul reminded us that "we are His workmanship, created in Christ Jesus *for good works*, which God prepared beforehand that we should walk in them" (Ephesians 2:10, emphasis added). We are saved by faith alone, but faith that saves is never alone.

Remember, it is a faith that works that pleases God.

CODE WORD: FRUIT

The only fruit you can produce in the Christian life is because of the outcropping of the One life of Christ in you abiding. Abide in the Vine today.

Lord, I desire today to glorify You by bringing forth good fruit. In Jesus' name, amen.

Against You, You only, have I sinned.

PSALM 51:4

K ing David had killed Uriah and taken his wife. When Nathan helped David realize that he had done evil in God's eyes, David's eyes were opened, and his heart was broken. Anyone who reads his Psalm 51 prayer of repentance can see a person crushed by the terrible consequences of his own sin.

When Nathan boldly asked, "Why have you despised the commandment of the LORD, to do evil in His sight?" (2 Samuel 12:9), David accepted full responsibility for his wrongdoing. Genuinely repentant, the humbled king admitted to God, "Against You, You only, have I sinned" (Psalm 51:4) and then pleaded, "Create in me a clean heart, O God, and renew a steadfast spirit within me" (v. 10).

David's experience shows us that, by God's grace, we can know cleansing and forgiveness for our sin. Sin is always evil in God's sight, and the sin you attempt to cover, God will uncover. Just ask David. But there is good news. What you uncover and confess, God will cover and forgive.

CODE WORD: RENEW

How refreshing is that word, *renew*? That is exactly God's desire for you today . . . to "renew a steadfast spirit" in you. And He will if, like David, you come to Him in true repentance.

Lord, help me see today that my own sin is so serious it necessitated the cross, and if I had been the only one who ever sinned we would still have the story of the cross. Forgive and cleanse me. In Jesus' name, amen.

Know that the LORD your God, He is God, the faithful God who keeps covenant and mercy for a thousand generations with those who love Him and keep His commandments.

DEUTERONOMY 7:9

We all understand the importance of rules. Can you picture the freeway without rules of the road? Or a football game without sideline markers? Imagine if the running back could leave the playing field, run up the stadium steps, go out through the parking lot, enter the field from another door, and score a touchdown!

Rules and boundaries are foundational to a civilized society as well as our everyday life. Consider that a train can move only when it stays on the tracks that have been set out for it. The same is true with us. Like the train, we move most freely when we have clearly defined tracks or standards by which to live. And that's what God has given us.

And if we get the command to love God right, then obedience to the others will come more easily.

CODE WORD: TRACKS

Think about a train. When is it most free . . . when it is going through a field or when it stays on its tracks? God has given you tracks—instructions—upon which to run. Stay on track.

Lord, You said, "If you love Me, keep My commandments" (John 14:15). Help me. In Jesus' name, amen.

God said to Moses, "I AM WHO I AM." And He said, "Thus you shall say to the children of Israel, 'I AM has sent me to you. . . . The LORD God of your fathers, the God of Abraham, the God of Isaac, and the God of Jacob, has sent me to you.'"

EXODUS 3:14–15

Before issuing the Ten Commandments, God declared: "I am the LORD your God" (Exodus 20:2). Those first two words—"I am"—are significant to the Hebrew people.

Think back to Exodus 3 when, speaking from a burning bush, God called Moses to lead His people out of Egypt. At one point Moses asked the Lord, "When I go back to the Israelites and they ask who sent me, what shall I say? What is Your name?" God replied, "Tell the people that I AM has sent you."

God is ever present, existing from eternity past through eternity future. For a brief thirty-three-year span in history, He stepped out of space into our physical realm. But He has always been and always will be the great I AM.

CODE WORD: PRESENT

Present . . . as in present tense, not past or future. He is the great I AM and not the great I WAS or the great I WILL BE. He is with you right now—present tense.

Lord, You are always in the moment, in the present, with me right now and always. In Jesus' name, amen.

OCTOBER 31

If we walk in the light as He is in the light, . . . the blood of Jesus Christ His Son cleanses us from all sin.

1 JOHN 1:7

In this verse, *sin* is singular because it refers to our sin nature that Christ dealt with on the cross. First John 1:9 deals with our sins—which we are to continually confess when we are made aware of them through conviction in our hearts. We need to distinguish between the root (sin) and the fruit (sins).

Our sin was dealt with on Calvary. When we were converted to Christ, we did not have to confess all our sins. Jesus' death and resurrection dealt with our sin, and we are able to be in an unbreakable relationship with our holy God. Our sins, however, interfere with our ongoing fellowship with Him.

God dealt with our sin once and for all on the cross. He now deals with our sins by cleansing us in response to our confession. When we confess our sins, He faithfully and graciously forgives us.

CODE WORD: ROOT

Sin (singular) is the root of our problem. Sins are the fruit issuing from it. If we had to confess every sin we committed, who of us could be saved? Make sure you have dealt with the root issue, your sin nature, by opening yourself to Christ and receiving His forgiveness.

Lord, thank You for taking my personal sin and shame on the cross. I repent and believe. In Jesus' name, amen.

NOVEMBER

*Now may the God of
hope fill you with all joy
and peace in believing,
that you may abound in
hope by the power of the
Holy Spirit.*

ROMANS 15:13

"The light has come into the world, and men loved darkness rather than light."

JOHN 3:19

W hile we are in the darkness of our sin . . .

- We are "dead in trespasses and sins" (Ephesians 2:1) and therefore unresponsive to God's offer of salvation.
- We are unperceptive: the gospel "is veiled to those who are perishing, . . . who do not believe" (2 Corinthians 4:3–4).
- We are unteachable: "The natural man does not receive the things of the Spirit of God, for they are foolishness to him; nor can he know them, because they are spiritually discerned" (1 Corinthians 2:14).
- We are unrighteous: "I was brought forth in iniquity, and in sin my mother conceived me" (Psalm 51:5).

We can do nothing in and of ourselves to reach our holy God. He must therefore be the initiator of our salvation—and He is! The Bible is the story of God's love for His chosen people.

CODE WORD: HOPELESS

Hopeless—that is you and me in and of our own selves before a holy God. But there is hope! He comes to us and turns on the light of salvation in our hearts and minds.

Lord, thank You for taking the initiative and knocking on my heart's door. Come in today. Come in to stay. In Jesus' name, amen.

The law was our tutor to bring us to Christ, that we might be justified by faith.

GALATIANS 3:24

As He prepares to deliver the Ten Commandments, the Almighty declares that He is "the LORD *your* God" (Exodus 20:2, emphasis added). In the original Hebrew, *your* is singular, indicating that the God of the universe desires a personal, one-on-one relationship with you. Still, many people believe that Christianity is about religion or mere ritual. But the Christian life is really about a relationship—a dynamic, life-giving, and personal relationship with the Lord Jesus Christ.

So God issued the Ten Commandments, fully knowing that none of us can perfectly keep those—or the rest of the six hundred others in the Old Testament. Making matters worse, Scripture teaches that, if we break just one law, we are guilty of breaking all of them (see James 2:10). And that is why—to use Paul's metaphor—the law is an effective "tutor." The law shows us how we all fall far short of meeting God's standards and, consequently, how much we need a Savior.

CODE WORD: TEACHER

We all remember our favorite teacher. Think of God's law as your personal tutor, your teacher, revealing the utter hopelessness of thinking you can gain God's favor by keeping all the law. You can't. It's all about grace.

Lord, teach me today at the point of my greatest need. I'm open to learning. In Jesus' name, amen.

I will remember the works of the LORD;
Surely I will remember Your wonders of old.
I will also meditate on all Your work,
And talk of Your deeds.

PSALM 77:11–12

The almighty God reminded Moses that He was the One who "brought you out of the land of Egypt, out of the house of bondage" (Exodus 20:2). He was the One who sent the plagues upon Egypt. He was the One who parted the Red Sea. He was the One who led the people of Israel with a cloud by day and a pillar of fire by night. He was the One who fed them daily with manna. He was the One who brought water from the rock. How prone we all are to forget both how powerful our God is and all He has done for us in the past.

When we remember what awesome things our powerful and loving God has done for our salvation and in our own lives, we can have peace in the present and confidence in Him for the future.

CODE WORD: REFLECT

It is wise to glance from time to time in the rearview mirror to reflect upon where you have been and to remember what God has done for you, to meditate awhile on it, and then to talk of His deeds.

Lord, You are with me today, and You are the same yesterday, today, and forever. In Jesus' name, amen.

NOVEMBER 4

He has not dealt with us according to our sins,
Nor punished us according to our iniquities.

PSALM 103:10

Have you heard this argument? Either God is all powerful but not all good (therefore He does not stop evil), or He is all good but not all powerful (thus He cannot stop the evil around us). That statement sounds logical, but not so fast.

The truth is, God could absolutely eradicate all evil in an instant. But suppose He were to decree that, at midnight tonight, He would radically stamp out all evil. On the surface that appears a wonderful idea, but is it? If He did, do you realize that not one of us would be here at 12:01? How thankful we can be that "He has not dealt with us according to our sins, nor punished us according to our iniquities" (Psalm 103:10).

But God has done something dramatic, costly, and loving about the problem of evil. He surrendered His only Son to die in the place of sinful, evil human beings.

Code Word: LOGIC

There are times in the Christian life when issues that seem so logical on the surface turn out, in the light of His will and way, to be so illogical. God is good. And powerful. And never makes a mistake.

Lord, when I cannot figure it all out, I know whatever the question may be—You are the answer. In Jesus' name, amen.

Count it all joy when you fall into various trials.

JAMES 1:2

The English doesn't show it, but "count it all joy" is in a tense that indicates when we are to do that counting—and that is when the trial is in the rearview mirror. James wasn't saying the trial itself should be considered a joy. *Consider* (sometimes *count*) literally means "to think ahead, to think forward."

Joseph did not "count it all joy" to be sold into slavery by his brothers or to be falsely accused and put in an Egyptian prison. But he trusted in God's sovereignty: Joseph thought ahead to a better day.

Our Lord looked beyond His intense suffering. As Hebrews 12:2 says, "for the joy that was set before Him [He] endured the cross." Thinking ahead, Jesus bore up under the stress of the cross.

James was not telling us to try to find some kind of superficial joy during life's trials. What James told us is to look beyond them—as Jesus did—for "joy comes in the morning" (Psalm 30:5).

CODE WORD: AHEAD

Look forward. Look beyond. Look ahead. You may not be experiencing joy right now. Weeping may endure for the night, but look ahead. Joy is on its way. It is coming in the morning.

Lord, help me to see beyond my need. This too shall pass. In Jesus' name, amen.

Lord, teach us to pray.

LUKE 11:1

According to the Bible, the disciples asked our Lord to teach them to do only one thing. They never asked Jesus to teach them to preach or evangelize or heal the sick. Their one request? "Lord, teach us to pray" (Luke 11:1).

The disciples knew that prayer was the lifeblood of Jesus' ministry, of His very existence. They knew He slipped away to pray and occasionally to pray all through the night. They saw Him pray before every great undertaking and after every great accomplishment. They knew that if they could experience the power of prayer, they would know how to preach, how to evangelize, and how to do all that carrying out their calling in life would require.

In response to their request, Jesus offered the model prayer. Found in Matthew 6:9–13, with a briefer version in Luke 11, this prayer is a model for our own prayer life. It contains a prayer for God's glory and a prayer for our good.

CODE WORD: MODEL

Life lessons are easier learned when you have a model to follow. Read and memorize this model prayer Jesus left for us to pray.

Lord, You have given me all I need to live a victorious life. You are my model. In Jesus' name, amen.

"In this manner, therefore, pray:
Our Father in heaven, hallowed be Your name."
MATTHEW 6:9

Jesus' model prayer begins with worship: "hallowed be Your name" (Matthew 6:9). *Hallowed* means "sanctified; that which is set apart." We are to enter into prayer with a reverent attitude: we are coming before the holy One, the King of kings.

The prayer involves our submission to God's sovereignty: "Your kingdom come" (v. 10). We pray for people who have not yet entered God's kingdom of grace, for those who have not yet been born again. We also join saints through the ages in anticipating the "glorious appearing" (Titus 2:13) when Jesus comes again to set up His eternal kingdom.

Jesus' prayer calls for our personal submission: "Your will be done" (Matthew 6:10). Rather than going to God in prayer bent on our way and our will, we are to go to Him humbly, joining Jesus in praying, "Not my will, but Yours, be done" (Luke 22:42).

CODE WORD: REVERENCE

God is not some sort of a "good buddy" to whom you can give a high five or a slap on the back. He is holy. Enter His presence with reverence.

Lord, I am coming to You, my King . . . Your grace and power
are such I can never ask too much. In Jesus' name, amen.

"Give us this day our daily bread."

MATTHEW 6:11

T he model prayer Jesus gave us begins with prayers for God's glory—that His name be hallowed, His kingdom come, and His will be done. The remainder of this model prayer consists of our personal petitions that result not only in God's glory, but in our own good.

First, we ask for our heavenly Father's provision: "Give us this day our daily bread" (v. 11). Rather than approaching Him with an independent and groundless spirit of self-sufficiency, we acknowledge our dependence on Him to meet our basic needs.

It is also important to note that the petition is for daily bread. Remember that the manna fell daily for the children of Israel in the wilderness, and it was edible only on that day. Just as God wanted His people then to look to Him daily, He wants us to look to Him each day for our daily bread—the food we need—and for the sustenance of His Word, the Bread of Life.

CODE WORD: DAILY

Yesterday's victories will not suffice for today's commitment. You need *daily* bread.

Lord, I need You not just every day . . . not just every hour . . . but all the time. In Jesus' name, amen.

"And forgive us our debts,
As we forgive our debtors."

MATTHEW 6:12

I n His model prayer Jesus began with prayers for God's glory. Then came requests for God to meet our personal needs. First, we ask for daily bread. Second, we ask the Lord to "forgive us our debts, as we forgive our debtors" (v. 12).

Seeking God's pardon like this, we are to go before Him in prayer with a spirit of penitence as well as dependence. We cannot pridefully go into the presence of our holy God with unconfessed and therefore unforgiven sin in our lives.

Then, when we ask God to forgive us "as we forgive our debtors," do we really mean this? We need to think deeply about what we are praying. Some of us say, "Well, I will forgive her, but I won't have anything to do with her ever again." That kind of "forgiveness" is not really the kind of forgiveness we want from God.

CODE WORD: AS

This little two-letter, one-syllable word cuts deep. "Forgive me *as* I forgive others." Be careful how you pray this model prayer.

Lord, help me to let go and totally forgive that someone today . . . as You have forgiven me. In Jesus' name, amen.

[The lawyer], wanting to justify himself, said to Jesus, "And who is my neighbor?"

LUKE 10:29

I f we truly love the Lord, then our actions will reveal that love as we love others. In fact, our love for the people around us will be as natural as water running downhill.

When the lawyer asked this question, Jesus answered with the story of the good Samaritan. He concluded this story of putting love for others into action with the admonition to "go and do likewise" (Luke 10:37). Love is always equated with action. Love is something we do. If our attitude is wholehearted love for Christ, then we will act with love for those around us.

Jesus said we are to love our neighbors as we love ourselves (Matthew 22:39). People who know they are loved by Jesus and who have fallen in love with Him are able to love like this. They have an endless supply of God's love to share with others exactly as He commands.

CODE WORD: ACTION

Love is something you do, not something you feel. Jesus said, "If you love Me, you will keep My commandments" (John 14:15 NASB).

Lord, You loved so much that You gave Yourself. Put someone in my path to whom I can give away Your love today. In Jesus' name, amen.

How shall they believe in Him of whom they have not heard?
And how shall they hear without a preacher?

ROMANS 10:14

We can read Romans 1–3 for a complete explanation of how we are all guilty before a righteous Judge. Those who have never heard the gospel are condemned, not because they have neglected or rejected Christ. They, like all of us, are "condemned already" because creation speaks of Him (John 3:18, Romans 1:20) and because our own conscience testifies of Him as well (Romans 2:15–16).

But men and women are saved when they hear and accept the truth about Jesus, His death and resurrection, and His plan of salvation. Only two times in human history has the entire population known of God's plan of redemption. Adam and Eve knew, and Noah, his wife, their sons, and their wives knew. Along the way we have failed to take the gospel to all people on the planet who don't yet know Jesus or God's plan of redemption. This is still our Great Commission from Christ.

CODE WORD: DUTY

We are only a generation away from a lost world. The gospel has been passed on from generation to generation for two millennia. Now, it's our duty to do the same. Someone you know needs to know Christ today.

Lord, lead me to that someone today with whom You desire that I share Your love. In Jesus' name, amen.

They sang a new song, saying:

> *"You were slain,*
> *And have redeemed us to God by Your blood*
> *Out of every tribe and tongue and people and nation."*

REVELATION 5:9

O ur limited minds can scarcely grasp the fact that Christ redeemed us with the purchase price of His blood. As the writer of Hebrews put it, "Not with the blood of goats and calves, but with His own blood He entered the Most Holy Place once for all, having obtained eternal redemption" (9:12).

Peter elaborated on the point, saying, "You were not redeemed with corruptible things, like silver or gold, from your aimless conduct received by tradition from your fathers, but with the precious blood of Christ, as of a lamb without blemish and without spot" (1 Peter 1:18–19).

It is no wonder we will be singing this "new song" in heaven. Jesus alone—the One who was slain and who redeemed us by His blood—is worthy to be the object of our worship.

CODE WORD: LAMB

Shepherds don't drive sheep, they lead them. Jesus, who Himself was "led as a lamb to the slaughter" (Isaiah 53:7), will lead you, but He will never drive you.

Lord, You know the way through the wilderness . . . all I have to do is follow. In Jesus' name, amen.

He has sent redemption to His people.

PSALM 111:9

O ur only hope of being redeemed from our sin is Christ—and only Christ. As Paul said, "In Him we have redemption through His blood, the forgiveness of sins, according to the riches of His grace" (Ephesians 1:7).

Redemption is the scarlet thread that runs through the entire Bible. The word *redemption* comes from *agora*, the Greek word for "the marketplace." In Revelation 5:9, the word indicates that Jesus Christ entered the marketplace and purchased us to be His very own. Our redemption—your redemption—had a large price tag affixed. The cost was Christ's own blood—and He paid it.

Revelation 5 describes one of the great worship experiences of all time as every creature—in heaven, on the earth, under the earth—sang, "Blessing and honor and glory and power be to Him who sits on the throne" (v. 13). And only the blood of the Lord Jesus enables us to come before His throne and worship. Our only hope of redemption is Christ and His shed blood.

CODE WORD: BLOOD

You are not redeemed by His teaching, though He taught as no one ever had . . . or His life, as perfectly as it was lived . . . but by His shed blood. Without the shedding of blood there is no remission of sin (Hebrews 9:22).

Lord, I have worth. You went into the marketplace and purchased me . . . with the price of Your own blood. In Jesus' name, amen.

The LORD redeems the soul of His servants,
And none of those who trust in Him shall be condemned.

PSALM 34:22

T he Revelation 5:9 new song of heaven declares that the scope of God's redemption extends to "every tribe and tongue and people and nation." Jesus reaches out to those in the most remote regions of our world. His redemption knows no language barrier. It is for every tongue, yes, it is for every people, and for every nation.

In order to redeem us, Jesus came down, past solar systems and constellations, through the immeasurable cosmos. Down still farther He came, a divine seed planted in the womb of a young virgin. Down yet farther, born in the filth of a Bethlehem stable. Then down even farther, doing good only to be beaten and mocked, spit upon and scorned, bleeding in order to redeem you.

This is the message of the gospel. And one day we will join that celestial choir in singing, "You are worthy . . . for You were slain and have redeemed us to God by Your blood" (Revelation 5:9).

CODE WORD: UNIVERSAL

Jesus didn't come to earth to usher in a cultural Christianity, but to redeem every people group of earth . . . every tribe and every language. His gospel is universal.

Lord, help me to see past my cultural bias to look at each person I see today through Your eyes. In Jesus' name, amen.

"Will you lay down your life for My sake?"
JOHN 13:38

I n the early church, the question Jesus asked—"Who do you say that I am?" (Matthew 16:15)—became synonymous with "Will you lay down your life for My sake?" (John 13:38). Choosing to follow Jesus rather than renounce their faith, hundreds of thousands of faithful ones answered yes and died a martyr's death at the hands of Roman oppressors.

In our increasingly pluralistic culture that affirms all truth claims as equal, Jesus still asks people, "Who do you say that I am?" Jesus does not ask, "Who do you think I am?" or "Who do you wish I were?" Jesus asks, "Who do you say that I am?" When respondents get that right, then He asks, "What are you telling this lost world about Me?" We must rise up and proclaim, "You are the Christ, the Son of the living God" (Matthew 16:16).

This truth about Jesus is most important; the truth He proclaims will matter throughout eternity. Man's opinions fade into insignificance next to God and His infallible Word.

CODE WORD: SACRIFICE

You hold the Word of God in Your hand today partly because millions of martyrs have died to preserve these truths. Our modern talk of sacrifice seems insignificant. He is still asking, "Will you lay down your life for Me?"

Lord, in the midst of my own Christian comforts, let this question sink deep within me today. In Jesus' name, amen.

"For I, the LORD, love justice."

ISAIAH 61:8

God is love (1 John 4:8), and in Isaiah 61:8 we hear our all-loving God say that He loves justice. In order to be true to His flawless character, then, God must judge us, the very sinners whom He created and whom He loves. He must judge you and me for our rebellion and disobedience, for our pridefully going our own way—and judgment for that sin is separation from our holy God.

But this is where Jesus steps in! He is the holy and sinless God-man, who came into this sin-filled world to suffer God's wrath and judgment for our sin. He did that when He died on the cross.

According to His gracious and perfect plan, in the body of His only Son hanging on the cross, God's love and His justice kissed.

CODE WORD: SUBSTITUTE

God is a God of love and doesn't want to punish you for your sin. This is where your Substitute, the Lord Jesus, steps in to die in your place. Focus on the fact that Jesus satisfied the righteous demands of the law in your place.

Father, I am sinful and therefore unable to stand before You and meet Your just demands. But I praise You that You will not see my sin when You look at me, forgiven and cleansed by the blood of Jesus, my eternal Substitute. In Jesus' name, amen.

Enter into His gates with thanksgiving,
And into His courts with praise.
Be thankful to Him, and bless His name.

Psalm 100:4

Thanksgiving week is when Americans set aside time for the express purpose of offering our thanks to God for His many blessings upon us and upon our nation. Sadly, this original purpose seems overshadowed by parades and pies, football and feasting. How many of us pause to offer heartfelt thanks to God for His many blessings and great faithfulness?

One day Jesus encountered ten lepers. When they called to Him, He stopped and healed all ten, but only one of them returned to thank Jesus. The Lord asked the healed leper—and us—a poignant and penetrating question: "Were there not ten cleansed? . . . Where are the nine?" (Luke 17:17).

Are you like the nine who rushed off? Or do you, like the one, make time to "enter into His gates with thanksgiving" (Psalm 100:4)? When God blesses you, always "be thankful to Him, and bless His name" (v. 4).

Code Word: GRATITUDE

There is a liberating effect in a life lived in the environment of thanksgiving. Make sure you possess an attitude of gratitude.

Lord, thank You for Your "indescribable gift" (2 Corinthians 9:15) to me in Christ and Your many blessings. In Jesus' name, amen.

344

When desire has conceived, it gives birth to sin; and sin, when it is full-grown, brings forth death.

JAMES 1:15

Temptation is like a weed growing in the midst of flowers in a garden: left unchecked it takes over. Now, a weed has three distinct features. It has a root, a shoot, and a fruit. Left alone, the root produces a shoot that bursts forth out of the ground and immediately produces a fruit that, in turn, produces more weeds. This is exactly what James was describing in the verse above.

The evil desires within us "conceive" (they take root), then they "give birth to sin" (they shoot up), and finally they become "full-grown" (they produce a dangerous fruit).

The root of temptation is a selfish desire, the shoot is a sinful decision, and the resulting fruit is a sure defeat. Or, as James put it, "When desire has conceived, it gives birth to sin; and sin, when it is full-grown, brings forth death." And any law of Scripture is as certain and sure as the law of gravity.

CODE WORD: PROGRESSION

Make certain today that every desire that enters your heart is in line with God's Word. If not, do not give it a room in which to dwell. This is the place to avoid this destructive progression.

Lord, as I delight in You, may the desires of my heart be only the ones You have planted there. In Jesus' name, amen.

The fear of the LORD is the beginning of wisdom,
And the knowledge of the Holy One is understanding.

PROVERBS 9:10

I n parenting our children, we need wisdom. We need to pick our battles. Is it more important to be able to say you never changed your mind about a decision or that your child's room was always clean—or to see your children grow up with virtue and values, convictions and commitments? Sometimes we parents definitely need to discipline our children. But at other times we need to keep the big picture in mind and extend grace. Losing a few little battles is not as important as winning the larger war.

The Lord will give us wisdom if we ask.

CODE WORD: BATTLE

Those who need your love the most often deserve it the least. Be willing to lose a few little inconsequential battles in order to win the much bigger war.

Lord, give me wisdom to choose my battles wisely and leave
some of them alone. In Jesus' name, amen.

After my skin is destroyed, this I know,
That in my flesh I shall see God,
Whom I shall see for myself.

JOB 19:26–27

In Jerusalem today there is a beautiful garden and in it lies a famous tomb, but there are many famous tombs in the world. The pyramids of Egypt are famous for the pharaohs who lie inside. The Cave of Machpelah in Hebron is famous for holding the bones of Abraham, Isaac, and Jacob. In London, Westminster Abbey contains the bodies of Browning, Tennyson, Livingston, and other great Englishmen and -women. In Mecca is the tomb of Muhammad, the prophet of Islam. All those tombs are famous for who is inside them. But the Garden Tomb, just outside the city walls of Jerusalem, is famous for whom it doesn't contain! Job's answer to life's question is pointed: "I know that my Redeemer lives" (Job 19:25)!

So Job said, "I have lost everything. So what if death comes? I know that my Redeemer lives and that in the end He will restore me. He lives, and I will live again also."

CODE WORD: EMPTY

Let everything you see today that is empty (a cup, a pen, etc.) be a reminder to you that Christ's tomb is still empty. Because He lives, you will live again also.

Lord, my eternal hope rests securely in Your empty tomb. In Jesus' name, amen.

If a man dies, shall he live again?

JOB 14:14

I n the midst of his great difficulties, Job found hope in his confident expectation that he would see God in the next life. In
heaven, we will never see a hospital: there will be no sickness. We
will see no funeral homes: there will be no more death. We will
see no more counseling centers: there will be no more depression,
heartache, or mental illness. We will see no more boxes of tissues,
for there will be no more tears. And whatever takes the joy out of
life for you will be gone forever for those of us who can say, "I know
that my Redeemer lives" (Job 19:25).

"If a man dies, shall he live again?" (Job 14:14). Yes . . . somewhere! "In torments in Hades" (Luke 16:23) or "carried by the
angels to Abraham's bosom" (v. 22). Those who have placed their
hope in Christ, their Redeemer, will live with Him in heaven forever. For the believer, death is not about leaving home. It's about
going home!

CODE WORD: HOME

This world is not your final home. You are simply passing through
it on your way to your home "not made with hands, eternal in the
heavens" (2 Corinthians 5:1).

*Lord, home is not really a place, it is a person . . . You! In
Jesus' name, amen.*

Show me your faith without your works, and I will show you my faith by my works.

JAMES 2:18

F aith alone is the channel of God's saving grace, and the proof of faith is our good works.

But when Paul spoke of works, he was generally speaking of the works of the law, like observing the Sabbath. When James spoke of works, he was referring to the fruit of genuine faith. Remember their audiences: Paul was addressing people who thought they could be saved by keeping the law through their own human effort, so Paul emphasized grace. James's argument is for those who adhere to a cheap faith that says, "I am saved and under grace, so I can live any way I desire."

It's possible to have no faith and no works. It's also possible to have works and no faith. But it's impossible to have true saving faith and no works. Yet biblical Christianity is not about faith and works either. Salvation begins with faith alone, but genuine Christianity is about a faith that works.

CODE WORD: VALIDATION

"Show me." Most of the world is waiting to see faith in action. The proof is not in what you say, but in what you do and how you do it.

Lord, if faith is good enough to save me, it is good enough to live by today. I trust You. In Jesus' name, amen.

NOVEMBER 23

The Spirit and the bride say, "'Come!" And let him who hears say, "Come!" And let him who thirsts come. Whoever desires, let him take the water of life freely.

REVELATION 22:17

The Spirit of God and the bride of Christ both cry out, "Come!" And they are calling to the Lord Jesus, who is the long-awaited Bridegroom of the church.

Jesus said, "Come" when He walked this earth: He called to thirsty people who had not yet accepted the water of life He so freely gives. And now those of us who have found our thirst quenched in Jesus—we who are His church—call out to Him, "Come!"

The bride is a symbol of the church in the New Testament, that body of born-again believers who one day will be reunited with their Bridegroom, the Lord Jesus Christ. It is the supreme task of the church to call people to come to Christ that others may join us in waiting and calling for Jesus when He returns again as victorious King.

CODE WORD: COME

This is one of the simplest words in the English language. A little child understands it. Can you hear Christ's voice whispering to your heart right now . . . "Come unto Me"?

Lord, just as I am . . . I come. In Jesus' name, amen.

Hosanna to the Son of David!
Blessed is He who comes in the name of the LORD!
Hosanna in the highest!

MATTHEW 21:9

As Jesus neared Jerusalem, people lined the road, carpeting it with their coats and waving palm branches as they shouted their praise: "Hosanna!"

What prompted their joy? Look at the crowd and you'll see. There's Bartimaeus, who was blind and begging just last week. But Jesus gave sight to his darkened eyes.

And the man with tears of joy streaming down his face? It's Lazarus, who not long ago was lying in a grave, until Jesus gave him new life.

Nearby is the once-crippled man who, for thirty-eight years, could be found lying by the pool of Bethesda. Now he is dancing and shouting, "Hosanna to the King!"

And Mary Magdalene, freed from seven demons . . .

Do you and I have any less reason to shout our own hosannas today? We have seen Jesus' greatest miracle ever: we were dead in our sin until He brought us new life through His death and resurrection.

CODE WORD: PRAISE

God inhabits the praises of His people (Psalm 22:3). If you want God to feel at home in your heart, offer Him your praise. He lives and settles in, in the praises of His people.

Lord, I praise You today for Your love, Your patience with me, and Your presence in me. In Jesus' name, amen.

[Jesus] Himself bore our sins in His own body on the tree, that we, having died to sins, might live for righteousness—by whose stripes you were healed.

1 PETER 2:24

The Bible is very straightforward: "All have sinned and fall short of the glory of God" (Romans 3:23). You and I were born with an inherent sin nature passed down by our relatives, Adam and Eve. Our parents never had to teach us to disobey; that came naturally. Our moms and dads had to teach us to obey!

So why did God permit His only Son to die on the cross? Love and justice were His primary motives. Sin cannot go unpunished. But in His great love for us, God poured out His justice on Christ, who took our punishment and died in our place.

As the prophet Isaiah said, "By His stripes we are healed" (Isaiah 53:5).

CODE WORD: UNDESERVED

Grace has been defined as getting what we do not deserve—and none of us deserves the forgiveness of sins made possible by the shed blood of Jesus on the cross and His resurrection from the dead. Think today of the great gospel blessing that is yours, a blessing so undeserved.

Father, I am fully aware that I do not deserve eternal life and that, in fact, every breath I breathe is a gift from You. Keep me mindful of this truth, that I may walk in faithfulness to You today and always. In Jesus' name, amen.

"As Moses lifted up the serpent in the wilderness, even so must the Son of Man be lifted up, that whoever believes in Him should not perish but have eternal life."

JOHN 3:14–15

I n Numbers 21, the people of Israel were complaining about the way God was treating them—and He responded by sending fiery serpents that bit the people. They ran to Moses, confessed their sin, and asked him to pray for their deliverance. When Moses did, God made a strange demand. Moses was to make a bronze serpent and place it high up on a pole. When the people looked at that serpent, they lived.

That healing serpent lifted above the people and bringing healing foreshadowed Jesus. Our Lord was lifted high on a Roman cross so that all could see Him, and to this day, everyone who looks to Him for healing from their sin—for salvation—lives . . . and lives eternally.

CODE WORD: LOOK

Look—and live! Look to Jesus today. Keep your gaze and focus on Him who is not on a cross. Far from it! Jesus is seated at the right hand of the Father and in control of everything that comes your way.

Lord, You said, "Blessed are those who have not seen and yet have believed" (John 20:29). I am one of those: I live "by faith, not by sight" (2 Corinthians 5:7) until that day when my faith shall be sight. In Jesus' name, amen.

As many as received [Jesus], to them He gave the right to become children of God, to those who believe in His name.

JOHN 1:12

Since the beginning of the church, the Spirit of God has worked in the church and through it. God has chosen to use the church to call men and women around the world to faith.

Remember when Jesus raised Lazarus from the dead? Shortly after Jesus arrived at the gravesite, He told people to roll away the large stone that sealed the tomb. Jesus spoke, saying, "Lazarus, come forth!" (John 11:43). And he did!

The church today is called to roll away any and all stones that keep people in the dark about knowing Jesus—stones of indifference and unbelief, stones of presumption, pride, and even procrastination that keep people dead in their sins. God uses our apologetics and our witness to make people more sensitive to Christ's call to their hearts.

And then these new brothers and sisters in the Lord join us and the Spirit in calling to Jesus, "Come!"

CODE WORD: STONE

Only Jesus can give life as He did to Lazarus. But there is something for you to do as well. Roll away the stone today to help others hear His voice calling them forth.

Lord, put someone in my path today with whom I can testify of Your saving grace. In Jesus' name, amen.

Hear me, O Lord, hear me, that this people may know that You are the Lord God, and that You have turned their hearts back to You.

1 KINGS 18:37

When Israel's King Ahab abandoned the worship of the true God in favor of the false god Baal, the prophet Elijah called for a confrontation between God and Baal on Mount Carmel.

Both sides would build an altar, both would offer sacrifices to their respective gods, and the God who answered by fire would be recognized as the true God.

Baal was tested first. The 850 false prophets of Baal whooped and wailed for hours . . . and nothing happened. Then Elijah repaired the broken altar of the Lord, prayed, and "the fire of the Lord fell and consumed the burnt sacrifice" (1 Kings 18:38). When the people saw the fire from heaven, they began to loudly profess, "The Lord, He is God! The Lord, He is God!" (v. 39).

When we get to heaven, we will be surprised at how little we really had to do with getting there. It is God who takes the initiative and turns our hearts to Himself.

CODE WORD: CONTROL

God is in control. Do you believe that? He is not wringing His hands over your situation. Nothing takes Him by surprise. Never once in the gospel did Jesus say, "Wow, I didn't see that coming!"

Lord, when I get to heaven I will see clearly how I had little to do with so many things. You are the One who turns my heart. In Jesus' name, amen.

Beloved, let us love one another, for love is of God; and everyone who loves is born of God and knows God. He who does not love does not know God, for God is love.

1 JOHN 4:7–8

Jesus commanded us to love one another as He loved us. To be more specific, our love for one another is to reflect His unlimited, unchanging, unselfish, and unconditional love. Loving others like this is impossible in our own strength. When we love God above and beyond all else, though, His love overflows through us to the people around us.

Jesus taught that all the commandments boil down to this: love. We who are His followers are to love God supremely and to love people around us. Recognizing the role of love in God's kingdom, the apostle Paul later wrote, "The greatest of [faith, hope, love] is love" (1 Corinthians 13:13).

Love truly is the oxygen of God's kingdom. And love is to be the distinguishing characteristic that shows the world that we belong to Him.

CODE WORD: OXYGEN

You can't live a minute without it. Love is the oxygen of the kingdom. Love breathes life into who we are and what we do. Of the themes men have known, one supremely stands alone—love!

Lord, You are love. That is who You are. Immerse me in Your love this moment. In Jesus' name, amen.

Therefore, as we have opportunity, let us do good to all, especially to those who are of the household of faith.

GALATIANS 6:10

Perhaps John Greenleaf Whittier, the Quaker American poet of the nineteenth century, framed it best: "For all sad words of tongue and pen, the saddest are these, 'It might have been!'"

A carpe diem—"Seize the day!"—attitude prevents "It might have been."

Commercial fishermen James and John left their nets when Jesus Christ called them to join his team—"and immediately, they left the boat and their father, and followed Him" (Matthew 4:22). Carpe diem!

Four friends cut a hole in a roof in order to lay their sick friend at Jesus' feet—and Jesus healed that faithful four's friend (see Mark 2:1–12). Carpe diem!

A woman who had been bleeding for twelve years reached out and touched Jesus' garment—and "immediately her flow of blood stopped" (Luke 8:44). Carpe diem!

As we call to Jesus to return soon, may we look for opportunities to share His gospel truth and seize the day. We don't want any reason to say, "It might have been."

CODE WORD: OPPORTUNITY

Look around you today. Opportunities are everywhere if you will have eyes to see. Seize them while you can.

Lord, help me take advantage of Your opportunities today so I might never have to live with "what might have been." In Jesus' name, amen.

DECEMBER

But without faith it is impossible to please Him, for he who comes to God must believe that He is, and that He is a rewarder of those who diligently seek Him.

Hebrews 11:6

The book of the genealogy of Jesus Christ. . . . And Jacob begot Joseph the husband of Mary, of whom was born Jesus who is called Christ.

MATTHEW 1:1, 16

There is no one like you. You are unique. No one has a fingerprint like yours, a DNA that exactly matches yours. Roots are important, and not just to plants. Your DNA shows what proclivities you may have regarding disease, intellect, temperament, and so much more.

There are forty-seven names listed in Matthew 1, most unpronounceable. Some are great, some not so great. From paupers to princes, shepherds to slaves, kings to harlots, spanning twenty-one centuries of human experience, the list ends in a stable on a starlit night with one name that is above every other name: Jesus!

The family tree of our Lord does not end with His ancestors, because His descendants—you and I—have been born again into His forever family.

Code Word: ROOTS

Can you tell me the full name of your great-grandfather? Or anything about his life? Chances are your own children's grandchildren will not even know your name. What really matters is this: are your true roots in Jesus' family tree?

Lord, may I be more concerned this season about being on Your list than on any other Christmas invitation list. In Jesus' name, amen.

Abraham begot Isaac. . . . David the king begot Solomon by her who had been the wife of Uriah.

MATTHEW 1:2, 6

Talk about heartbreak, sorrow, misery, and grief—all those things are woven through the fabric of our Lord's family tree. Can you feel their grief behind these words? The grief of Abraham leaving all he had known to go to a land where he had never been. And what about King David? He had a son who died in infancy because of David's own sin. His son Absalom killed his brother Amnon, and if that were not enough to break a father's heart, Absalom led a revolt against his own dad.

But all these names in Christ's family tree don't hold a candle to grief this Christmas season. Jesus understands the grief in His ancestors and His descendants. Perhaps your own heart is heavy. Perhaps you have been misunderstood. Jesus was. He says, "I understand." Perhaps you are lonely. Jesus says, "I know the loneliness of Gethsemane's garden." He will bear your griefs and carry your sorrows . . . if you will let Him.

CODE WORD: GRIEF

The month of December holds more grief than any other. In the midst of all the tinsel and trappings, loneliness haunts so many. Jesus understands your grief. Behind the lives of all these men and women in His family tree, we see grief, but they made it . . . and so can you.

Lord, thank You for bearing my grief and carrying my sorrows. I am leaning on You. In Jesus' name, amen.

Salmon begot Boaz by Rahab, Boaz begot Obed by Ruth.

MATTHEW 1:5

I f time permitted, we could stop at each of the dozens of names in Christ's genealogy and speak of the grace behind their lives. But there are four obvious testimonies of grace that should catch our eyes. They are all women, and in that ancient world it was unheard of to see women listed in genealogy tables.

First is Tamar (Matthew 1:3). Who was she? Let me introduce her. She once dressed as a prostitute, seduced her father-in-law, and had an illegitimate child (Genesis 38). We also read of Rahab (Matthew 1:5). She was the town prostitute of ancient Jericho. Next comes Ruth (v. 5). She was a member of a race that began in incest and worshipped pagan gods. Finally we meet Bathsheba (v. 6). She lived in adultery with King David.

How did these women find their way into Jesus' own family tree? Only one word: grace! God's unmerited favor.

CODE WORD: FAVOR

There is good news this Christmas. Where sin abounds, grace much more abounds . . . for you. What is the Lord telling us? I don't think He is speaking softly—"If anyone is in Christ, he is a new creation; old things have passed away; behold, all things have become new" (2 Corinthians 5:17).

Lord, thank You for giving me what I never deserved . . . an amazing gift: grace! In Jesus' name, amen.

And Jacob begot Joseph the husband of Mary, of whom was born Jesus who is called Christ.

MATTHEW 1:16

Note carefully what today's verse says . . . and doesn't say. It does not say, "Joseph begot Jesus." Here the repetition of the "begots" ends. The "whom" in Greek is feminine singular, referring only to Mary and not to Joseph. Can you see God the Father right here in the family tree of Jesus? Jesus was the virgin-born son of Mary, in whose womb the Father implanted His Son. Hundreds of years earlier, the prophet Isaiah had said the virgin birth would be the "sign" of the long-awaited Messiah (Isaiah 7:14).

It is because Jesus was Mary's seed (the seed of a woman, see Genesis 3:15) and not the seed of Joseph that entitles Him to be your Savior and Lord. The virgin birth is the bedrock of His authority.

Some see only grief. But look closer and you will find grace. And, if you look close enough, you will see the hand of God molding, making, forming, and fashioning you. He has been there all along.

CODE WORD: BOOK

The only book that ultimately matters is the Lamb's Book of Life, where the names of all those who have put their trust in Christ are listed. Is your name in that book? Jesus said, "Do not rejoice . . . that the spirits are subject to you, but rather rejoice because your names are written in heaven" (Luke 10:20).

Lord, thank You that You are working in my life this very moment, forming and fashioning me into Your very image. In Jesus' name, amen.

DECEMBER 5

She brought forth her firstborn Son . . . and laid Him in a manger.
LUKE 2:7

I f you are like me, you type hundreds of words each day on your laptop. Let me ask you a question. Are the keys you type on black, grey, or white? Think about it. The truth is, most people cannot give a definitive answer without looking at the keys . . . even though they look at them several times every single day. The point? There are a lot of things in life we see but don't really see.

Take the nativity scene. You have seen it depicted thousands of times, but have you really *seen* it? I love the feature on my mobile phone that allows me to crop my photos. Recently we took a family picture. Susie and I are in the middle, with the grandkids and their parents flanking us on either side. We have a common "enemy" with our grandkids—their parents! I cropped them out of the picture and now have a beautiful photo of Susie, me, and the grandkids!

Let's crop the nativity. Look at the entire nativity scene. It is a worship service. Crop it a bit and you find a family in the middle: Joseph, Mary, and the Christ. Crop it more, and in the center you see Jesus only.

CODE WORD: CROP

Take a picture of the nativity set in your home. Crop out everything but Jesus. Christmas is about Jesus. Keep Him in the middle of your Christmas this year.

Lord, in the midst of all the hustle and bustle of this season, help me focus on You. In Jesus' name, amen.

DECEMBER 6

Glory to God in the highest, and on earth peace, goodwill toward men!

LUKE 2:14

L ook at the nativity, and you see a worship service. Angels hover over it like drones. Common, smelly shepherds and sophisticated wise men bow down. Worship flows from everyone toward the child.

It is difficult to imagine any greater contrasts than what we see at the nativity. They were different socially. Shepherds were low on the socioeconomic scale. Wise men were so socially acceptable they entered the king's palace. They were different educationally. Shepherds had no formal education, while the wise men were famed for knowledge. God is telling us that no matter who you are or where you are from, any and all can come to Christ and worship Him.

Christmas, first and foremost, is about worship. Those at the manger were not there simply admiring this Child. They were worshiping Him. Make sure worship is first on your Christmas list.

CODE WORD: MANGER

Think about it: "She . . . laid Him in a manger" . . . a feeding trough for the animals (Luke 2:7). Had He been born in a palace, only the elite would have access. But any and all can approach a manger. Jesus is still accessible to you and anyone who will join the shepherds in bowing before Him.

Lord, help me keep the worship of You in the heart of my Christmas this year. Glory to God in the highest. In Jesus' name, amen.

So it was, that while they were there, the days were completed for her to be delivered.

LUKE 2:6

Look in the middle of the nativity and you find a little family. Christmas is about family. God entrusted His own Son to a human family, just like yours. He could have circumvented the family, but He didn't. God put His own stamp of approval on the family.

Family is important to God. Think about it. He instituted the family long before He did the church. He placed His own Son in a family with relationships and domestic responsibilities. So Jesus was raised in Nazareth in a family unit.

Later, while hanging on the cross, He spotted Mary and instructed John to care for her. Jesus was a family man. His was a blended family, when you think about it. Family is precious to Him.

The nativity has a family in the middle of it for good reason. God is pro-family. Christmas has its own unique way of drawing families together.

CODE WORD: FAMILY

Where do we most want to be at Christmas? Home. We drive long distances to sleep on couches and floors to be home for Christmas. Make sure you hold your family close to your heart and don't be hesitant to say, "I love you."

Lord, thank You for family, and help me do my part in drawing my family closer this Christmas. In Jesus' name, amen.

There is born to you this day in the city of David a Savior, who is Christ the Lord.

LUKE 2:11

I love Rembrandt's portrayal of the nativity. One great beam of light falls upon the baby Jesus so that all the other participants are somewhat shrouded in shadow. He wanted nothing to take away from the significance of Christ.

Christmas is really about Christ. And, primarily, Christ alone. Not only is He the center of the nativity scene, He is the center of all of human history. His birth divided all of human history into "before" and "after" Christ. And, if you don't believe this, just think about it at the end of this month when you change your calendar. His birth points the way for all men and women to see that the road to our eternal home is through Him.

If the nativity were your own life, who or what would be in the center? He longs to be the center of your life this holiday season.

CODE WORD: TRANSPORT

If you could transport yourself back in time to that stable, would you see yourself standing somewhere off to the side, observing? Or would you find yourself on your knees, joining the angelic choir saying, "Glory to God in the highest!" (Luke 2:14)?

Lord, my desire is to be a worshipper. And You alone are worthy of my worship. In Jesus' name, amen.

DECEMBER 9

Let us now go to Bethlehem and see this thing that has come to pass, which the Lord has made known to us.

LUKE 2:15

It was a dark night . . . yet there was light! The Light of the world had come. Bethlehem almost missed it. No room. So the young, pregnant Jewish girl found herself without the decency of even a clean sheet or a simple cot. In her hour of labor, her bed was straw in a stable. And, when the babe was born, she herself, with trembling fingers, wrapped Him in cloths and laid Him in the feeding trough.

Down the hillside a group of shepherds had a surprise visit from heaven. They rushed to the stable, found the babe, and returned "glorifying and praising God" (Luke 2:20).

Let's become Bethlehem ourselves. We find in this little village a place of potential, providence, and privilege. The Lord longs for you to become a Bethlehem in your own right. That is, to awaken to the fact that you are a person of potential, providence, and privilege.

CODE WORD: SURPRISE

Can you imagine the surprise of the shepherds that night when heaven burst open before them and the angelic chorus in perfect harmony declared the Lord's birth? This is usually the way it happens . . . being surprised by God. Be prepared for Him to meet you in a surprising way this Christmas.

Lord, help me live in anticipation of a heavenly surprise this day. In Jesus' name, amen.

"But you, Bethlehem . . . though you are little among the thousands of Judah, yet out of you shall come forth . . . the One . . . whose goings forth are from of old, from everlasting."

MICAH 5:2

T hink of it. Of all the places for the Messiah to be born, God chose Bethlehem. One would have thought it might be in a much more prominent place, like Jerusalem. Bethlehem reminds us that in God's economy the small shall become great and the last shall be first. Bethlehem was a place of potential, and even though you may feel insignificant, like Bethlehem, you are a person of potential!

As the Lord looks at you, He doesn't see you for what you are, but for what you could become. This is the message of Bethlehem. God did not come to Caesar's palace to be born, nor to Herod's court. He arrived quietly, almost unannounced, in a seemingly insignificant village.

God is reminding you today that in His eyes you have potential for greatness. See yourself as a Bethlehem. You, too, are a person of potential.

CODE WORD: PROSPECT

Your prospects are limitless. God sees you not for who you are, but for who you can become. When He first saw Peter, He said, "You are a small pebble but will become a great rock" (John 1:42, author's paraphrase). Peter believed it and later became the leader of the early church.

Lord, help me see today what You see—incredible potential in me. In Jesus' name, amen.

"But you, Bethlehem Ephrathah,
Though you are little among the thousands of Judah,
Yet out of you shall come forth to Me
The One to be Ruler in Israel,
Whose goings forth are from of old,
From everlasting."

MICAH 5:2

Long centuries before His birth, the prophets foretold that Christ would be born in Bethlehem. But how? Joseph and Mary resided seventy miles north, in Nazareth. God put the whole world in motion to fulfill His Word. A decree went out from Caesar Augustus that everyone was to go to the place of their family lineage to pay taxes. So Joseph, because he was in the line of David, left Nazareth with his very pregnant wife on a long journey.

Many of the things in our lives that on the surface appear inconvenient may just be the hand of God's providence getting us to our own Bethlehem.

Bethlehem reminds us what God promises, He performs—no matter what. Bethlehem is a place of providence, and so are you.

CODE WORD: PROVIDENCE

God is at work, behind the scenes in your life, right now. He has not abdicated His throne. He is at work in your life when you are not even aware.

Lord, what You have promised You will perform. Make me a Bethlehem today. In Jesus' name, amen.

My little children, for whom I labor in birth again until Christ is formed in you . . .

GALATIANS 4:19

W hat an awesome privilege to be the handpicked city to cradle the Son of God. Why Bethlehem? Why not Jerusalem, the seat of religious power? Or Rome, the center of political power? Or Athens, the center of intellectual power? God was sending a message. The hope of our world is not in religion, politics, or philosophy. God privileged the little village of Bethlehem to send the message—the hope of the world is in a Savior!

This Christmas could become a Bethlehem moment for you. Like Bethlehem, you can awaken to a brand-new world. The same Christ born in Bethlehem can be born again in you. Paul put it this way: "I labor in birth again until Christ is formed in you." If you think Bethlehem is privileged to be His birthplace, what a greater privilege for Christ to be born in you.

Thinking of Bethlehem, Phillips Brooks wrote, "The hopes and fears of all the years are met in thee tonight."

CODE WORD: EXPECTATION

One of the code words of Advent is *hope*—that sense of expectation, the feeling that something good is going to happen. Bethlehem almost missed the moment. But you can awaken to a brand-new hope by allowing your life to become a Bethlehem—the great privilege of having Christ born again in you.

Lord, thank You, not just for hope but for the realization that You are truly alive in me, in this moment. In Jesus' name, amen.

You shall call His name JESUS. . . . They shall call His name Immanuel.

MATTHEW 1:21, 23

There is an interesting psychology in the naming of our children. Some are named with family names to retain a family heritage. I am often asked what *O. S.* stands for, and I am quick to say, "Omar Sharif." But the truth is, my initials represent family names—Otis Swafford. And now you know why I used O. S. on the cover of this book. Others are named for an attribute their parents desire their child to achieve in life: Faith or Hope, for example.

In the Bible, names have specific meanings. Jesus changed Simon's name to Peter because he saw the potential for him to be a "rock." Joseph's name was changed to Barnabas (which means "Son of Encouragement) because every time he had center stage, he was encouraging the early believers.

During these days let's pause to think of the names given to our Lord. The mission of Christmas is in His name: Jesus. And the message of Christmas is in His name as well: Immanuel.

CODE WORD: NAME

What does your name mean? The next time you sign a check or a note and look at your name, think about it. Names matter . . . and the one name that is above all others is *Jesus!*

Lord, help me wear the name "Christian" with integrity and honor today. In Jesus' name, amen.

She will bring forth a Son, and you shall call His name Jesus,
for He will save His people from their sins.

MATTHEW 1:21

The name *Jesus* is a transliteration of the Hebrew name *Joshua*, which means "Jehovah saves." His very name, Jesus, tell us of the mission upon which He came from heaven to earth—to "save His people from their sins."

Jesus is our Lord's intensely personal name. Have you noticed how difficult it is for some people to say this name, Jesus? They find it much easier to refer to Him as God or Lord or Christ or "the man upstairs." But there is something about speaking the name Jesus. Say it now. Out loud. Jesus is His most personal name, and only those who truly know Him in the free pardoning of their sin find it easy to speak His name.

He came for the purpose of saving you from your sins. Open your heart to Him. He said, "I came to seek and to save those who were lost" (see Luke 19:10).

CODE WORD: LOST

Say that word: *lost.* Say it again, out loud. Without Christ, that is what we are—lost beyond hope, lost beyond time, lost beyond eternity, lost, forever lost. But when we open our hearts to Him, we begin to know Him by His up close and personal name: Jesus!

Jesus, thank You for coming on a mission for the express pur-
pose of saving me. In Jesus' name, amen.

"And they shall call His name Immanuel," which is translated, "God with us."

MATTHEW 1:23

The name *Immanuel* is a translation of two Hebrew words expressing "God is with us." *God* with us. Not some prophet or teacher or holy man. But God Himself clothed in human flesh— *with us!* He came to where we are so we could go eternally to where He is. God . . . always with us.

God—that is majesty. With us—that is mercy. God—that is glory. With us—that is grace. He came to be with us, to give us what we never deserved and to not give us what we did deserve.

He could not be Jesus without being Immanuel. That is, in order to save us, He first had to come and be with us, taking on human flesh. At Bethlehem we see God with us. At Calvary we see God for us. At Pentecost we see God in us.

CODE WORD: WITH

It is one thing to be *for* someone but another to be *with* someone, to stand by his or her side in good times as well as bad, times of sorrow as well as times of joy. This is our Lord's name: Immanuel. He is with you, right now. And when He left this earth, He did so with these final words: "Lo, I am with you always" (Matthew 28:20).

Lord, nowhere I go today will I be without You. You are with me always. In Jesus' name, amen.

The Lord Himself will give you a sign: Behold, the virgin shall conceive and bear a Son, and shall call His name Immanuel.

ISAIAH 7:14

What is a sign? It is something that is intended to do two things: grab your attention and then tell you something. You may be driving on a hazardous mountain road and see a flashing sign warning you to slow down for a sharp curve ahead. Billboards are designed to grab your attention, to do it fast, and then to leave you with a message you won't soon forget.

The Bible tells us there is a "sign" regarding the promised coming Messiah. And this sign, designed to get our attention and tell us something, is that a "virgin shall conceive and bear a Son." This is humanly impossible. It would take a divine miracle.

Jesus was virgin-born. He was not God and man. He is the God-man, the "only begotten Son . . . of the Father" (John 1:18), who put His own seed in a young virgin girl.

CODE WORD: SIGN

Today, as you do your Christmas shopping and see a hundred signs grabbing your attention to tell you something, let each one be a reminder that the "sign" that Jesus is Lord is the virgin birth, the bedrock of your salvation.

Lord, if I could understand it all, there wouldn't be much to it. I believe . . . by faith. In Jesus' name, amen.

She brought forth her firstborn Son . . . and laid Him in a manger.

LUKE 2:7

These words grab my heart more than any others: she "laid Him in a manger." Not a nice little wooden cradle we see in a manger scene. But a rock-hewn cattle trough in a cavelike stable where your sandals squashed in the dung as you walked and the nauseating smell of the animals filled your nostrils. She laid Him in a manger. Think of it. Sickness, disease, death were likely possibilities.

How desperately alone from family and friends Mary must have felt when she realized the babe would be born far away from home. In her hour of pain, her bed was straw in a stable, and when the baby was born, she herself, with trembling fingers, "wrapped Him in swaddling cloths, and laid Him in a manger" (Luke 2:7).

"No room" was not just the message of Bethlehem but the theme of Jesus' life. But those who find Him and make room in their hearts for Him understand the true message of Christmas.

CODE WORD: ACCESS

Had Jesus been born in a palace like most kings, few could have reached Him without gaining permission. But no one, no matter how poor or how rich, has difficulty accessing a stable. What access is behind those beautiful and welcoming words: "She . . . laid Him in a manger."

Lord, thank You that anyone may come to You . . . and that includes me. In Jesus' name, amen.

But Mary kept all these things and pondered them in her heart.

LUKE 2:19

M ary. A young girl playing in the streets of Nazareth with her friends one day and finding she is pregnant, though a virgin and unmarried, the next. Her initial response? "How can this be?" (Luke 1:34).

After Jesus was born, it all began to sink in, Mary "pondered" all these things in her heart. The word picture is of a cake, with all the ingredients in a bowl, being stirred up. She was putting it all together, stirring it up in her mind . . . the prophecies . . . the angel's message . . . the virgin birth.

She knew those chubby little hands would never be adorned with expensive gold or silver rings. They were destined for other things, like touching lepers, forming spittle for blind eyes, and eventually being pierced with Roman spikes. But she also knew that millions of us would follow in His steps. She "pondered" all these things and kept them to herself.

CODE WORD: BAKE

As you bake and enjoy a host of pastries this Christmas season, let each bite remind you of Mary pondering all those things in her heart. Get by yourself, contemplate it, meditate on it, and ponder the wonder of Bethlehem.

Lord, I honor You in pausing to give honor to the woman You chose to nurture Your own Son. Help me to be a ponderer this season. In Jesus' name, amen.

An angel . . . appeared to him, . . . saying, "Joseph, . . . do not be afraid to take to you Mary your wife, for that which is conceived in her is of the Holy Spirit."

MATTHEW 1:20

Joseph is the one person in the Christmas drama seldom mentioned and never quoted, yet the entire narrative hinges on his faithfulness. Mary is quoted. As are Elizabeth, Zacharias, the shepherds, the wise men, Herod, Simeon, and even the angels. But there is no record of anything Joseph ever said.

We hear a lot of carols at Christmastime. There are songs about Mary, the wise men, the shepherds, the angels, the star. Everyone has a carol about them, except Joseph. Hardly anyone sings of him.

But there is a reason God chose Joseph to mentor and raise His own son. He was faithful. Each time God sent him a message through an angel, he obeyed immediately (Matthew 1:18–25; 2:13–15; 2:20–22). Our legacy from this often overlooked man at the manger is not in what he said but in what he did. The entire story hinges on his obedience to God.

CODE WORD: ORDINARY

Maybe no one takes notes on what you say. Perhaps you have never written a book. Like me, you are just an ordinary person. Learn a lesson from another one of us, Joseph, a common carpenter. God uses ordinary people. He chooses people like you and me to do as He commands.

Lord, help me see today that what I do speaks louder than anything I might say. In Jesus' name, amen.

DECEMBER 20

Then the shepherds returned, glorifying and praising God for all the things they had heard and seen, as it was told them.

LUKE 2:20

How can you make the most of Christmas? For some it is all about decorating the house or tree, getting that special gift, seeing relatives, or getting invited to that certain someone's party. But making the most of Christmas is so much more than any of these things.

Join the shepherds this year in making these next few days a time of "glorifying and praising God," a time of celebrating all that Christmas is and means. God inhabits the praises of His people (Psalm 22:3). This is where and when God feels at home—in the midst of your praise.

Note the shepherds "returned." Where? To their homes and businesses. What an impact this must have had on those who knew them best. May God give you the grace to follow these shepherds and make the most of Christmas this year.

CODE WORD: JOY

Another of the code words of Advent is *joy*. Celebrate Christ above all other things this holiday season. Sing it—"Joy to the world, the Lord has come!"

Lord, thank You for the joy only You can give. Let's celebrate Your birth! In Jesus' name, amen.

Now when they had seen Him, they made widely known the saying which was told them concerning this Child.

LUKE 2:17

Don't just celebrate Christmas this year; circulate it! The shepherds became verbal witnesses of what they had seen and heard. They had seen God in human flesh. Their own eyes had looked upon the One the prophets had foretold for centuries. They heard the music of heaven. And they could not help but speak to others about what they had seen and heard.

God chose a bunch of simple shepherds to be the first to circulate the good news of Christ's coming. Others in Bethlehem were of more importance and higher prominence. Surely their testimony would have borne more weight. But God still has His ways of confounding the wise.

Christmas is just another warm and fuzzy, sentimental story unless you circulate it. Christmas provides a great opportunity to share the good news with family and friends whose hearts will be more open than at any other time of the year.

CODE WORD: TELL

Jesus tells us to go and tell (see Matthew 28:19–20). We seem to find it much easier and safer to change this to "come and hear." Ask God to give you the boldness of the shepherds this Christmas to make "widely known" the true message of Christmas.

Lord, I want to deliver Your good news. And the headline reads, "Jesus saves." In Jesus' name, amen.

"I have come . . . to do Your will."

HEBREWS 10:7

All over our world, churches large and small are presenting Christmas plays and pageants. What amazes me is how much goes on backstage before the curtain ever rises. There are props to be made, costumes to be sewn, music to be rehearsed, lines to be memorized, and so much more.

On this Christmas, with all the attention on Bethlehem and the manger, think for a minute about what was transpiring backstage . . . in heaven, that is. Our Lord was saying a farewell to His Father. Laying aside His glory, He stepped over the portals of heaven into a smelly Eastern stable.

What would He say to the Father as He departed, when the curtain rose on the greatest event in human history? "I go to do Your will."

That for which we had been waiting and to which the prophets had been pointing was coming . . . and for the express purpose of doing the Father's will.

CODE WORD: BACKSTAGE

All of heaven was backstage, looking over those portals that starlit night in Bethlehem. The "fullness of the time" (Galatians 4:4) had come. Although most on earth were oblivious, those in heaven were watching and worshipping. Remember: what is onstage is not always the whole story.

Lord, to think of what You left to come to give me life moves me to want to "do Your will." In Jesus' name, amen.

When He came into the world, He said: . . . "A body You have prepared for Me."

What a step—from the splendor of heaven to the womb of a woman and finally to a stable in Bethlehem. There is so much behind those words "a body You have prepared for Me." God is Spirit, and yet He stepped into a body of flesh to identify with you and, ultimately, to be your own sin-bearer.

This is condescension of the first and finest order. God became as helpless as a tiny seed planted in the womb of a young virgin girl. Then, as helpless as a baby totally dependent on someone else's care.

Look at Mary. To paraphrase the master wordsmith Max Lucado, she is in labor . . . her back is aching . . . her feet are swollen . . . she is sweating profusely . . . and having rapid contractions. The baby's head appears as she groans and pushes Him into the world. And He arrives! God in flesh has come to visit us: "A body You have prepared for Me."

CODE WORD: BODY

Pinch yourself. Flesh, that is what God became . . . for you. So that He might say, "I understand." He came down to take a physical body so that one day you could go up and have a spiritual body. He came to be with you so that you could one day go to be with Him.

Lord, there is nothing I go through that You don't understand. In Jesus' name, amen.

When He came into the world, He said: . . . "I have come . . . to do Your will."

HEBREWS 10:5, 7

Jesus not only comprehended the Father's will; He came to perform it. This is the primary purpose of His Advent, to do the Father's will. He commenced this theme here on Christmas Eve and concluded with it thirty-three years later in Gethsemane's garden: "Not My will, but Yours, be done" (Luke 22:42).

There are two very important one-syllable, two-letter words in our scripture for the day: "I have come *to do* Your will." The Lord didn't come to find the will of the Father but "to do" His will. His journey to Golgotha was not primarily to save us, but to be obedient to His Father's will.

Should we do less this Christmas season? True success in your life comes not in knowing the will of God, but in doing it.

CODE WORD: PEACE

Peace is one of the most beautiful attributes of Advent. And doing the Father's will is what brings true peace to this special night. No wonder we call Him the "Prince of Peace."

Lord, put Your peace on me now, the peace You give that the world cannot take away. In Jesus' name, amen.

DECEMBER 25

Thanks be to God for His indescribable gift!
2 CORINTHIANS 9:15

It's the Christmas miracle: "The Word became flesh and dwelt among us" (John 1:14).

Jesus was the unique God-man. As God, He walked on water, calmed the storm, healed the sick, and rose from the dead. As man, He got thirsty and tired; He felt sorrow and pain.

Jesus came to earth as a helpless, tiny seed planted in the womb of a young Jewish virgin. Forty weeks later, Jesus was born in a filthy stable.

Jesus was born in Bethlehem. Its name meaning "the house of bread," Bethlehem was the birthplace of the Bread of Life. God wanted people to know that the hope of the world is a Savior.

On this Christmas Day, in the midst of family and friends, gadgets and gifts, join Paul in exclaiming, "Thanks be to God for His indescribable gift!" (2 Corinthians 9:15).

CODE WORD: LOVE

The very definition of our Lord is this: "God is love" (1 John 4:8). This Advent season comes to a close with this word: *love*. Love is the oxygen of the kingdom. Without it, there is no Christmas. "For God so loved the world that He gave His only begotten Son" (John 3:16). Believe on Him.

Lord, I love You on this Christmas Day because You first loved me. Happy birthday, Jesus. In Jesus' name, amen.

Fear God.

1 PETER 2:17

W hy is the fear of the Lord ignored or forgotten by so many believers today? Perhaps the reason is that we have lost a sense of God's holiness.

When Isaiah saw the holiness of God, he said, "Woe is me!" (Isaiah 6:5). When John saw the Lord in His glory, he fell down like a dead man (Revelation 1:17).

All through the Bible, believers lived in the fear of the Lord. Noah was "moved with godly fear" to build the ark (Hebrews 11:7). The Proverbs 31 woman "fears the LORD" (v. 30). Young Mary sang that God's "mercy is on those who fear Him" (Luke 1:50). At Pentecost "fear came upon every soul" (Acts 2:43). To the Romans Paul wrote, "Stand by faith. Do not be haughty, but fear [God]" (11:20). In Ephesians 5:21, Paul stated, "[Submit] to one another in the fear of God."

The fear of the Lord is characteristic of God's people throughout time. Yet it seems a forgotten subject today. Again, perhaps we need to recover a sense of the holiness of God.

CODE WORDS: BOTTOM LINE

What is the bottom line? Solomon completed the book of Ecclesiastes saying, "Let us hear the conclusion of the whole matter: Fear God and keep His commandments, for this is man's all" (Ecclesiastes 12:13).

That's it . . . fear God.

Lord, You are holy. When I see You for who You are, like Isaiah, I see myself for who I am. In Jesus' name, amen.

The LORD commanded us to observe all these statutes, to fear the LORD our God, for our good always.

DEUTERONOMY 6:24

What does it mean to live in the fear of the Lord? Does fearing God mean living in constant dread that if we say something wrong or do something wrong, God will hit us with a big club of retribution? Nothing could be further from biblical truth.

The most common Old Testament word for *fear* means "to stand before God with reverence and respect." The most common New Testament word for *fear* means "living with a reverential awe that becomes the controlling motivation of our lives."

When I was a young believer, my pastor taught me that the fear of God is not the worry that He would put His strong hand of discipline on me. The fear of God is not that He will put His hand on me, but the fear that He might take His hand of mercy off me. May the Lord use that truth to guide our steps.

CODE WORD: DETERRENT

When you walk in the fear of the Lord, it is a deterrent to sin, and God will give you a supernatural ability to overcome your sinful desires. Where do we get that? How about Proverbs 16:6: "By the fear of the LORD one departs from evil." Did you hear that? "God has come to test you, and that His fear may be before you, so that you may not sin" (Exodus 20:20).

Lord, give me power today to overcome my own sinful desires. In Jesus' name, amen.

DECEMBER 28

If you receive my words,
And treasure my commands . . .
So that you incline your ear to wisdom,
And apply your heart to understanding;
Yes, if you cry out for discernment,
And lift up your voice for understanding,
If you seek [wisdom] as silver,
And search for her as for hidden treasures;
Then you will understand the fear of the LORD.

PROVERBS 2:1–5 (EMPHASIS ADDED)

I n your devotional reading of the Bible, begin marking every time you encounter the idea of the fear of the Lord. God will use His Word to help you walk in the fear of the Lord—for your good and His glory.

And remember that the fear of God is not the fear that He might put His hand of retribution on you, but the fear that He might take His hand of blessing and anointing off you.

Again, the wisest man who ever lived, inspired by God's Spirit, gave us this as his final advice: "Fear God and keep His commandments, for this is man's all" (Ecclesiastes 12:13).

CODE WORD: UNDERSTAND

You can understand the fear of the Lord *if* you receive His words, treasure His commands, apply your heart, cry out for it, and seek and search for it.

Lord, hear my cry to You today from my whole heart. In Jesus' name, amen.

Give to Your servant an understanding heart to judge Your people, that I may discern between good and evil.

1 KINGS 3:9

This was King Solomon's response to God's saying, "Ask! What shall I give you?" (1 Kings 3:5). Pleased, God gave Solomon not only a "wise and understanding heart," but also incredible wealth (v. 12).

Unfortunately, there is a sad postscript to Solomon's story. Solomon was blessed with great power and God-given wisdom, yet his focus and priorities began to change. When he was an old man, he wrote bitter words about the folly of learning, laughter, liquor, lust, luxury, and everything else that seems so important in life. Solomon's ultimate and sober conclusion was this: "Vanity of vanities . . . all is vanity" (Ecclesiastes 12:8).

In the final chapter of Ecclesiastes, we hear from an old man whose heart can no longer hear from God. But listen to the hard-won wisdom of Solomon's words: "Hear the conclusion of the whole matter: Fear God and keep His commandments, for this is man's all" (12:13).

CODE WORD: ASK

Be careful for what you ask . . . you just might get it. What you want may not be what you need . . . but it is a good indication of where your heart is. When Solomon asked for the best, God threw in all the rest.

Lord, give me a wise and discerning heart that I may make good decisions. In Jesus' name, amen.

Whoever calls on the name of the LORD shall be saved.

ROMANS 10:13

As you have read this book, has God's Spirit been encouraging you to put your faith and trust in Jesus?

We are sinners who fall short of God's perfect standards. He is a God of love and does not want to punish us for our sins, but He is also a God of justice and must punish sin.

But Jesus, the sinless God-man, suffered the consequences of our sin when He died on the cross. So we must confess our sins, receive the forgiveness made available through Jesus, and, acknowledging Jesus is God's Son and the impossibility of us earning our way to heaven, name Him our Savior and Lord.

Dear Jesus,

I have sinned. Thank You for dying on the cross for me and forgiving me for my sins. Please come into my life right now as Savior and Lord. I accept Your free gifts of forgiveness and eternal life right now. Thank You.

Tell someone that you have received Christ as your own personal Savior!

CODE WORD: SALVATION

Ultimately it will not matter who you know, how many worldly goods you have been able to accumulate, how high you may have climbed in worldly circles, or how many people know your name . . . all that will ultimately matter is what you have done with Jesus Christ.

Lord, I believe; help my unbelief. In Jesus' name, amen.

Every good gift and every perfect gift is from above.

JAMES 1:17

Anything and everything good in our lives comes from God. Think back over the year, and identify some of the many gifts your gracious and generous God gave—gifts both tangible and intangible; experiences and insights; changes and transitions; and times that didn't seem like gifts as they unfolded.

The year undoubtedly had hard times as well. Life always has its shadows, but they are never caused by God's turning away. Your heavenly Father's love for you never wavers.

The prophet Jeremiah framed it like this: "Through the LORD's mercies we are not consumed, because His compassions fail not. They are new every morning; great is Your faithfulness" (Lamentations 3:22–23).

CODE WORD: FAITHFUL

God is faithful. Looking back over time, we often see that things we thought were unfortunate were really the hand of God leading us to something better for us. As you look to the new year, remember, all you need He will provide . . . Great is His faithfulness.

Lord, thank You for another year of life and Your steadfast faithfulness to me. In Jesus' name, amen.

EPILOGUE

I t may be that, while you have journeyed through these pages, God's Spirit has been nudging you to put your faith and trust in Christ for the forgiveness of your sin and the gift of eternal life. Heaven, eternal life, is God's personal and free gift to you; it cannot be earned, nor will you ever deserve it. Your part is to receive this gift by faith.

The power of the gospel does not bring about a *changed* life as much as it brings about an *exchanged* life. We confess our sin and hand over to God our old life; in exchange, He gives us one that is brand-new. Christ comes to live in us, never to leave us, empowering us to serve Him and others. Once we are filled with this Spirit of Christ, we can begin the great adventure and find our true purpose for which we have been created in the first place. There is a reason no one else on the planet has a DNA like yours. You are valuable to God. He knows you . . . where you live . . . your e-mail address. And He loves you and has a wonderful plan for your life.

In fact, this new life is God's free gift to us. The Bible says, "The wages of sin is death, but the gift of God is eternal life in Christ Jesus our Lord" (Romans 6:23). We cannot earn our salvation, and we certainly do not deserve it. God gives us a transformed and eternal life because of His love and grace, and we receive this gift through faith in Him alone. We are all sinners who have fallen short of His holy standards and can do nothing, apart from Him, to save ourselves.

God is a God of love who loves us despite our sins, but, at the same time, He is a God of justice who must, therefore, punish sin. This is where Jesus steps in! He is the holy and sinless God-man who came into this sin-filled world to take your sin in His own body and, on your behalf, to suffer God's wrath and judgment for your sin on the cross.

But, just knowing this good news, this gospel, is not enough. You must transfer your trust in this life from yourself and your own human efforts, no matter how noble, to Christ alone, believing that His death and resurrection can achieve for you God's forgiveness and your own personal salvation.

Jesus said, "Behold, I stand at the door and knock. If anyone hears My voice and opens the door, I will come in to him" (Revelation 3:20). Picture, for just a moment, an imaginary door on your heart. Jesus is knocking on that door . . . right now. If you would like to receive God's free offer of eternal and abundant life, you can respond to Jesus . . . right now . . . open that door to your heart and invite Him to come in. And, when you do, you can stand tall on His promise to you—"Whoever calls on the name of the LORD shall be saved" (Romans 10:13).

If this is the desire of your heart as you read these words, the following is a prayer you can pray. Go ahead—in your heart—pray it . . . right now.

Dear Lord Jesus,

I know I have sinned. I know I do not deserve eternal life. Please forgive my sin. Thank You for taking all my sin upon Your own self and dying on the cross in my place, the very death I deserved. I trust that You are the one and only One who can save me from eternal separation from a holy God. So, I ask You now to be the Lord and King of my life. I turn my face to You, accepting Your gracious gift and offer of forgiveness and eternal life. Thank You, Lord, for coming into my life as my Savior and my Lord. In Jesus' name I pray, amen.

A simple prayer can never save you, but Jesus can—and He will—if this prayer expresses the desire of your heart. You can now claim the promise Jesus made to all who would follow Him: "Most assuredly . . . he who believes in Me has everlasting life" (John 6:47)!

Now, you are ready for the great adventure for which you were created in the first place: to know Christ and walk with Him daily from this day forth. And, as you do, His Spirit, now abiding *in* you, will be at work to continue transforming you, making you more like Him in character and integrity.

One more thought. If it is great to get a blessing, it is much greater to *be* a blessing. If *The Believer's Code* has blessed your life, become Christ's hand extended by giving a copy to a family member or a friend. And . . . it might well be that you will want to make another journey through it yourself in the coming year.

ABOUT THE AUTHOR

For more than twenty-five years, O. S. Hawkins served pastor-ates including the First Baptist Church in Fort Lauderdale, Florida, and the First Baptist Church in Dallas, Texas. A native of Fort Worth, he has three earned degrees (BBA, MDiv, and DMin) as well as several honorary degrees. He is president of GuideStone Financial Resources, which serves 250,000 pastors, church staff members, missionaries, doctors, nurses, university professors, and other workers in various Christian organizations with their retire-ment and benefit service needs. He is the author of more than thirty books, including the bestselling *The Joshua Code*, *The Jesus Code*, and *The James Code*, and preaches regularly at conferences, uni-versities, business groups, and churches across the nation. He and his wife, Susie, have two married daughters and six grandchildren.

Follow O. S. Hawkins on Twitter @oshawkins.
Visit www.oshawkins.com for free resources.

MISSION:DIGNITY

All the author's royalties and any additional proceeds from the "Code" series (including *The Believer's Code*) go to the support of Mission:Dignity, a ministry that enables thousands of retired ministers (and, in most cases, their widows) who are living near the poverty level to live out their days with dignity and security. Many of them spent their ministries in small churches that were unable to provide adequately for their retirement. They also lived in church-owned parsonages and had to vacate them upon their vocational retirement as well. Mission:Dignity tangibly shows these good and godly servants they are not forgotten and will be cared for in their declining years.

All the expenses for this ministry are paid out of an endowment that has already been been raised. Consequently, anyone who gives to Mission:Dignity can be assured that every cent of their gift goes straight to one of these precious saints in need.

Find out more by visiting www.guidestone.org and click on the Mission:Dignity icon or call toll-free 888-984-8433.

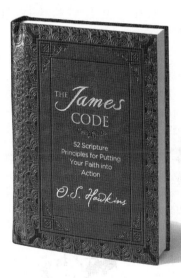

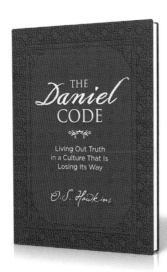

JOURNEY THROUGH

Advent

Grow close to the Lord this Advent season with 25 insightful and meaningful devotions from *The Christmas Code* by bestselling author O. S. Hawkins. Trace the birth of Jesus from its roots in the Old Testament to the ultimate gift of God: salvation. With a short reading each day leading up to Christmas, this devotional will be the perfect way to keep daily focus on the true meaning of Christmas.
ISBN: 978-1-4003-0924-5

One hundred percent of the author's royalties and proceeds go to support Mission:Dignity—a ministry providing support for impoverished retired pastors and missionaries.

THOMAS NELSON
Since 1798